# the world's best
# spicy
# food

## where to find it
## & how to make it

lonely planet

Melbourne * London * Oakland

# Contents

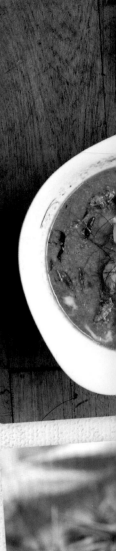

# \* Condiments \*

# * Introduction *

By Tom Parker-Bowles

**It started with a drop, beguilingly red and devilishly scented, poured from a small, elegant bottle onto the back of my hand.**

'Go on, try it,' my sister implored, her eyes glittering with glee. 'All the grown ups drink the stuff. How dangerous can it be?' So I closed my eyes tight, and plunged my tongue into the unknown. The first taste was sharp but not unpleasant, like the vinegar that we splashed on our chips. I smiled, and sighed with relief. Much ado about nothing. And then it hit, a fierce, brutally burning sensation that started in my mouth before spreading, like a raging forest fire, across my lips and down into my throat.

My eyes brimmed with tears and I tried to scream but to no avail. I'd never felt pain like this. It was worse than stinging nettles and grazed knees and the slap of a cold football on rain-drenched flesh. I fell to the floor, clutching my belly, convinced that this damned liquid, this evil draught, was noxious poison, the killer of small boys.

Then, as suddenly as it had begun, the agony abated. I opened my eyes and looked about. The light seemed somehow brighter, every colour suddenly more vivid. Sure, my tongue still throbbed and my lips smarted too. But my whole body was enveloped in a warm glow. My sister, of course, was sheet-white and trembling, convinced that she was the architect of her brother's demise. I, though, was in love. One drop of Tabasco sauce, and I've never looked back since.

Soon, I was splashing this beautiful Louisiana hot sauce over everything that was put before me, from toast and egg to steak and shepherd's pie. And this was just the start: Tabasco was the gateway drug of an addiction that would take over my life. Curries followed, each more potent than the next, madras first, then the great leap to vindaloo. I began to cook with chillies, moving quickly from dull, generic long green things to the fruity insanity of the Scotch bonnet. Before long, I was a subscriber to Chile Pepper magazine, scouring the streets for my next spicy hit.

Visits to Thailand followed, som toms with enough bird's-eye punch to floor a rampaging bull elephant, let alone a rather pasty Brit. Tom yam gungs, fragrant with heat and fish sauce, nam phrik pla flowing like monsoon-bloated rivers. I just couldn't get enough: it was pain,

AUSTIN BUSH | GETTY IMAGES

of flavour and texture and joy. The smoky heft of a chipotle chilli, the verdant tang of a fresh jalapeno. But the reason why the chilli pepper is so damned addictive lies in its active ingredient, capsaicin, a nasty little irritant alkaloid. The hotter the chilli, the more of this chemical it contains, hitting the taste buds hard, sending them reeling in pain. So the body reacts, and sends in the Special Forces (better known as endorphins). That's why the agony of really hot chilli burn is followed by that blissful state of dreamy joy. As these endorphins flood the system, putting out the fires, we experience a truly natural 'high'.

But this book is not about chillies alone, rather 'spicy' food in its every guise. The pungent, nose-clearing honk of wasabi, mustard and horseradish; pepper's pep (black, white, pink and Sichuan) and paprika's punch; the warming allure of cinnamon and mace, the bracing crunch of piccalilli. These are dishes to make the taste buds punch the air with elation, flavours that kickstart the palate and infuse every sense with joy.

As you'd expect, there are a huge number of dishes from Thailand, India and Mexico, the three great chilli cuisines, alongside Sichuan Chinese and Korean too. But we also feast upon herrings from Norway, Turkish kebabs, Czech sausages and African chicken. Trindadian souse sits alongside Hungarian goulash, katsu curry shares space with Spanish grilled peppers. This book is a celebration of spiciness in every form: ingredients that turn the bland to the brilliant, the dreary into the divine.

And, like all food, it's the finest way to experience any foreign culture. Forget the funereal silence and air-conditioned gloom of those insipid 'international' restaurants, with their second-rate approximations of dreary Western fare. This is real food, pulsing with vibrancy and delight, bringing a truly happy tear to one's eye. Best of all, you need nothing more than a healthy appetite, an open mind and a handful of the local currency. Spice. One word, a million different thrills.

sure, but exquisite pleasure too. There were dhals eaten in India at roadside shops, little more than ten pence a portion, but thick with great lengths of dried Kashmiri chilli. And Indonesian sambals, in every hue and pong.

I visited hot-sauce shows in Albuquerque, New Mexico: entire conference centres devoted to fiery foods. And fell in love with the chile con carne of Texas, plus the entire cuisine of Mexico, from birrias and ceviches to tortillas, tacos and tostadas. I huffed and puffed my way through incendiary, but impossibly crisp, hot chicken at Prince's in Nashville, Tennessee, breakfast burritos smothered with green chile in Santa Fe, New Mexico. And bought Caribbean hot sauces bottled in old Lucozade bottles from roadside stalls in Antigua. Then there's kimchi in Korea, harissa-spiked couscous, Sichuan chilli hotpots and everything else in between.

I love the chilli more than any other fruit, pretty much more than any ingredient there is. It's not all about heat, rather, huge complexities

# * Dishes *

## Legend

### Recipe

(E) **Easy** - A very basic recipe, eg, putting together a sandwich or tossing salad ingredients.

(M) **Medium** - Suitable for the average home cook.

(C) **Complex** - Several parts to make, or lots of ingredients to prepare, or a specific technique involved that may take some practice.

**Note** Definitions for words in blue in the recipes can be found in the glosssary on page 214.

## Utensils

 **Hands**

 **Knife * Fork * Spoon**

 **Chopsticks**

 **Drinks**

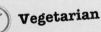 **Hot**   **Medium**   **Mild**

**Vegetarian**

# * Adana Kebab *

## TURKEY

**Smoky, spicy and supremely satisfying, it's worth a trip to the off-the-beaten-track city of Adana just to taste Turkey's fieriest lamb kebab on its home turf.**

## What is it?

Coarsely ground lamb meat – ideally from a male sheep and with a robust addition of tail fat – is mixed with finely chopped red peppers and onions, and spices including chilli flakes, coriander and cumin. Shaped onto skewers, the kebabs are charcoal grilled and served with warm pita bread alongside a zingy salad of parsley, sliced red onions and sumac (a citrus-tinged spice used in Middle Eastern cuisine).

## Origin

Spicy lamb kebabs packed full of heat and flavour – and the essential unctuous tail fat – have long been popular across southeastern Anatolia, Syria and Iraq. But only in the Turkish city of Adana has the dish blending Turkish and Arab culinary influences been patented. Locals are so serious about it that sidewalk traders and more formal restaurants selling the dish are even subject to random inspections by the Adana Chamber of Commerce.

## Tasting

All your senses are aroused as you make your way through the busy labyrinth of Adana's old town to dine on the city's signature dish. The call to prayer of the muezzins drifts from Adana's mosques and fragrant aromas waft from simple eateries concealed deep within the city's bazaar. Take a window seat with views of the compelling chaos outside and request *bir porsiyon* (one portion). Adana kebab is not a dish to be rushed and don't go making plans for dinner. Tear off some gossamer-thin bread, place some of the smoky, chargrilled lamb inside, and then stuff full of the zesty salad of parsley, onion and sumac. Repeat leisurely until you're supremely satisfied; request a side order of grilled red peppers for an additional fiery hit.

## Finding It

Head to Adana's bustling Öz Asmaalti eatery for the city's finest kebab. Expect to pay 15 Turkish lira (around US$8).

* **TIPS** * Wash down an Adana kebab with a cooling glass of tangy *ayran* (drink made with yoghurt and salt), or a refreshing serving of *salgam suyu* (turnip juice). If you're a dedicated spicy food fan, ask for a further sprinkling of chilli on the juice. For dessert, order *kadayif* (dough soaked in syrup and topped with clotted cream).

* By Brett Atkinson *

# Recipe Adana Kebab

## INGREDIENTS

500g (1lb) ground lamb

500g (1lb) ground veal

1 red pepper

1 yellow onion

2 cloves of garlic, crushed

2 tsp red chilli flakes

2 tsp ground coriander

2 tsp ground cumin

2 tsp black pepper

3 tsp salt

2 red onions

1 tsp sumac

2 tsp lemon juice

1 cup (250mL) yoghurt

8 pieces of pita bread

4 tsp olive oil

Handful of parsley leaves

## METHOD

1. Mix the lamb and veal together in a large bowl.
2. Combine with finely chopped red pepper, yellow onion and one clove of garlic.
3. Add in the chilli flakes, coriander, cumin, pepper and two teaspoons of the salt.
4. Cover the mixture and leave in the refrigerator, ideally over-night, but at least for a few hours.
5. Slice the red onions thinly, mix in the sumac and half the lemon juice; refrigerate overnight.
6. Mix the yoghurt with the remaining lemon juice, garlic and a teaspoon of salt, to create a sauce.
7. When it's time to cook, shape the lamb and veal mixture into cylinders around kebab skewers. Your cylinders should measure about 15cm x 6cm (6in x 2in).
8. Place on a hot grill and cook for around 3 to 4 minutes on each side. When the kebabs are ready, they should be slightly spongy to the touch.
9. Baste the pita bread with olive oil and place on the grill to warm through.
10. Place the kebab in the warm pita bread, add the sliced onions with sumac to the parsley, and garnish with the yoghurt sauce. If you like, serve with chargrilled tomatoes and red peppers.

SERVES 4 TO 6

# * Assam Laksa *

PENANG, MALAYSIA

**This is not your average laksa. *Assam* laksa (aka Penang laksa) is a fish-based noodle soup that tastes like no other. Made famous by food-crazy Penang-ites, this is one unique dish.**

## What is it?

Unlike the coconut-milk-heavy curry version you'll find almost everywhere, *assam* laksa is an explosive combination of tamarind-laden fish broth and rice noodles, topped with a mound of chopped vegetables and chillies. This is street food at its best: flavoursome and moreish, served in one dish. Its pungent, sour taste makes it a good wake-me-up at lunchtime.

## Origin

Its precise origins are unknown, but variations of *assam* laksa can be found along coastal Malaysia and also in Borneo, leading some to believe that the dish originated from Malaysian fisherfolk. One might imagine these people using leftover, unsold fish to make a noodle soup, adding tamarind and other spices and topping it with vegetables and whatever other scraps they had on hand. The dish evolved through the years, and recently achieved superstar status when *CNNgo* named it number seven in the top 50 best foods in the world.

## Tasting

You'll find the tastiest versions of *assam* laksa at low-fi coffee shops in Penang: the sort of place where you jostle with other punters for the first available seat regardless of how grimy the interior looks. The laksa broth is made with mackerel, a fiery spice paste and tamarind: it's a potent combination of sour, spicy and pungent fishiness. The strong flavour of the soup is offset with a fresh, zesty topping of chopped mint, pineapple, cucumber, onion and fresh chillies. In short, your first taste or two might make you grimace – but your third and fourth will set you slurping it all down and raising your hand for seconds.

## Finding it

Head to Penang and sniff out *assam* laksa at Nan Guang coffeeshop in Balik Pulau (near the corner of Jln Tun Sardon and Jln Balik Pulau). It's around RM6 (US$2) a bowl.

* **VARIATIONS** * A great accompaniment to the dish is *otak-otak* – a strip of cake made with spiced fish paste, wrapped in a banana leaf and grilled over a charcoal fire. You'll find it across Malaysia, Singapore and even Indonesia. The Penang version is wrapped in banana leaves before being steamed in coconut milk.

* By Shawn Low *

# Recipe Assam Laksa

## INGREDIENTS

1 kg fresh mackerel, gutted

⅓ cup (80mL) tamarind juice (soak tamarind pulp in hot water for 5 minutes, squeeze for juice)

3 pieces tamarind peel

Salt and sugar, to taste

1 packet of dried laksa rice noodles*

## Spice Paste

10 dried red chillies, soak in water for 5 minutes, press dry

5 fresh red chillies

8–10 small shallots

1 piece galangal

1 piece ginger

2 tsp belacan (Malay shrimp paste) *

2 stalks lemon grass, white part only

1 ginger flower

## Vegetable Garnish

1 cucumber

½ pineapple

1 onion

3 small fresh red chillies

½ cup Vietnamese mint

½ cup mint

## Optional

Hae ko (prawn paste)*


\* Available at any good Asian grocer

## METHOD

1. Prepare the vegetable garnish. Julienne the cucumber and pineapple, finely chop the onion and chillies, and coarsely chop the mint.

2. Boil the fish in a pot with enough water to cover it until it's cooked through (10-15 minutes).

3. Remove the fish from the stock, debone it, and put the fish head and bones back into the stock to simmer for another 15 minutes. Strain the stock to get rid of bones and other small bits.

4. Coarsely flake the fish and set aside.

5. Combine the spice paste ingredients and blend in a food processor.

6. Add the spice paste, tamarind juice and tamarind peel to the stock, season to taste with salt and sugar and simmer another 15 minutes.

7. Turn the heat off and return fish flesh to the stock.

8. Meanwhile, cook the rice noodles as per packet instructions and drain.

9. Divide the noodles into bowls, top with the fish stock and garnish generously with vegetables.

10. If desired, dilute hae ko paste with water to a syrupy texture and dollop a teaspoon on top of each dish before serving.

SERVES 6

# * Black-Pepper Crab *

## SINGAPORE

**Everyone knows about Singapore's chilli crab but the other – arguably tastier – crab dish worth seeking out in the Lion City is the version cooked in a sticky, spicy, black-pepper sauce.**

## What is it?

The dish is surprisingly simple to prepare. Fresh crab is stir-fried in a buttery pepper sauce – the secret is in the freshness of the crab, liberal use of black pepper and a good wok that can withstand high heat. It's typically served in seafood restaurants as a shared main course.

## Origin

The dish's more famous cousin, chilli crab, had its origin back in the 1950s when Madam Cher's husband asked her to try cooking crabs at home differently. Instead of steaming them, she stir-fried a batch in tomato sauce. Her husband suggested adding chilli to offset the sweetness of the tomatoes, and the resulting dish was so good that Madam Cher started a pushcart serving seafood by the beach. Business boomed, and Palm Beach seafood restaurant was born. A rival restaurant, Long Beach, came up with the black-pepper version in 1959, presumably to compete with Palm Beach. Both versions have since proved their popularity and longevity and are possibly Singapore's most famed dishes.

## Tasting

While there's a certain romance in having seafood on a beach, good food can always trump the setting it's served in. Fresh crab, inherently sweet, tender and juicy, is coated with a sticky, buttery pepper sauce – a hot wok is the key to combining the two elements. Of course, eating black-pepper crab is a messy affair: it's all fingers on deck when you crack the shell to slurp out the succulent flesh. While doing that, the peppery sauce tantalises your lips and tongue. Leave your white shirt at home and don't forget to wear a bib – it will get messy!

## Finding it

Compare the version at Singapore's Long Beach Seafood (1018E East Coast Parkway) and Eng Seng Restaurant (247 Joo Chiat Place). Book ahead or come early for the latter, and expect to pay around S$40–50/kg (US$30–40).

---

**\* VARIATIONS \*** Why stop at black-pepper crab? It's not uncommon for locals to order chilli crab in addition to the black-pepper version. If you do order both, ask for some fried *mantou* (bread bun) – use it to mop up all the delicious sauce the crabs are cooked in. The local Tiger beer makes a refreshing palate cleanser.

* By Shawn Low *

# Recipe Black-Pepper Crab

## INGREDIENTS

5 tbs coarsely ground black peppercorns

2 large crabs, quartered (Dungeness, Sri Lankan or mud varieties)

6 tbs unsalted butter

6 cloves garlic, chopped

½ tsp ground white pepper

Pinch of Chinese five-spice powder

1 tbs oyster sauce

3 tbs Chinese rice wine

3 tbs water

Peanut oil

## METHOD

1. In a wok, dry fry the ground peppercorns on low heat to bring out the fragrance. Set aside.

2. Heat oil in a large wok over high heat until it starts shimmering.

3. Add the crab, ensuring that the heat remains high. Cook for four to five minutes and set aside. Drain the oil from the wok.

4. Reduce the heat to medium. Add the butter and fry the garlic, being careful not to burn them both.

5. Quickly add the black peppercorns, white pepper, five spice powder, oyster sauce, rice wine and water and mix.

6. Return the crab to the wok and stir to completely coat the crab in sauce. Remove and serve.

SERVES 4

# * Buffalo Wings *

## USA

**No American bar menu, Super Bowl party or backyard barbecue is complete without these fiery chicken snacks served with a smooth blue-cheese sauce and crunchy celery sticks.**

## WHAT IS IT?

A favourite accompaniment for a cold beer or an ice-cold soft drink, the humble chicken wing is jointed, slathered in a finger-licking, lip-smacking, tear-inducing hot butter sauce and then deep fried to crispy perfection. A pungent, creamy blue-cheese dip and refreshing celery sticks provide a soothing foil to the tangy and spicy sauce.

## TASTING

Like spaghetti and tacos, Buffalo wings are a definite no-no on those all-important dining occasions such as a first date. There is simply no way to savour the delectable wings other than digging in, using your fingers to generously coat piquantly hot and sticky chicken with the unctuous blue-cheese dip. Cooling celery sticks provide the perfect foil to the fiery, peppery sauce. Typically served in platters, the addictive combination of hot chilli and soothing blue cheese means it is virtually impossible to stop at one chicken wing. Serious Buffalo wing aficionados enter eating and cooking competitions across the country and debate the merits or otherwise of deep-frying versus grilling; how hot the butter sauce should be; or whether to use bottled blue-cheese dressing or a home-made version.

## ORIGIN

Buffalo wings are said to be the invention of Teresa Bellissimo, part-owner of her family's Italian-American restaurant in Buffalo, New York called Anchor Bar. The restaurant exists to this day and family legend has it that Teresa whipped up the impromptu recipe, from an oversupply of chicken wings, as a late night snack for her son's friends 50 years ago. The hot sauce has since evolved into a number of blends with different degrees of fieriness, but the original recipe remains a closely guarded family secret.

## FINDING IT

Your best bet is the annual National Buffalo Wings Festival in Buffalo, New York where you can take a stab at the world record of eating 191 wings in one sitting. Jumbo chicken wings sell for US$1 each.

**\* VARIATIONS \*** A 'true' Buffalo wing is simply deep fried and slathered in hot butter sauce but variations include breaded and crumbed versions similar to that other famous fried chicken.

\* By Johanna Ashby \*

# Recipe Buffalo Wings

This grilled version is less fiddly than the deep-fried original but no less tasty. Anchor Bar does publish the recipe for the original blue-cheese dip on its website.

## INGREDIENTS

10 chicken wings, wing tip removed and jointed into 20 pieces

½ cup (125mL) hot sauce

50g butter, melted

1 tbs Worcestershire sauce

1 tbs Tabasco sauce

1 tsp cayenne pepper

1 cup (250mL) sour cream

½ cup (125mL) mayonnaise

150g (5oz) blue cheese, crumbled

1 tbs white vinegar

Juice of 1 lemon

Celery sticks for serving

## METHOD

1. Marinate the chicken wings in a mixture of the hot sauce, butter, Worcestershire sauce, Tabasco sauce and cayenne pepper, preferably overnight.

2. Deep-fry or grill the wings until cooked and golden brown on both sides.

3. Make the blue-cheese dip by combining the sour cream, mayonnaise, blue cheese, white vinegar and lemon juice. Season to taste.

4. Lay out the wings on a platter and serve with the dip and the celery sticks.

SERVES 4 (5 PIECES PER PERSON)

# * Bunny Chow *

## DURBAN, SOUTH AFRICA

**Durban's home-grown dish has its roots in the subcontinent,
but this fragrant curry comes served not with rice, roti or naan,
but ladled into a hollowed-out loaf of bread.**

## What is it?

Bunny Chow, you might be pleased to find, has nothing to do with fluffy rabbits. The oddly-named dish is Durban's favourite takeaway food, a flavoursome – but not fiery – curry served in an edible container, a half-loaf of fresh white bread. The classic Bunny is made with beans, although it comes in chicken, vegetable and mutton versions, the latter being particularly popular.

## Tasting

At first glance Bunny Chow seems an odd dish and you can't help wondering how to attack it without the use of a knife and fork. But this fusion of Indian flavours with European bread is a culinary symbol of South Africa's melange of cultures. Eating it like a local presents a way to quickly assimilate into Durban life. Meat is often served on the bone, lending flavour and tenderness but presenting an extra hurdle when your only utensil is bread. As you munch through your Bunny, subdue the heat with the traditional can of cream soda, or spice it up with atchar (spicy pickles) or sambal (a salsa-like condiment featuring tomato, onion, carrot and chilli). As you finish you use your 'virgin', the fluffy chunk of bread originally scooped out of the loaf, to mop up spilt juices – as a first-time Bunny eater, expect a little spillage.

## Origin

Myth and lore surround the origin of Bunny Chow. Its geographical roots are clear, of course, influenced by Durban's sizeable Indian population. But why did someone decide to scoop curry into a loaf of bread? Was it thought up by Indian golf caddies in need of a quick lunch in Tupperware-less times? Did sugar plantation workers with no time to bake traditional Indian breads invent it? Or was it a resourceful restaurateur catering to people forbidden from eating in certain establishments during apartheid? In any case it is undeniably born of ingenuity.

## Finding it

Grab a Bunny to go at Durban's ultimate takeout joint, the 24-hour Sunrise Chip 'n' Ranch in Overport, ZAR 15–50 (US$1.50–5).

* TIPS * **The Bunny, as it is known, comes in a full, half or quarter loaf, depending on your appetite. Order simply as a 'full mutton', 'half chicken' or 'quarter beans' to sound like a local. And don't expect or ask for any cutlery – chowing down on a Bunny means getting your hands dirty, ripping off pieces of loaf to scoop out the saucy centre.**

* By Lucy Corne *

# Recipe Bunny Chow

## INGREDIENTS

800g (1lb 10oz) stewing lamb, preferably boneless

2 potatoes

2 onions

2 large tomatoes, coarsely chopped

2 tsp fresh ginger, grated

4 cloves garlic, grated

4 cardamom pods

1 tin garden peas

1 stick cinnamon

4 curry leaves

2 tsp turmeric

4 tsp garam masala

2 tsp leaf masala

1 tsp ground coriander

2 tsp ground cumin

1 tsp salt

½ cup (125mL) water

Fresh coriander leaves to garnish

Sunflower oil

Loaf of fresh white bread, unsliced

## METHOD

1. Cut the lamb into bite-sized pieces.
2. Peel and cube the potatoes and coarsely chop the onions.
3. Combine the grated ginger and garlic.
4. Add a generous glug of oil to a deep pan and fry the onions for four to five minutes on a medium heat.
5. Add the cardamom pods, cinnamon stick and curry leaves and fry until the onion begins to brown.
6. Add the turmeric, garam masala, leaf masala, ground coriander and cumin, then the ginger and garlic. Stir to coat the onion.
7. Cook for another couple of minutes, stirring constantly, then add the meat. If the oil has been soaked up by the spices, you can add a little extra oil.
8. Once the meat is starting to brown, add the tomatoes, potatoes and about ¼ cup of hot water to start with, making sure that the potatoes are just covered with liquid.
9. Simmer for 30 to 40 minutes, until the meat and potatoes are tender.
10. Add more liquid and salt in small quantities as required.
11. Prepare the bread, taking care to leave the crust intact, keeping a narrow lining of fluffy bread.
12. Add the tinned peas to the curry and heat for five minutes.
13. To serve, ladle the curry into each bread container and serve with a sprinkle of fresh coriander and the 'virgin' on the side.

SERVES 4

# * Camarones a la Diabla *

## MEXICO

**Fresh shrimp (*camarones*) are plucked from the salty sea and cooked with a fiery sauce of tomato and spicy chillies, earning the name '*a la diabla*' – devil-style!**

## What is it?

Seafood cooked *a la diabla* is a favourite preparation in coastal Mexico. The sauce generally consists of diced tomatoes, butter, garlic and onions, and various types of chillies – piquant *árbols* and serranos are popular. The shrimp are usually served as part of a *platillo* (main course), along with rice, beans, salad and tortillas.

## Origin

Chillies, native to the New World, have been cultivated in Latin America for some 6000 years. Tomatoes, another main ingredient in *camarones a la diabla*, are also native New World fruits. Garlic and onions, however, didn't make it to Mexico until the arrival of the Spaniards, who also introduced dairy cattle for butter and cheese. Though the precise origins of the *a la diabla* preparation are unknown, it is especially popular in the coastal regions of the Yucatan peninsula and the West Coast.

## Finding it

Near Veracruz, the beach town of Boca del Rio is famed for its row of beachfront *palapas* (palm huts) serving seafood straight from *el mar* (approximately US$5 a main).

## Tasting

Imagine sitting at a beach cantina in, oh, say, the Yucatan town of Tulum or the Oaxacan coastal hamlet of Mazunte, your bare feet skimming the warm, white sand. You're a few margaritas in when the waiter brings you a plate of *camarones a la diabla* – fat pink shrimp swimming in a brilliant red sauce, its surface gleaming with the richness of butter. You tear off a piece of hot corn tortilla and scoop up a bite. The fiery kick of the chilli contrasts with the firmness of the fresh shrimp; you can cool everything down with a bite of rice or a mouthful of *frijoles refritos* (refried beans) flecked with creamy crumbles of white queso fresco (fresh cheese).

**\* TIPS \* Kick it up a notch by chasing your *camarones a la diabla* with a *michelada*, a picante Mexican thirst-quencher of a beer spiked with lime, salt and hot chilli.**

* By Emily Matchar *

# Recipe **Camarones a la Diabla**

## INGREDIENTS

1kg (2lb) peeled shrimp

1L water

5 medium tomatoes, chopped

2 medium red onions, sliced

6 cloves garlic

400g (14oz) canned chipotle chillies

700mL ketchup

1 tsp salt

2 tbs vegetable oil

## METHOD

1. Put water, tomatoes, half an onion and garlic cloves in a large pot.

2. Bring to the boil over high heat, then reduce to a simmer and cook until tomatoes are soft.

3. Remove from heat and allow to cool for two minutes.

4. Pour tomato mixture into a blender, adding chillies, ketchup and salt. Blend until smooth.

5. Saute remaining onion in a pan with the vegetable oil over medium-high heat until golden brown. Add shrimp and cook for two minutes.

6. Pour tomato sauce over shrimp and simmer for eight minutes.

7. Serve over rice.

SERVES 6

# * Caribbean Curry Goat *

## CARIBBEAN

**A party in Jamaica or Trinidad is not considered complete without a steaming pot of curry goat, a highly spiced stew of goat meat spiked with flaming-hot Scotch bonnet chillies.**

## What is it?

Chunks of goat meat, sometimes with the bone still in, are slow-simmered in a sauce of allspice-heavy curry powder, with Caribbean-grown Scotch bonnet chillies added for heat. Coconut milk is optional, as is the addition of vegetables like potatoes and carrots. The curry is generally served over rice.

## Tasting

While curry goat is on the menu of many home-style Caribbean restaurants, it's best known as a party dish. Any large gathering – a birthday celebration, a village dance, a Christmas party – necessitates the presence of a curry goat 'specialist' to prepare and stir the stew as the festivities begin to roll. Party-goers, tired from dancing and rum-guzzling, grab paper plates piled with rice and hot curry to revive them as steel drums pound in the background. The slow-stewed meat is pleasantly chewy, the sauce deep and complex. The heat comes on slowly, rolling from the back of your tongue to the front, building to a crescendo. Revellers muffle the heat with rice, or, in Trinidad, Indian-style roti bread.

## Origin

The ubiquity of curry in Caribbean countries like Jamaica, Trinidad and Guyana is thanks to a large population of Indo-Caribbeans, mostly descendants of indentured sugarcane workers brought to the region in the days of colonial rule. Common Indian curry spices – turmeric, coriander, cumin – were supplemented with native Caribbean allspice, which gives the dish a unique, warm flavour. The heat derives from the Scotch bonnet chilli, known in Guyana as the Ball of Fire, which is about three times hotter than the tongue-scorching cayenne.

## Finding it

Moby Dick Restaurant in downtown Kingston, Jamaica, is the locals' top curry spot (US$10 for a bowl).

* VARIATIONS * In Jamaica, the bits of the goat not used in curry – intestines, penis, brains – are sometimes turned into 'mannish water', a supposedly aphrodisiac soup sometimes served to the groom on his wedding night. Don't worry, ladies, you can try it, too.

* By Emily Matchar *

# Recipe Caribbean Curry Goat

## INGREDIENTS

1kg (2lb) goat stewing meat, cubed

2 tsp curry powder

½ tsp allspice

2 onions, diced

2 spring onions, roughly chopped

½ tsp salt

½ tsp pepper

2 Scotch bonnet chillies (or 4 jalapeño chillies), thinly sliced

1 tbs grated fresh ginger

1 tbs butter

2 medium potatoes, diced

2 medium carrots, sliced

## METHOD

1.  Combine curry powder, allspice, onions, spring onions, salt, pepper, chillies, ginger and half a cup of water in a blender and blend for approximately 30 seconds.

2.  Rub the mixture over the meat and refrigerate in a plastic bag or sealed container overnight.

3.  Drain the meat, reserving the remaining marinade.

4.  Melt butter in a large pan over medium-high heat then brown the goat pieces.

5.  Add potatoes, carrots, marinade and enough water to cover the meat.

6.  Bring to the boil then simmer until tender (one to two hours).

7.  Serve with steamed rice.

SERVES 4

# * Carne Deshebrada en Salsa Roja *

## JALISCO, MEXICO

**Enjoyed as breakfast, or even for lunch, this spicy stew of shredded beef in  Guajillo sauce is your best friend after a night on the tequila.**

## What is it?

This is comfort food Mexican-style. Slow-cooked, tender shredded beef is bathed and simmered in a *guajillo* chilli sauce that calls for warm corn tortillas and soupy black beans. Ladle it onto a tortilla and eat as a taco or use the tortillas to scoop up all its savoury greatness – it offers a reward in every bite.

## Origin

Since the early days of the Aztec civilization Mexican cooks have shredded beef, chicken or turkey, simmering it slowly in an incredible array of salsas in traditional earthenware *cazuelas* (pots). This gives a delicious spicy dish, known as *guisados*, resembling the traditional stews found in other world cuisines, but with the use of native ingredients like ground pumpkin, tomatoes, a great variety of dry or fresh chillies, spices and herbs such as coriander, epazote, and bay leaves.

## Finding it

Las Hermanas Coraje, an eatery next to the train station in Guadalajara (Chicago Street 1280) serves a great version of the dish every day. For US$2 you get the full treatment.

## Tasting

This hearty, warm, and spicy breakfast stew comforts the spirit at the start of a long day. The juicy shredded beef, cooked to extreme tenderness, is only part of the incentive. The real deal here comes from the *guajillo* chillies, a not-very-spicy pepper with an intense bloodshot color that adds a fruity flavor to the simmering salsa. And then there is the punch from the *chiles de árbol*, a pepper as red as *guajillo* but with a much higher spice rank. Have corn tortillas on hand as the toasty corn makes a perfect sidekick to the salsa.

**\* VARIATIONS \* If you can shred it you can eat it and all over Mexico you will find variations of this dish. In central Mexico *tinga poblana* is shredded pork shoulder cooked with chipotle chillies. Shredded chicken in *escabeche* is a dish found in the Yucatán Península where chicken is cooked in vinegar, chillies and spices and served cold. *Machaca*, or shredded beef jerky with scrambled eggs and chilli, is a popular breakfast in the northern lands.**

**\* By Mauricio Velázquez de León \***

# Recipe Carne Deshebrada en Salsa Roja

## INGREDIENTS

### Beef

1.4kg (3lb) skirt steak, in one piece (flank or brisket work well too)

1 onion, quartered

3 cloves of garlic

1 bay leaf

¼ tsp black peppercorns

3 allspice, whole

1 clove, whole

1 tsp salt

Water

### Salsa

340g (¾lb) tomatoes, quartered (about 2–3 medium tomatoes)

3 tbs vegetable oil

85g (3oz) dried *guajillo* chillies, wiped clean (approximately 12–15 chillies)

¼ tsp black peppercorns

¼ tsp cumin seeds

3 allspice, whole

1 clove, whole

½ cup onion, chopped

3 large cloves of garlic

5 dried *chiles de árbol*, wiped clean, stemmed and seeded

1 tsp salt

## METHOD

### Beef

1. Put all the ingredients in a large pot with enough water to cover the beef. Simmer, partially covered, until tender. Depending of the thickness and the type of meat this could be 30 minutes (for skirt steak) to 2 hours (for brisket). Skim off any foam.
2. Remove the beef, let it cool, then shred.
3. Strain broth through a fine-meshed sieve into a bowl, discard the solids and skim off any fat.
4. Reserve the broth.

### Salsa

1. Preheat the grill.
2. Toss tomatoes with 1 tbs of the oil in a baking tray. Grill the tomatoes 3 to 4 inches from heat until softened and charred, around 5 minutes. Set aside.
3. Slit *guajillo* chillies lengthwise, then stem and seed them and open them flat.
4. Heat a dry frying pan over a medium heat until hot. Toast the chillies in two batches, turning and pressing with tongs, until pliable and slightly coloured, about 30 seconds per batch.
5. Transfer the chillies to a bowl, cover in hot water and soak until softened, about 10–20 minutes.
6. Toast peppercorns, cumin seeds, allspice and clove in the same frying pan over a medium heat, stirring constantly until fragrant and a shade darker, 30 seconds to 1 minute. Transfer to a blender.
7. Drain soaked *guajillo* chillies and puree in blender with toasted spices, tomatoes, onion, garlic, 5 *chiles de árbol*, 2 cups of the reserved broth, and 1 tsp salt until smooth, about 2 minutes.
8. Heat the remaining 2 tbs oil in a deep pot over a medium heat until it shimmers. Gradually stir in the sauce from the blender.
9. Simmer for 5 minutes, stirring frequently.
10. Add the beef and 1 cup of broth and cook over a medium-low heat, stirring, until the meat is heated through (a few minutes).
11. Serve with warm corn tortillas, white rice and black beans.

# * Ceviche *

## PACIFIC COAST, PERU

**Combining a Spanish-influenced zesty citrus punch with marinated fish and chillies used in Incan times, Peru's national dish has now been adopted and adapted across Latin America.**

### What is it?

Raw fish – often corvina or Pacific sea bass – is marinated in lime juice and cured or 'cooked' by the citric acid of the juice. Added to the tender chunks of fish are seasonings including coriander (cilantro), garlic, red onion and fresh chillies. *Ceviche* is most commonly served at lunch to best showcase the fresh fish landed just hours before.

### Origin

The roots of *ceviche* go back to Incan times when *chicha*, a marinated corn drink, was used to marinate fish prior to cooking. The lime was introduced to Latin America by Spanish conquistadores, proving a sublime match for the fleshy white fish of South America's Pacific coast. Some also believe that ocean-going navigators from the Polynesian islands of the South Pacific introduced a version of the dish to Rapa Nui (Easter Island) and continental South America. Dishes such as Rarotonga's *ika mata* are very similar.

### Tasting

On a continent where food can be heavy with carbs – rice, beans and potatoes anyone? – the lightness of flavour of *ceviche* is a revelation. Visually, it's also a diverse treat with red and green accents of chilli and coriander standing out on the neutral canvas of white fish. Your first mouthful will boldly announce the super-fresh crunch of red onions and the sharp punch of lime juice. Then the chilli fire hits, but it's balanced with the freshness of the fish and a subtle sweetness from a touch of sugar.

### Finding It

Avenida del Mar in Lima's Miraflores district is the city's *ceviche* hub. Amid the scattered eateries is the more upmarket Pescados Capitales with *ceviche* from around 35 Peruvian nuevo sol (around US$12.50).

* **VARIATIONS** * *Ceviche* is popular across Latin America, but the Pacific Ocean coast of Peru is considered its heartland. There's even a national Peruvian holiday celebrating the vibrant dish. Regional variations include using shrimp and adding salted popcorn and tomatoes in Ecuador, and using halibut or toothfish in Chile. In the Amazon basin, the river fish dorade is used.

* By Brett Atkinson *

# Recipe Ceviche

## INGREDIENTS

1kg (2lb) fillets of firm white fish (eg sea bass) cut into large bite-sized chunks

1 red onion, thinly sliced

1 pinch red chilli flakes

3 cloves garlic, finely chopped

½ cup (8 tbs) fresh lime juice

3 tbs olive oil

2 tsp rice vinegar

¼ tsp caster sugar

1 Peruvian *aji limo* chilli, seeded and chopped (substitute a small red chilli if not available)

2 sweetcorn cobs cut in half

2 sweet potatoes, peeled and sliced thinly

3 tbs chopped coriander (cilantro) leaves

Salt

Ground black pepper

## METHOD

1. Preheat grill to medium heat.

2. Layer half of the sliced onions in a glass bowl and lay the fish on top. Sprinkle on the chilli flakes and chopped garlic and cover with lime juice.

3. Cover the bowl and place to marinate in a refrigerator for two hours. During this time spoon the lime juice over the fish two more times.

4. Whisk together the oil, rice vinegar and caster sugar until smooth, and then add the chopped fresh chilli.

5. After the fish has been marinated, drain and discard the lime juice and mix in the mixture of chilli/oil/rice vinegar/caster sugar, blending well.

6. Brush the sweetcorn and sweet potato with oil and place under a medium-heat grill for around 10 minutes.

7. When cooked, divide the *ceviche* into six servings. Top with chopped coriander and the remaining sliced red onion, and season to taste with salt and ground black pepper.

8. Serve with the grilled sweetcorn and sweet potato.

SERVES 6 AS A STARTER

# * Chilli Dogs *

## USA

**Take an old-world European food (the Frankfurter, aka the hot dog), add spices indigenous to the American Southwest, serve in excessive portions on rolls made from refined white flour and – voila! – quintessential Americana.**

## What is it?

The traditional version of this dish – found in county fairs, carnivals and food courts from sea to shining sea – is a ladle-full of spicy-as-hell beef chilli served on top of an all-American hot dog. It's usually garnished with condiments, raw onions for crunch and extra bite and perhaps some extra-sharp shredded cheddar for zing of a different sort.

## Origin

Frankfurters hail from Frankfurt, but the resemblance between these and the American hot dog may only be skin deep. Chilli has been around in some form since prehistoric man (or woman) discovered that mixing spicy chilli peppers into past-its-best meat made it taste better. Where the marriage between the two first occurred is debated: California, Michigan and Brooklyn's Coney Island all claim the honour.

## Tasting

Traditional Tex-Mex chilli is an explosion of meat and spice, one offering a mix of deep flavours and heat. A good chilli dog offers a fiery meat overload, beef dogs slathered in smoky, spicy chilli, tempered slightly by cheese with an added crispy tang of raw red onion. Though easy to find (in America, at least) making your own chilli dogs allows you to indulge in variation. Not a fan of processed meats? Use sausages prepared by a local butcher. Red meat not your thing? The entire dish can be made with turkey. Vegetarians can even use soy-dogs and chilli made with texturized vegetable protein (TVP). Whatever you chose, it can be grilled or boiled; buns can be grilled or toasted. Some folks split the dog down the middle, but keeping them intact gives a more satisfying juicy meat-bomb mouth-feel.

## Finding it

Try Nathan's in Coney Island, Brooklyn. For the real chilli dog experience, head to a carnival or county fair anywhere in the American Southwest! A chilli dog in either place shouldn't set you back more than US$6.

**\* VARIATIONS \* Folks in New Mexico have their own version of chilli dogs, spelled Chile Dogs. This variation of the dish eschews the chilli (considered a 'Tex-Mex thing') for New Mexico's ubiquitous green and red chile peppers. It's a slower – some say purer – burn. But don't be fooled by the smaller heft of the New Mexico Chile Dog: New Mexico's chiles are known for their fiery disposition.**

* By Joshua Samuel Brown *

# Recipe Chilli Dogs

## INGREDIENTS

500g (1lb) ground beef

20 hot dogs and buns

6 cloves of garlic

1 large yellow onion

Olive oil

2 tbs cayenne pepper

2 tbs chilli powder

2 tbs smoked paprika

1 tbs cumin

1 tsp salt

225g (8oz) can of tomato sauce

2 tbs honey

1 large red onion (for garnish)

110g (¼lb) shredded cheese

## METHOD

1.  Sauté chopped garlic and yellow onion in a bit of olive oil, adding ground beef and spices after the onion and garlic mixture is clear.

2.  After browning the meat over a medium heat – 10 minutes generally suffices – add tomato sauce and honey and simmer for an hour.

3.  Hot dogs can be grilled or boiled, and buns can be grilled or toasted.

4.  Add chilli to hot dogs then garnish with chopped red onion and cheese.

SERVES 10

# * Chongqing Hotpot *

CHONGQING, CHINA

**Think Swiss fondue, but replace the bread with raw meats and Chinese vegetables, then swap the melted cheese for a boiling broth of chilli-laced madness.**

## What is it?

The ultimate DIY dish for spice junkies, Chongqing hotpot (or *huoguo*, literally 'fire pot') allows you to boil ingredients of your choice for as long as you dare in a bubbling broth of chillies and, crucially, mouth-numbing Sichuan peppercorns. Sliced raw meats, fish, vegetables, plus some more obscure offerings (duck intestine, anyone?) are dunked by diners and then, once cooked, fished out, dipped in a sesame paste and eaten with a cold beer at hand.

## Origin

Chinese hotpot is thought to have originated from the mutton-based (and nonspicy) Mongolian hotpot, which spread south during the Tang Dynasty (618 AD to 907 AD). The Chongqing variation is said to have first been eaten by boatmen on the Yangzi River before its popularity spread into Sichuan province (it is sometimes referred to as Sichuan hotpot) and beyond. As well as the number of chillies used, and the popularity of unusual dipping ingredients such as eel, tripe, duck intestine and pig brain, what separates Chongqing hotpot from other types is the liberal use of lip-tingling Sichuan peppercorns to create that *ma-la*, or 'numb-and-spicy' sensation.

## Tasting

In boisterous restaurants, groups of diners dunk raw ingredients in no particular order and then the fun begins: each person uses their chopsticks to fish out spicy delights before embarking on a personal journey into the bizarre world of the *ma-la* mouth sensation. The Sichuan peppercorns hit first, making lips tingle. Soon the chillies kick in – brows sweat, noses run – before the peppercorns take over again: this time a complete numbing of the mouth ensues, which tricks you into thinking the chillies aren't that spicy after all. They are. And they soon bite back: eyes stream, mouths burn. Eventually, after more and more rounds of *ma* (numb) and *la* (spice), your whole body becomes consumed: arms and legs tingle; hot flushes increase; palpitations begin. Welcome to Chongqing-flavoured spice insanity.

## Finding it

In-the-know locals sneak into the unassuming Yefu Huoguo (夜富火锅), a no-nonsense hotpot joint, renowned for piling on the Sichuan peppercorns like no other restaurant in Chongqing. The hotpot broth is free; you just pay for raw ingredients. Expect around ¥30 (US$5) per person, all in.

* TIPS * The broth of a Chongqing hotpot can be ordered with differing levels of spice: mild (微辣; *wei la*), medium (中辣; *zhong la*), very spicy (特辣; *te la*) or extra, extra spicy (加嘛加辣; *jia ma jia la*). Choose wisely. Sometimes you can order a half-spicy, half-clear split pot (鸳鸯锅; *yuanyang guo*), but you'll still have to state how spicy you want the spicy half.

By Daniel McCrohan *

# Recipe Chongqing Hotpot

## YOU'LL NEED

### Equipment

Electric-heated hotplate

Hotpot – wide but not too deep, to allow for easy food fishing

Chopsticks and/or straining ladle, for fishing out cooked items

### Broth

4L water

1kg (2lb) beef/pork/chicken bones

3 slices fresh ginger

1 spring onion, sliced

3–4 bay leaves

### Spice Paste

5–10 dried chillies (soaked until soft)

1–2 tbs Sichuan peppercorns

4 slices fresh ginger

4 cloves garlic, sliced

3 tbs Sichuan spicy bean paste*

1 tsp white sugar

1 cinnamon stick

3–4 star anise

½ cup (125mL) rice wine

4 tsp peanut or vegetable oil

### Sesame Paste

4 tsp sesame paste

8 tbs water

4 tsp vegetable oil

chopped spring onions, chives and fresh coriander, half cup (or 1 tbs of each)

* a paste made from fermented broad beans, soybeans, salt, rice and various spices. Called *la douban jiang* (辣豆瓣酱) in Chinese, available in many Chinese supermarkets in the West

## METHOD

Raw ingredients to be cooked at the table may include wafer-thin slices of frozen lamb or mutton, thin slices of fresh beef, strips of duck intestine, strips of tripe, strips of eel, cabbage leaves, tofu slabs, lotus root slices, chrysanthemum stalks, mushrooms, slices of potato or sweet potato, water spinach and, added last, noodles.

1. Combine all the ingredients for the broth stock into a large pot, bring to the boil then simmer for three hours.

2. To make your spice paste, lightly fry the chopped chillies, ginger and garlic in the peanut oil, then add the Sichuan spicy bean paste and cook over a low heat for 10 minutes until fragrant, stirring continually.

3. Add the rest of the spice paste ingredients to the pan and simmer over a low heat for about 30 minutes.

4. Combine with the stock and transfer to your hotpot, which should be kept simmering on the electric hotplate throughout the meal. (Note, during eating it's fine to top up the broth with extra water as the liquid starts to evaporate.)

5. Mix the sesame paste ingredients together until smooth, then serve in individual bowls.

6. Once the broth has come to a boil, add raw ingredients to the hotpot as desired.

7. When cooked through, lift each piece out, dip into the sesame paste and eat.

# * Chorizo *

SPAIN/PORTUGAL

**A gloriously fatty cured Iberian pork, garlic and paprika sausage, available cooked, raw, sweet or hot. Slice into sandwiches, fry with eggs, or grill on its own... it's one of the world's great bangers.**

## What is it?

Who could resist chopped pig, speckled with fat, then heavily seasoned with salt and paprika? It's devoured all over Spain and Portugal, as well as the various Central and South American countries that were conquered by these once-great empires. The 'fresh' versions are cured for no more than a couple of days, and have to be cooked, while the 'cured' version can be sliced and eaten like salami.

## Origin

While sausages have played a starring role in Iberian cuisine since Roman times, the chorizo is a post-Columbian snag, appearing sometime in the 17th century. This is because the main flavouring, paprika, is a New World spice. Still, it's changed little since its inception: paprika-spiced pig meat and fat stuffed into a large or small intestine.

## Tasting

Ah, the charred snap of a perfectly grilled chorizo. The meat should be charred and glistening with scarlet juice, the flesh suitably piggy and the paprika strong, but never overwhelming. It has a rich majesty that lingers for minutes after, as well as a satisfyingly chewy texture. Some like theirs *picante* (or hot), with a subtle kick, while others prefer *dolce* (sweet), where the flavours are a little softer and more muted. If you can find shops and restaurants that specialise in their own recipe, so much the better. The difference between a cheap, mass-produced version and a handmade beauty is huge. The cooked version is thinly sliced and crammed into *boccadillos* (small sandwiches). It, too, can vary in taste and pungency. But for the true experience of chorizo, they're best eaten burning hot, straight from the grill.

## Finding it

It may be a touristy cliché these days, but lunch at Barcelona's Cal Pep (Plaça de les olles 8) is one of those things that has to be done at least once. Or twice. Old-school waiters give fast, often brusque service but the chorizo dishes are spot-on.

* VARIATIONS * **Mexican chorizo is rather different, in that the meat is ground, rather than chopped, and the sausage fresh, rather than cured. The red colour usually comes from red chilli, rather than paprika, and you'll find it cooked in tacos, burritos and fried up with eggs.**

* By Tom Parker-Bowles *

# Recipe Fabada

This is a rich, Spanish bean stew featuring chorizo, traditionally from the Asturia region. Enjoy with traditional accompaniments of crusty bread and apple cider.

## INGREDIENTS

1 cup dry haricot (navy) beans, soaked overnight

6 cloves of garlic

2 medium onions, quartered

1 bay leaf

4 tbs extra virgin olive oil

450g streaky bacon

160g (6oz) black pudding

3 chorizo sausages

1 small rump roast or several small pork ribs

Pinch of saffron threads

1 tbs sweet paprika

Salt (optional)

## METHOD

1. Drain the beans and place in a large pot of cold water (cover beans by about 5cm/2in) with the garlic, onions and bay leaf and bring to the boil.

2. Add the olive oil, bacon, black pudding, chorizo, rump roast/pork ribs, half-cover the pot with a lid and simmer for 1½ hours.

3. Add the saffron threads and paprika and simmer for another 1 to 1½ hours.

4. Taste and add salt if necessary, but you may be okay, given the saltiness of the sausage and bacon.

5. Remove the sausage, black pudding and roast from the pot, cut them into serving-size pieces then return to the pot.

6. Ladle into soup bowls and eat steaming hot.

SERVES 6

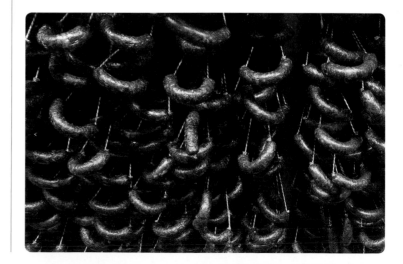

# * Çiğ Köfte *

## TURKEY

**Çiğ köfte is a gritty, raw-meat and cracked-wheat experience, buzzing with the scorching *isot* pepper of the Mesopotamian plains and served up in a crisp lettuce leaf.**

## What is it?

Translated literally as 'raw meatballs', *çiğ köfte* is the finest lean raw beef (or sometimes lamb), ground together with onions, tomato paste and bulgur (cracked wheat) and laced with trademark *isot* pepper from the city of Urfa in southeastern Turkey. This dark, fiery flaked pepper imparts an intense flavour and is said to 'cook' the raw ingredients. Served atop a lettuce leaf, *çiğ köfte* is a smooth-yet-crunchy mouthful of intense spiciness.

## Origin

*Çiğ köfte* is said to originate from the era of Biblical heroes and villains. In Urfa, on the edge of the Mesopotamian plain, King Nimrod piled all of the area's firewood into a massive execution pyre for his nemesis, the prophet Abraham. Left with no fuel for cooking, a local woman prepared a mixture of raw meat, bulgur and spices, grinding them together with mortar and pestle. According to the story, Abraham walked from the flames unharmed, and the dish gained lasting fame from its walk-on role in the legendary tale.

## Tasting

Generally served as a communal appetiser, *çiğ köfte* requires its own eating technique. Dishes of *çiğ köfte*, fresh lettuce, lemon segments and *isot* pepper are set out. Taking a lettuce leaf, spread it with the spicy-meaty mixture, drizzle with lemon juice, then – if you dare – add more *isot* pepper, and eat. The crisp lettuce is your first encounter, before you experience the creamy, meaty essence of the ground beef that is the core of the dish, also noticing the slight grittiness of the bulgur. Soon the peppery fire of *isot* will dawn on you, a slow smouldering that builds to a furnace-like intensity. This is your cue to reach for more cooling lettuce, or extra drizzles of lemon. Or to embrace the fire and wolf down more.

## Finding it

Due to the hygiene issues with preparing raw meat, it's difficult to find *çiğ köfte* in restaurants. Your best bet is to befriend a Turkish family and be invited home for dinner.

* **VARIATIONS** * Everyone has their own take on *çiğ köfte*. Other ingredients may include vinegar, pomegranate molasses, raw garlic or walnuts, and sprigs of fresh mint or parsley may be added to serve. An Ethiopian equivalent, called *kitfo*, consists of raw minced beef that has been blended with a chilli-based spice mix and doused in melted, clarified butter.

* By Will Gourlay *

# Recipe Çiğ Köfte

Making *çiğ köfte* is simple enough, but it is time consuming and labour intensive. And you must be prepared to get your hands dirty.

## INGREDIENTS

300g (11oz) bulgur

300mL water

1 large onion, chopped

300g (11oz) beef (or lamb), finely ground and as lean as possible

2 tbs tomato paste

Bunch parsley, chopped

1 tbs cinnamon

1 tbs cumin

Juice of 1 lemon

100g (3oz) *isot* pepper, or ground chilli flakes

1 lettuce (to serve; cos lettuce works well)

Lemon segments (to serve)

## METHOD

1.  In a large mixing bowl place bulgur, water and chopped onion. Mix together with your hands for up to 15 minutes until the bulgur softens.

2.  Add minced beef, tomato paste and chopped parsley, mixing to ensure all ingredients are evenly dispersed.

3.  While continuing to roll and knead for up to 30 minutes, progressively add cinnamon, cumin, lemon juice and *isot* (or chilli flakes). Experienced *çiğ köfte* makers will turn and fold their mixture constantly, periodically adding more *isot*, chopped parsley or lemon juice, and working to get as smooth a consistency as possible.

4.  Serve by placing a dollop of the mixture on lettuce leaves and dressing with a squeeze of lemon (and more *isot* if you are bold).

# * Crab with Kampot Pepper *

## KAMPOT, CAMBODIA

**Stir-fried crab served with Kampot pepper is one of Southeast Asia's tastiest dishes, best enjoyed to the sounds of the sea in close proximity to the source of its super-fresh ingredients.**

## Origin

Pepper has been cultivated in Cambodia for more than a thousand years, and from French colonial times to the 1960s, Kampot's aromatic pepper was regarded as the world's finest by Parisian chefs. The Vietnam War and the era of the Khmer Rouge halted production, but Kampot pepper is now reassuming its global renown. Most pepper is exported in dried form, but the just-picked unripe berry has a zingy, citrusy flavour that's perfect with stir-fried crab.

## Tasting

When Cambodia was a French colony, sleepy Kep was a beach escape for the French residents of Phnom Penh. With a compact waterfront corniche, it still retains a Gallic ambience but the town's famous crab market could only be in Southeast Asia. Fresh crabs are landed by fishermen in the morning and then it's just a short distance to hot woks. Eating crab initially looks challenging, but using a tiny fork makes it easy to extract the tender meat inside the shell and legs. The overriding flavour is the fragrant zing of green peppercorns, with a subtle saltiness and sweet notes coming from fish sauce and palm sugar. Ocean breezes from the Gulf of Thailand drift into the open-sided eateries and a chilled Angkor beer completes one of Cambodia's best dining experiences.

## Finding it

From lunch to evening, Kep's above-the-water eateries serve Kampot peppercorns with local crab and other seafood. Try the Kep Thmey or Kimly restaurants. A heaving plate should cost around 25,000 riel (US$6).

## What is it?

Briny-fresh crab is flash-fried in a steaming wok with ginger and garlic, married with fresh and zesty green peppercorns. It's a hearty dish that demands a back-to-basics approach to eating: find a breezy, rustic eatery in Kep's renowned crab market and tuck in with your fingers.

* **VARIATIONS** * Lots of other seafood is also tastily combined with Kampot peppercorns in southern Cambodia. Make your way along the rickety labyrinth of the Kep crab market to purchase prawns, squid and fish to accompany the region's world-renowned produce. Simply take your pick of the fresh seafood and within minutes it will be transformed into a spicy feast.

* By Brett Atkinson *

# Recipe Crab with Kampot Pepper

## INGREDIENTS

4–6 whole crabs (ideally mud or blue swimmer crabs)

2 tbs peanut oil

3 cloves of garlic, coarsely chopped

3 tsp ginger, finely chopped

4 Kampot green peppercorn vines (available in Asian grocery stores or online), or 2 tbs green peppercorns in brine, drained and carefully rinsed

1½ tsp fish sauce

2 tbs soy sauce

2 tsp palm sugar

6 spring onions, trimmed on the ends and sliced diagonally into chunks

## METHOD

1. Heat the oil over high heat in a hot wok until it's almost smoking. Add the whole crabs and stir-fry for around 5 minutes until almost cooked.

2. Add the garlic, ginger and peppercorns, and stir-fry for a minute until soft and fragrant.

3. Add the fish sauce, soy sauce and palm sugar and stir-fry for around two to three minutes until the sauce thickens.

4. Remove from the heat and stir in the sliced spring onions until they wilt.

5. Serve over steamed rice.

SERVES 2 TO 4

# * Dan Dan Noodles *

## CHINA

**This classic Sichuan dish is a tangle of yellow al dente egg noodles tossed in a fiery red chilli, Sichuan pepper and sesame sauce. The familiar nutty taste fronts the tingling pepper sensation in a rare meeting of hedonistic flavours.**

## What is it?

Yellow egg noodles are poached then doused in a sauce made from sesame paste, chilli and sesame oil, chilli paste and Sichuan peppers. This combo is topped with minced pork (or beef) fried with ginger, garlic and spring onions, and finished with a sprinkling of dry-roasted peanuts. The dish is commonly served as a side in a communal Sichuan spread. All hail the Sichuan staple.

## Origin

In Chinese days of yore, street vendors carried their kitchens in baskets hanging on *dan dan* – bamboo poles slung across their shoulders. At the request of hungry passersby, this mobile kitchen could be unharnessed for a fast-food noodle feast. The unique spicy-nutty noodle concoction soon became known as *dan dan* noodles, or *dan dan mian*, which translates as peddler's noodles. Today no Sichuan chow down is complete without a bowlful.

## Tasting

It's not unusual to have a sweaty brow and watering eyes before you've sat down in a Sichuan restaurant. They're packed with punters as keen for a chilli-hit as they are for sustenance. Bowls bubbling with chilli concoctions fill the room with piquant scents. Take a deep breath. Locals like to see a foreigner reeling after a chilli-oil–drenched mouthful of their native food. And if this is the case, *dan dan* noodles is a good option. Its mid-range spiciness is right on the money, with the different textures of noodles, meat and sauce contributing to varying levels of heat. The comfort of the nutty satay flavour lays the groundwork for overlapping chilli flavours. The punch to watch for is the Sichuan pepper. It creeps up on the palate like a tourist to a panda, creating a tingling or anaesthetised *ma-la* sensation, which is as addictive as the chilli hit. Seeing red? Water won't help – the only answer is to keep slurping.

## Finding it

Try Yu's restaurant, 4 Yiu Wa Street, Causeway Bay, Hong Kong. Expect to pay HK$76 (US$9) for the tasting set.

**\* VARIATIONS \* When made for the Western palate, the familiar nutty taste of sesame paste can win out over the chilli hit. The Taiwanese version, found at globally famed Din Tai Fung (dintaifung.com.au) restaurant, is probably the best example of this. American-Chinese versions, where peanut butter is often a substitute, are slightly sweeter.**

**\* By Penny Watson \***

# Recipe **Dan Dan Noodles**

## INGREDIENTS

300g (11oz) fresh egg noodles

2 cloves garlic

5cm (2in) piece of fresh ginger

3 spring onions, white and green parts

2 tbs peanut oil

200g (7oz) minced fatty pork (or beef)

1 tbs Shaoxing Chinese rice wine

Salt

1 handful dry-roasted peanuts, roughly chopped

## Sauce

3 tsp water

2 tbs light soy sauce

3 tbs tahini or sesame paste

1 tbs Chinese black rice vinegar

2–3 tbs chilli oil (adjust for chilli hit)

2 tsp sesame oil

1 tsp sugar

1 tsp ground Sichuan pepper

## METHOD

1. Bring a large pot of lightly salted water to the boil.

2. Cook the noodles for three to five minutes until al dente.

3. Rinse under cold water, then drain and tip into a serving dish.

4. In a small bowl whisk together all the sauce ingredients.

5. Pour the sauce over the noodles and toss. Set aside.

6. In a mortar, pound the garlic, ginger and two of the spring onions.

7. Heat the oil in a frying pan over medium-high heat. Add the garlic, ginger and spring onions, and fry briefly until fragrant. Add the meat and stir-fry until it is no longer pink and the pan gets sticky.

8. Deglaze with rice wine.

9. Season with salt.

10. Spoon the cooked meat mixture over the noodles, sprinkle with remaining chopped spring onions and peanuts. Serve straight away.

SERVES 2

# * Devil's Curry *

## SINGAPORE & MELAKA, MALAYSIA

**For those who haven't got the picture, this curry's name is derived from its hellfire-like spiciness. A mash-up of Asian spices with Portuguese elements, this dish will test your tastebuds.**

## What is it?

This is a curry made with a melange of meats – pork and/or chicken with sausages – cooked in a fiery chilli paste comprised of familiar Southeast Asian ingredients such as candlenuts, ginger and lemongrass.

## Origin

Devil's curry originated with the Kristang people, a Eurasian group of Portuguese and Malay descent that arose in the 16th century. Their cuisine is a blend of Portuguese and Malay styles and is particularly notable in Melaka (Malaysia) and Singapore. Legend has it that this dish, with its multiple meats, first came into being as a way of dealing with Christmas dinner leftovers.

## Tasting

Devil's curry looks like a sloppy mess. And the contents? Traditionally an unholy marriage of leftovers, where sausages are tossed in with the roast chicken. Yet devil's curry somehow comes together in beguiling fashion. The key to the dish is the complex curry paste made with a heap of red chillies combined with shallots, lemongrass, garlic, galangal, ginger and turmeric. The essential ingredients, though, are mustard seeds and vinegar, which together impart a sour and tangy flavour that cuts through the heat of the chillies. These days, short of crashing a Eurasian Christmas dinner in Singapore or Melaka, to sample devil's curry you'll have to find a Eurasian restaurant or cook it yourself. Like most curries, it develops further overnight, so cook a big pot and leave some for leftovers.

## Finding it

In Singapore, try it at Quentin's (www.quentins.com.sg). In Melaka, visit Restaurant Nyonya Makko (123 Jalan Merdeka, Taman Melaka Raya). Expect to pay US$15 to $20.

**\* VARIATIONS \*** Modern-day devil's curry is made with fresh meat. Though of Malay origin, the Kristang people aren't Muslims and have no qualms cooking it with pork instead of chicken. If you're a fan of offal, you're in luck as it tastes great in this curry. Some chefs add vegies such as cabbage, carrots, snowpeas and/or French beans in order to turn it into a one-dish wonder. You can reduce the amount of chillies to tone down the heat.

* By Shawn Low *

# Recipe Devil's Curry

## INGREDIENTS

1kg (2lb) chicken pieces (or pork, beef or offal; sausages can be added)

1 tsp soy sauce

3 tsp vinegar (any sort)

Vegetable oil

2 thick ginger slices, peeled and cut into matchstick lengths

2 large onions, peeled and quartered

6 large fresh red chillies, cut in half lengthwise

2 tsp mustard seeds

6 potatoes, peeled and quartered

Salt, sugar and extra vinegar to taste

2 tbs tamarind juice (soak 2 tbs tamarind pulp in ½ cup hot water and squeeze to extract juice)

### Curry Paste

2 tsp mustard seeds

30 shallots, peeled

5 cloves garlic, peeled

6 candlenuts, peeled (substitute blanched almonds or macadamias)

3 stalks lemongrass, white portion only, sliced

Thick piece of galangal, peeled and chopped roughly

¼ tsp turmeric

50 dried chillies, soaked in hot water for ½ hour and drained

### Optional

250g (9oz) vegetables (carrots, French beans, cabbage, etc)

## METHOD

1. Marinate the chicken with soy sauce and vinegar for ½ hour.

2. Blend all paste ingredients in a food processor until smooth. Add a little water if it's too dry.

3. Heat the oil in a large pan or wok over a medium-high heat. Add the ginger, onions and fresh red chillies. Fry until the ginger turns golden, remove and set aside.

4. Lower the heat to medium, add the mustard seeds and cook until they start popping. Add ginger, onion and chillies back to the pan.

5. Add the curry paste to the pan and fry, stirring constantly, until it turns dark with an oily sheen.

6. Add the chicken and potatoes and toss to coat well with the paste. Add the tamarind juice and enough water to cover the chicken.

7. Boil uncovered for 10 minutes, reduce heat to a simmer and cook until the chicken and potatoes are tender, about 30 minutes. The liquid should be reduced. Add the vegies, if using, and continue to cook until tender.

8. Season further to taste. Serve with jasmine rice.

SERVES 4

# * Doro Wat *

## ETHIOPIA

**Wrap some tangy *injera* (fermented pancake) around a morsel of *doro wat*, a chicken stew with a devilish hot fizz, pop it into your mouth and savour the tastes of highland Ethiopia.**

## What is it?

*Wat* is the catch-all name for a whole array of Ethiopian dishes that look like curries and act like curries, but often give a knock-out spice punch that few curries can match. *Doro wat*, which is virtually the national dish of Ethiopia, is a thick stew of chicken, egg and onion laced with the exotic-sounding *berbere* spice mixture.

## Tasting

There is an art to eating *doro wat*. Firstly, do away with plates, bowls and utensils and instead pile the *wat* on to a sheet of *injera*. On to what, you might ask? Unique to Ethiopia, *injera* can best be described as a large, thin, rubbery and rather sour-tasting fermented pancake made of *teff*, a cereal that grows only in the Ethiopian highlands. The *injera* serves as accompaniment, cutlery and, some would say, tablecloth to your *wat*; its bitter tang tempers the fire of the *wat*. In order to make your Ethiopian meal even more authentic, finish off with a brain-bendingly strong Ethiopian coffee (Ethiopia is the original home of the coffee plant).

## Origin

The history of *wat* and *injera* stretches back a long way, but like so much that is Ethiopian, the actual origins remain largely unknown. What we do know is that the ox and plough have been used in Ethiopia for at least 3000 years (in the rest of sub-Saharan Africa these items were unknown until just a couple of hundred years ago) and that *teff*, the essential behind *injera*, is probably as old. As for *wat*, that has been consumed in some variation for just as long, but the dish didn't gain its legendary bite until the arrival of the chilli with the first Portuguese.

## Finding it

Eat *doro wat* at the Dashen Traditional Restaurant (off Itegue Taitu St) in Addis Ababa. Budget Birr100–145 (US$5–8) for a meal.

**\* TIPS \* If your dining partner suddenly leans forward and, using their fingers, daintily places a morsel of *doro wat* and *injera* into your mouth, don't be alarmed. This is the Ethiopian custom of *gursha* and it's a sign of friendship or love.**

* By Stuart Butler *

# Recipe Doro Wat

## INGREDIENTS

### Berbere Spice Mixture

1 tsp ground ginger

½ tsp cardamom seeds

½ tsp fenugreek seeds

½ tsp ground coriander seeds

½ tsp ground cinnamon

¼ tsp ground cloves

¼ tsp allspice

2 tbs salt

½ cup cayenne pepper

½ cup sweet paprika

### Doro Wat

4 tbs *nit'r qibe* (Ethiopian spiced butter) or unsalted butter

2 large onions, roughly chopped

1 tbs garlic, freshly chopped

1 tbs fresh ginger, peeled and finely chopped

1–2 tbs *berbere* (to taste)

4 chicken legs

4 hard-boiled eggs

Salt

*Injera*

## METHOD

### Berbere Spice Mixture

1. Heat a large, heavy pan.

2. Add the ginger, cardamom, fenugreek, coriander, cinnamon, cloves and allspice; roast over a low heat for two minutes, stirring constantly to prevent burning.

3. Add the salt, cayenne pepper and paprika and roast over very low heat for a further 10 minutes.

4. Allow to cool; store in a sealed jar.

### Doro Wat

1. Heat the butter over low heat in a large wok or deep frying pan.

2. Add the onions and, stirring frequently for about 25 minutes, cook until caramelised.

3. Add the garlic and ginger and cook for five to eight minutes, until soft.

4. Add *berbere* and 2 cups of water. Stir well.

5. Season the chicken with salt.

6. Add the chicken to the wok, cover and simmer for about 40 minutes, stirring occasionally, until well cooked.

7. Uncover the wok and raise the heat to medium-high.

8. Simmer until the liquid has been reduced to a thick, gravy-like consistency.

9. Add eggs and stir to warm them through.

10. Taste and season with more *berbere* and salt.

11. Serve with *injera* and eat with the fingers.

SERVES 4

# * Ema Datse *

## BHUTAN

**Not so much a national dish as a national obsession: in Bhutan, *ema datse* is ubiquitous – a palpitation-inducing chillies-and-cheese combo that's much more than the sum of its two parts.**

## What is it?

Chillies with cheese. It's that simple: *ema* translates as chilli, *datse* means cheese. The chillies, green or red, are thrown into a pan with soft farmers' cheese, a little water, oil and onion till the cheese melts into a silky, sensuous coat for the hot peppers. Accompanied by rice, *ema datse* is an ever present at breakfast, lunch and dinner throughout the year.

## Origin

Chilli peppers hark from the Americas, of course, but spread rapidly through Asia from the 16th century, probably arriving in Bhutan a couple of centuries later. But whereas in India chillies are used mainly to add heat to dishes, in this long-isolated Himalayan kingdom they're considered vegetables – the core component of *ema datse* and an integral part of almost every other dish, though also served as condiments.

## Tasting

Whether you're at a swanky hotel restaurant or folding creaking knees to sit cross-legged by the *bukhari* (wood-burning stove) of a traditional farmhouse kitchen, *ema datse* will be arriving any moment now – it's not just customary, it's mandatory. Get ready to serve yourself as meals are invariably buffet-style affairs. Peer through the gloom (Bhutanese curtains are always closed) and pile rice on your plate, if you're lucky it's the favoured, nutty, red variety. Add a ladleful of dried beef stewed with – of course – chillies; in spring, you might also be treated to fresh asparagus or *nakey* (fern fronds). Finally, top with a hearty dollop of *ema datse*, and dive in. First, enjoy the crunch of sliced chillies, sweet and earthy; savour the contrast with the thick, rich cheese sauce as it folds around your tongue. Then reach for the Red Panda wheat beer and prepare to douse the oral conflagration. Repeat till sated and sweating profusely.

## Finding it

Plums Café on Chorten Lam, Thimphu, serves great *ema datse*. You'll pay 40–120 ngultrum (US$0.65–2), depending on whether fresh green chillies or dried red chillies are used (the latter are pricier).

* VARIATIONS * Takes on *ema datse* are diverse and personal. It tends to be drier and gloopier in the west of the country, runnier towards the east. Some people add garlic, tomatoes or other vegetables, particularly if they're trying to keep the heat down. Similar – but less fiery – dishes include *kewa datse* (potatoes in cheese) and *shamu datse* (mushrooms in cheese).

* By Sarah Baxter *

# Recipe Ema Datse

Choose chillies to suit your taste: large green ones give crunch and freshness, reds heat, dried chillies intensity. In Bhutan, home-made cows'-milk cheese is used, or rounds of cottage cheese bought at markets and roadside stalls; you can use pretty much any soft or medium-hard variety.

## INGREDIENTS

250g (9oz) large chillies, sliced lengthwise into 4

200g (7oz) soft cheese

1 medium onion or handful spring onions (scallions), diced

½ cup (125mL) water

4 tbs oil

Salt to taste

## METHOD

1. Place ingredients in a medium saucepan and cook on a low heat for 10–15 minutes till the cheese has formed a smooth sauce with the water and oil. Serve with rice. That's it.

2. For reduced tongue-burn, remove seeds from the chillies before cooking, and consider adding chopped tomato or other vegetables. Alternatively, if you'd prefer it turned up to 11, heat the water before adding the other ingredients.

SERVES 4

# * Enchiladas *

MEXICO & SOUTHWESTERN UNITED STATES

**In Spanish to *enchilar* something means to put chilli on it. When a chilli salsa is poured over a rolled, stuffed tortilla the dish becomes an enchilada. That's your cue to start smiling.**

## What is it?

Lightly fried corn tortillas are filled with shredded chicken, beef, pork or eggs and rolled like a taco. Three or four of these are then completely covered with a cooked, spicy salsa and garnished with thinly sliced onions, cheese (queso fresco or *añejo*), Mexican cream (*crema*), lettuce or cabbage, depending on the style of the *enchilada*.

## Origin

Dipping tortillas in salsa, or pouring over salsa, may have been an accident in pre-Hispanic Mexico (that is, before the arrival of Spanish conquistadores), or perhaps a genius move by hungry tribesmen. In any case, the domestic cultivation of maize or corn thousands of years ago allowed the creation of tortillas, and it is likely that somebody has been making some kind of *enchilada* ever since.

## Tasting

*Enchiladas verdes* (green *enchiladas*) are perhaps the most widely available *enchiladas* in Mexico. Often eaten for dinner at unpretentious restaurants, it's a dish whose apparent simplicity hides its complex blend of flavours and textures. Like most *enchiladas*, half the fun comes from the salsa and this one, made of tangy *tomatillos*, (a light-green berry), serrano or jalapeño chillies and a sprig of coriander (cilantro), has piquant potency and a hint of sweetness. The tortillas are filled with poached shredded chicken and topped with thinly sliced onions and sharp Mexican cheese (such as *queso añejo*) so that every bite offers six layers of greatness: tangy, spicy, a bit sweet, crunchy (from the onions and the fried tortillas), sharp (from the cheese) and soft juicy chicken that completes a delicious treat repeated in every bite.

## Finding it

El Bajío with ten locations in Mexico City is the place for enchiladas. The original location in Azcapotzalco (Av Cuitláhuac No. 2709, Mexico City) also offers a great traditional setting. Expect to pay about 80 Mexican pesos (US$9) a serving.

**\* VARIATIONS \*** There are as many kinds of *enchiladas* as regions in Mexico. But one of the most popular is the *enchiladas suizas* (Swiss-style *enchiladas*) in which the *enchiladas* include thick cream in the salsa and are baked in the oven instead of fried. A layer of melted jack cheese makes these *enchiladas* the ultimate-spicy casserole.

* By Mauricio Velázquez de León *

# Recipe **Enchiladas**

## INGREDIENTS

10 tomatillos, husked

3–4 serrano chillies or 2–3 jalapeños

2–3 sprigs of coriander (cilantro)

1 small onion, cut in chunks

1 clove of garlic

2 tbs canola oil

2 cups (500mL) chicken or vegetable stock

Salt

2 tbs canola oil

12 corn tortillas

1 large chicken breast, cooked and shredded

¼ cup (60mL) thick cream or sour cream

½ cup (125mL) *queso añejo* or mild parmesan

5–6 onions, sliced into rings

## METHOD

1. Boil the tomatillos and chillies in salted water for 10 minutes. Drain.

2. Puree the tomatillos, chillies, coriander, onion and garlic to make a salsa. This should make around makes 2½ cups of tomatillo sauce.

3. Heat the oil in a frying pan over a medium-high heat. Pour in the salsa and stir for 5 minutes; it will get darker and thicker.

4. Add the chicken or vegetable stock, add salt to taste, reduce heat and simmer for 10 minutes. Keep warm.

5. Heat the oil in a small frying pan and fry the tortillas quickly. You want to soften the tortillas but don't let them get too crispy. Drain on paper towels.

6. Pour a couple of tablespoons of the salsa onto a plate. Lay a tortilla over it and put some of the shredded chicken in the centre. Roll up. Repeat with 3 more tortillas.

7. Cover the enchiladas with salsa.

8. Sprinkle the enchiladas with cheese, a dollop of cream and onion and serve.

# * Fiš Paprikas *

## CROATIA

**Croatia's love for fresh fish meets Hungary's goulash traditions in this fiery fish broth from northeastern Croatia. This is a hot, hearty take on the traditional 'catch of the day'.**

## Origin

*Fiš paprikas* harks back to the Austro-Hungarian empire and is influenced by the cuisine of Croatia's northeastern neighbour, Hungary. In the Croatian region of Slavonia, fish such as trout, carp and catfish populate the Drava, Sava and Danuba rivers that carve up the land. The dish combines the resources available in the region – freshwater fish, homegrown paprika, farm-fresh chilli peppers and springwater.

## Finding it

*Fiš paprikas* country is Slavonia and Baranja, in northeastern Croatia, where you can find the dish in most traditional restaurants. Kovač Čarda, a little inn in the Baranja village of Suza, is rumoured to serve the best *fiš paprikas* of all.

## What is it?

River fish stewed in a paprika broth, served with noodles – the perfect antidote to a cloudy October day.

## Tasting

At the annual *fiš paprikas* competition held every July in Slavonski Brod, hundreds of participants line the river Sava with iron-cast cauldrons and buckets of freshly netted fish. Judges look for creativity as well as respect for the more traditional aspects of the recipe – cooking the dish over an open flame. If you don't own a cauldron, you can make *fiš paprikas* on a household burner or hob. You can also honour tradition by sticking to river varieties of fish. Catfish is a favourite in the region; afficionados say its flakes are softer in the mouth than those of carp or trout. The taste is enhanced by cut hot pepper and paprika, many varieties of which originate from the border region of Hungary and Croatia. Opt for a mixture of sweet and hot paprika if you can; for *fiš paprikas*, locals love the sweet, delicate *kulonleges* variety, mixed with the self-explanatory eros classification. The resulting dish is comforting and warming, with spice laced through the flakes of fish. Sometimes locals don a bib to avoid ruining their clothes in the heat of the moment.

**\* LOCAL FLAVOUR \* Connoisseurs of *fiš paprikas* like to make a two-course meal of it. They'll cook the broth and fish separately, tucking into the soup as a starter and the fish as a main course. And they won't hesitate to use their fingers to prise apart the cooked skins, fins and cheeks of the fish.**

# Recipe Fiš Paprikas

## INGREDIENTS

Olive oil

2 diced onions

2 tbs hot paprika

2 tbs tomato paste

Handful of cut hot pepper

1 bouillon cube

Packet of wide egg noodles

Pinch of salt

60mL white wine

Large freshwater fish, cleaned (trout, carp, catfish or pike)

## METHOD

1. Add the onions to a warm pan with a splash of olive oil and saute.

2. Add the tomato paste, salt, paprika, the cut fish, bouillon cube and 1.5Lt of water per kilo of fish.

3. Simmer over a medium flame for about 15 minutes.

4. Add the wine and cut hot peppers, and cook for another 30 minutes over a low flame. The sauce should have a rich broth-like consistency.

5. Cook the noodles in hot boiling water.

6. Pour the sauce over the noodles and serve.

SERVES 2

# * Fish Head Curry *

## SINGAPORE & MALAYSIA

**Though most Westerners shy away from dishes in which the main ingredient's eyes are included, food-mad Singaporeans swear it's the Peranakan fish's head that contains the sweetest meat.**

## What is it?

Somewhere between sour fish soup and hearty, spicy stew, fish head curry is among the most popular dishes in Singapore. Whereas reasonable copies of Hainanese chicken rice, chilli crab and other Singaporean favourites can be found around the globe, finding the genuine Peranakan variety of this dish outside of Singapore and Malaysia is trickier.

## Origin

As with many Peranakan dishes, the roots of fish head curry can be traced back to the early days of nautical migration and trade between East Asia, South Asia and the West. While today's dish might seem, at first glance, more heavily influenced by its South rather than East Asian roots, the Chinese fondness for fish head is well known, making the Peranakan version – like Singapore itself – a shining example of cultural cooperation.

## Tasting

Imagine: you're in an untouristy area of Singapore with restaurants known only to locals. The sun has just set and the temperature has dipped below sweltering. Now it's time to turn up the internal heat with this popular Singaporean dish which beautifully combines elements from across the continent.

Peranakan fish head curry has a sour-spice flavour that's reminiscent of *tom yum* (Thai seafood soup) and is more soup-like than traditional Indian curry. Eschew the Indian hand-to-mouth eating method; you'll want a spoon. The flavour comes from tamarind paste while the spice comes from chillies, the former acting as a brake on the latter, giving this dish a slow burn. Though the fish head is the dish's star, the fried tofu soaks up most of the flavour and okra adds crunch. For extra authenticity – or to impress your friends – try eating an eyeball. They are crunchy on the outside and gooey on the inside!

## Finding it

Restaurants throughout Singapore serve the dish for around US$15-30, but why not take a class from master chef Ruqxana Vasanwala at Singapore's Cookery Magic, *www.cookerymagic.com*.

---

**\* VARIATIONS \* Though the recipe traditionally calls for red snapper other types of fish create great results. Salmon is especially good, but use a bit less oil in the beginning as salmon tends to be a bit oilier than snapper. Cod also works nicely.**

* By Joshua Samuel Brown *

# Recipe Fish Head Curry

## INGREDIENTS

2 tbs oil

1 tsp fenugreek seeds

3 sprigs curry leaves

3 cloves garlic, finely chopped

2 onions, thinly sliced

6–8 small pickled red chillies, diced

3 tbs madras curry powder

2 tbs tamarind paste

Salt to taste

1 large (about 1kg/2lb) red snapper head

225g (½lb) fried tofu, cubed

8 large okra, cut lengthwise

2 big tomatoes cut into quarters

1 cup (250mL) coconut milk

1 tbs chopped coriander leaves

10 cups water

## METHOD

1.  Heat oil in a large soup pan over medium heat and add the fenugreek seeds and saute for one minute.

2.  Add the curry leaves and garlic and sauté for another minute.

3.  Add the onions and chillies and fry until the onions are light brown.

4.  Add curry powder and fry for another five minutes until fragrant.

5.  Add a splash of water and tamarind paste and salt and bring to boil.

6.  Reduce heat and simmer for 10 minutes.

7.  Add the fish head, okra, tofu, tomatoes and coconut milk and simmer until fish is cooked, about 10 minutes.

8.  Turn off heat and garnish with coriander leaves.

SERVES 4

# * Five Alarm Texas Chili *

## USA

In Texas, this slow-simmered beef dish with its fiery chilli paste is known as a 'bowl o' red'. The more 'alarms', the hotter the chili – five is the tongue-sizzling maximum.

## What is it?

Texas chili, also known as chili con carne ('chilli with meat' in Spanish), is a hearty meat and chilli stew, distinguished from other types of chili by its lack of beans or tomatoes. It's a staple of church cook-offs, backyard gatherings and football tailgate parties state-wide.

## Tasting

Though you can sample chili at nearly any greasy-spoon diner in the Lone Star State, attending a chili cook-off is undoubtedly the most authentic way to taste the spicy red stuff (and meet some authentic Texans to boot). On any given day in any given Texas town, someone is holding a cook-off – as a library fundraiser, a 4th of July celebration, or simply just for fun. Buy yourself a raffle ticket, grab a spoon, and get ready for some heat. The best chilis will be thick and never greasy, with tender chunks of meat and a slow-smoked flavour. The type of chilli used depends on the cook – popular bets are smoky *guajillos*; rich, dark *pasillas*; or singing-hot *árbols*. Cool your mouth down with a fat wedge of cornbread and a slug of Texas lager.

## Origins

Though chili is as humble a food as there is, its origin story is baroquely bizarre. According to legend, the recipe was invented by a 17th-century Spanish nun, Sister Mary of Ágreda, who, though she never physically left Spain, is said to have gone into trances and teleported to the American West, where she helped to evangelise the Native Americans. Supernatural tales aside, chili was probably invented by poor Texan settlers in the 1800s, who stewed tough chunks of beef into edibility.

## Finding it

The International Chili Championship in the ghost town of Terlingua, Texas, draws some 10,000 chili heads each November (US$5 a plate).

* VARIATIONS * Though the debate over whether beans can be included in 'authentic' Texas chili continues to rage, plenty of home cooks include pinto or kidney beans, as well as diced tomatoes, in their recipes.

* By Emily Matchar *

# Recipe Five Alarm Texas Chili

## INGREDIENTS

1kg (2lb) beef mince

250mL tomato passata

500mL water

½–2 tsp ground cayenne pepper
(depending on how spicy you want it)

1½ tsp salt

1½ tsp cumin

1½ tsp oregano

1½ tsp paprika

¼ small onion, minced

2 cloves garlic, minced

## METHOD

1. Brown beef in a large saucepan.

2. Add tomato and water and stir.

3. Add remaining ingredients and bring to a simmer.

4. Simmer for 45 minutes, stirring occasionally.

5. Serve with grated cheddar cheese and sour cream.

SERVES 4

# * Gaang Tai Plaa *

## SOUTHERN THAILAND

**For an authentic Thai curry that packs a potent punch, this fermented fish dish is a clear winner. Its unique curry paste simply explodes with flavour – and tongue-tingling heat.**

## What is it?

*Gaang tai plaa* overpowers almost every sense with its fiery curry paste, rich aroma and sunset-orange appearance. The paste seeps into fish chunks, vegetables and chilli to create a dish that is popular throughout Thailand, but is especially big down south. Available any time of year, it takes some skill to master but, done well, it is one of the true curry kings.

## Origin

Creative Thai cooks don't like to waste food – so they came up a novel way to involve every part of the fish in the cooking process. By fermenting the fish stomach (and sometimes other organs) they created *tai plaa*, a concoction that is vastly different from the more famous Thai curries and has its own special taste. In Southern Thailand coconut milk is often added to give it a local flavour; upcountry the coconut milk is usually omitted.

## Finding it

Krua Tong Na Tham, in Huai Yot, Trang offers excellent servings of *gaang tai plaa* for US$4 a dish.

## Tasting

Chances are you'll be perched on wooden benches with your toes in the sand somewhere in Southern Thailand when you sample the salty brilliance of this curry.

Like a good wine, it's worth taking in the powerful aroma first before ladling the *gaang tai plaa* over your rice. Let the curry soak in to the rice before pushing it onto your spoon, Thai-style. Enjoy the meaty fish chunks, the slight crunchiness of eggplant and long beans, and the admiring stares of locals who marvel at your ability to survive their local curry. Unlike other Thai curries, this one isn't simply laden with chillies; the peppers and paste give it an extra layer of heat.

## * TIPS *

Order *gaang tai plaa* with some less-fiery options to give your meal balance. Thais don't eat directly from the large serving bowl; they pour the curry over the rice that is on their own plates. The type of dried fish used can vary, but mackerel, tuna and saba are the most popular choices. In Southern Thailand it is also eaten with rice noodles.

* By Mark Beales *

# Recipe Gaang Tai Plaa

## INGREDIENTS

### *Tai plaa* paste

3 tbs fish stomach

1 handful of dried chilli pepper

2 tbs cumin

2 tbs sliced galangal

2 cloves of garlic

1 tbs chopped lemongrass

1 tbs black pepper

1 tbs of kaffir lime rind

2 red onions

Pinch of salt

### Curry

3–4 cups (750mL–1L) of water

1 cup of dried fish (tuna, Thai mackerel or saba)

1 tbs lime juice

1 cup of bamboo shoots

3 kaffir lime leaves

1 tbs of shrimp paste (*gra-bee*)

Handful of eggplant and long beans

1 cucumber, sliced

## METHOD

1. Clean the fish stomach then ferment it, with salt, for at least a week.

2. Take the resulting mixture and add it to a mortar and pestle, along with dried chillies. Bash it up, then pour in the other *tai plaa* ingredients and blend together.

3. Pour two cups of water into a wok and boil. Combine the *tai plaa* paste, chopped-up vegetables, shrimp paste and pound some more.

4. Add the dried fish with a little lime juice.

5. Let this simmer for around 5 minutes. Add water as needed to reduce saltiness.

6. Serve with boiled rice and a side salad of sliced cucumber.

SERVES 4

# * Gado Gado *

### INDONESIA

**This is the Indonesian street food of choice, a tasty and refreshing salad given added depth by its savoury peanut sauce, and eaten at all times of the day.**

## What is it?

*Gado gado* literally translates as '*mix mix*'. It's a salad of boiled and raw vegetables, sliced fried tofu and/or tempeh (fermented soy bean cake), potatoes and boiled eggs, with a generous portion of spicy peanut sauce stirred through. Finally, it's topped with crunchy *krupuk* (fried prawn crackers, a bit like potato chips on steroids) and a side-serving of *lontong* (rice cakes).

## Tasting

There's something authentic about wandering into a *warung* (small, family-run eatery) in Indonesia and not having to fuss with a menu in Bahasa Indonesian because it's so easy to say, '*Gado gado satu, terimah kasih*' ('One *gado gado*, thank you'). A *gado gado* is a study in texture and a medley of flavours. The base is warm (blanched vegies) and cold (fresh vegies) at the same time; soft yet crunchy. The peanut sauce that binds the dish together has a rich roasted nuttiness that's sweet, sour, spicy and crunchy all at the same time. The *krupuk* added to the salad adds a crispy savoury bite – just try not to lick your plate when you're done.

## Origin

The basic stuff that makes up much of modern-day Indonesian cooking – the chilli and nuts in particular – was brought to Indonesia by the Spanish and Portuguese around the 16th century. While no-one can truly trace the origins of *gado gado*, it's not hard to imagine its beginnings as a dish thrown together with available seasonal vegetables and dressed with something spicy. Indonesian celebrity chef William Wongso says that *gado gado* has 'probably been around for as long as we've had nuts and chillies.'

## Finding it

For around 30,000Rp (US$3), get it at Kartika Gado-Gado (Pondok Indah Plaza 2, Jln Sekolah Duta, Jakarta Selatan) in Jakarta.

---

**\* VARIATIONS \*** In Jakarta, sample the *betawi* version, served with tempeh, or the *boplo* version, which uses cashew nuts instead of peanuts: it's sweeter, finer and richer. Surabaya in East Java serves the *siram gado gado*: the salad is served with a bit of theatrical flair as the dressing is *siram* (poured) over the dish in front of the diner – try this version for a dinner party.

**\* By Shawn Low \***

# Recipe Gado Gado

## INGREDIENTS

### Salad

75g (3oz) bean sprouts

100g (3½oz) green beans, cut into 5cm lengths

200g (7oz) cabbage, sliced thinly

250g (9oz) tofu, fried till golden, quartered

2 eggs, boiled, quartered

1 medium cucumber, quartered lengthways then sliced into 3cm (1in) pieces

2 stalks Chinese celery, finely chopped

2 spring onions, finely chopped

20g (1oz) *krupuk* (prawn crackers)

### Peanut Sauce

2 cloves garlic

10 bird's-eye chillies

20g (1oz) *gula melaka* (palm sugar)

½ tsp salt

200g (7oz) peanuts, roasted

½ tbs shrimp paste

1 lime, juiced (or equivalent tamarind juice)

½ tbs *kecap manis* (sweet soy sauce)

1½ cups (375mL) water

### Optional

Fried tempeh, sliced into bite-size portions

## METHOD

1. For the sauce, grind the garlic, chillies, *gula melaka*, salt, peanuts and shrimp paste with a mortar and pestle until coarse. You can blitz this mixture in the food processor if you don't have a mortar and pestle.

2. Transfer the mixture to a bowl. Add the lime juice and *kecap manis*, mix well.

3. Slowly add the water, stirring the mixture at the same time. The sauce should have a gluggy consistency and not be too watery.

4. Prepare your salad by blanching the bean sprouts and green beans until they are cooked but still have crunch.

5. Combine all salad ingredients in a big mixing bowl. Add the peanut sauce, stir through to coat and serve.

6. Serve your *krupuk* on the side to crumble over the salad just before eating.

SERVES 4

# * Gan Guo *

## HUNAN, CHINA

**Dig into the sizzling, fiery red chillies of this signature dish
from central China to get to the main attraction – morsels
of tender beef, caramelised and crisp.**

## What is it?

*Gan guo*, or 'dry wok', describes how this dish is cooked. The dry wok method uses an intense flame and plenty of oil to bring out maximum flavour and spiciness. An alarming amount of chillies are tossed with ginger, garlic, crisp Chinese celery and beef, then served in a flash on a sizzling hot plate.

## Finding it

Huogongdian, 127 Pozi Jie, an institution in Hunan's capital Changsha since 1747, serves *gan guo* in various forms, including the popular *tian ji*, literally "land chicken" (also known as frog) for ¥40 (US$8).

## Tasting

For a full *gan guo* experience you will need one extra ingredient: an unbearably hot day. You'll already be sweating when you perch on your stool at a street stall, ready to dig in. Wait until the sizzling plate quiets, then take a bite. You'll be bowled over by the intensely savoury, sweet and spicy flavours of the beef, the crunch of celery, and the lingering kick of chilli. This is the magic of cooking over fast, high heat; dry wok cooking drives out the moisture from ingredients without burning them, lending a uniquely crisp and chewy texture. And as the sweat drips down your face and your eyes water, you'll have forgotten all about the scorching weather.

## Origin

Thousands of years ago, the culinary tradition known as Xiang grew out of the need to cope with the sweltering hot and humid climate of China's central region. To help eaters sweat it out, fiercely fiery Xiang dishes rely on liberal amounts of chilli and garlic cooked in lashings of oil. *Gan guo*, with its abundance of all three, is the most famous. Though simple in its ingredients, *gan guo* requires particular mastery over fire to ensure everything is cooked for just long enough and at the right temperatures to bring out flavours – without turning it into a slimy mess.

**\* VARIATIONS \* Hunan's neighbour to the northwest, Sichuan, puts its own spin on this dish by including its namesake pepper. *Huajiao* (Sichuan pepper), adds *ma* (a numbing heat) which, for better or worse, helps you to ignore the burning sensation of your tongue.**

# Recipe Gan Guo

## INGREDIENTS

1 tbs Shaoxing wine

1 tsp light soy sauce

1 tsp dark soy sauce

1 tbs cornflour

Pinch of salt

1 tbs water

340g (12oz) beef

5 tbs peanut oil

1 cup Chinese celery, very finely sliced

6 dried bird's-eye chillies, coarsely chopped

2 tsp dried chilli flakes

2 tsp ground cumin

1 tsp dark soy sauce

2 tsp minced ginger

1 tbs garlic, finely chopped

2 spring onions, very finely sliced

1 tsp sesame oil

Salt

Pepper

## METHOD

1. In a bowl, combine the wine, soy sauces, cornflour, salt and water to make the marinade.
2. Slice the beef across the grain into thin slices, then toss in the marinade.
3. Heat a wok over a high flame until a drop of water evaporates within a second or two of contact. Add 1 tbs of oil, then the celery, chillies, chilli flakes and cumin and stir-fry briefly until fragrant. Transfer the celery to a plate.
4. Add the remaining oil and heat until hot. Drain any excess marinade then add the meat.
5. Cook undisturbed for one minute, letting the beef begin to sear. Then stir-fry for one minute, until beef starts to release its juices and pan is sizzling as the liquid evaporates.
6. Reduce the heat to medium and continue stir-frying a few minutes until the beef is well browned and the wok is almost dry.
7. Swirl the soy sauce into the wok and stir fry for a few seconds until well combined.
8. Add the ginger and garlic and stir-fry for a few seconds until fragrant.
9. Add the celery again and stir-fry until warmed through and combined.
10. Add the sesame oil and spring onions, then salt and pepper to taste.
11. Remove immediately from the heat and serve.

SERVES 2 TO 4

# * Gong Bao Chicken *

SICHUAN, CHINA

**A fiery dance of chicken and peanuts, with a kick of dried chillies and a flourish of Sichuan pepper. Tamer versions abound, but it's most tantalizing in its authentic form.**

## What is it?

Gong Bao chicken is chicken breast stirfried with peanuts, dried red chillies and the highlight of the dish – Sichuan peppercorns which lend depth to the heat by creating a tingling feeling on the tongue. The dark-pink peppercorns, known as 'flower pepper' in Chinese, are also very aromatic. This simple, tasty and wholesome dish is eaten in Sichuanese restaurants all year round.

## Origin

The dish is named after Ding Baozhen, a Qing-era bureaucrat – Gong Bao was his title. While Ding was ruling Shandong, he crossed paths with the favourite eunuch and rumoured lover of the Empress Dowager. Eunuchs were banned from leaving the capital Peking under pain of beheading. Ding executed the protege and in accordance with tradition, put his naked body on public display for three days. His castration was plain to see, thus scotching the rumours and saving the Empress Dowager's reputation. Ding went on to become governor of Sichuan and it was there that he is said to have invented the dish.

## Finding it

Zhang Mama (張媽媽) at 4 Fensiting Hutong in Beijing serves a tantalising version for ¥15 (US$2.40).

## Tasting

The dish is characterised by *ma-la* or 'hot and numbing' spiciness unique to Sichuan. The *la* (heat) comes from the dried chillies while the Sichuan peppercorns provide the *ma* (numbing feeling). It's the contrast of chicken and peanuts that excites the palate – tender, succulent subtlety versus dry, crunchy roundedness. As you chew, the complex *ma-la* flavours in the oil are released and build up slowly into a tingling wave of heat. If you like chillies, the seared dried chillies pack a punch. The peppercorns, though deliciously aromatic, are better left alone. The dish is perfect with a bowl of fluffy white rice.

* VARIATIONS * Different variations have found their way to almost every Chinese restaurant outside Sichuan. One popular version features celery, bell pepper and a sweetish red chilli sauce. As the dish was deemed politically incorrect during the Cultural Revolution because of its association with the imperial court, it is sometimes also called hong bao chicken ('flash-fried chicken').

* By Piera Chen *

# Recipe Gong Bao Chicken

## INGREDIENTS

### Marinade

3 tsp light soy sauce

2 tsp Shaoxing wine

2 chicken breasts, diced into 1cm (½in) cubes

### Sauce

1 tsp dark soy sauce

1 tsp light soy sauce

3 tsp Chinese black vinegar

1 tsp sesame oil

1 tbs water

2 tsp sugar

A pinch of cornflour

### Stir-fry

12 dried red chillies

4 tbs oil

2 tsp whole Sichuan peppercorns

Ginger, a piece about 3x3cm, thinly sliced

3 cloves of garlic, thinly sliced

3 spring onions, cut into 2cm (1in) pieces

⅔ cup plain roasted peanuts

## METHOD

1. Mix together the light soy sauce and the Shaoxing wine to make the marinade. Pour it over the chicken, toss to coat evenly and marinade for 2 hours.

2. Mix together all the sauce ingredients.

3. Snip off the stems of the chillies. Leave the chillies whole if you want the dish to be really hot. If not, half them and remove the seeds.

4. Pour the oil into a wok or pan. When it is hot add the chillies and Sichuan pepper and stir-fry quickly for a few seconds until fragrant, taking care not to burn.

5. Add the chicken, ginger, garlic and spring onions, and continue to stir-fry until the meat is just cooked.

6. Pour the sauce into the wok or pan, stirring and tossing to coat the ingredients thoroughly. As soon as the sauce becomes thick add the peanuts.

7. Serve immediately.

SERVES 2

# * Goulash *

## HUNGARY

**Hungary's national dish has a proud history of providing a filling meal and sustaining early Magyar cattle herders – a tradition that continues in Hungarian households and restaurants today.**

## WHAT IS IT?

Hungarian goulash is a simple, hearty feast of tender beef chunks and root vegetables, flavoured with the semi-sweet and pungent local paprika. The medium sauce-like consistency of the brick-red broth makes it an intriguing cross between a soup and stew.

## TASTING

Long cold winters in Hungary require warming, slow-cooked, nourishing comfort foods such as goulash, which go perfectly with filling noodles or dumplings. Not to be confused with that other Hungarian staple *pörkölt* (a dry-fried meat stew), a soothing bowl of goulash is a one-pot wonder of beef and vegetables. It becomes a complete and satisfying meal when cooked with handmade egg noodles called *csipetke*. Unlike the smoky Spanish version or the mild generic versions found in most supermarkets, the Hungarian paprika used in traditional goulash provides an intense red capsicum flavour and deep red colour to the dish. The paprika can come in mild, sweet, semi-sweet and hot varieties, depending on the type of capsicum, but even the hot versions will have a more complex aroma and taste than cayenne or chilli powder, lending a more nuanced depth of flavour and colour to goulash.

## ORIGIN

Goulash was the staple meal of herders who drove cattle on Hungary's plains as far back as the 9th century. The herdsmen would cook the stew in iron kettles over a fire for sustenance, supposedly using animals that couldn't make the trip. The stew would be cooked until almost dry for storing in bags made of sheep's stomachs and later reconstituted with water into a stew. Paprika was not considered a crucial ingredient until the Turks introduced the spice to the country in the 18th century.

## FINDING IT

Enjoy an authentic goulash with homemade noodles in the atmospheric garden of Vár: a Speiz, one of Budapest's most charming traditional restaurants. Expect to pay around HUF1800 (US$8).

**\* VARIATIONS \*** Plenty of variations exist with each household generally having their own spin on the basic version, from additional ingredients such as *székegulyás* (with cabbage), *babgulyás* (with beans) and *birkagulyás* (with mutton), to different degrees of spiciness in the paprika, from mild to hot.

* By Johanna Ashby *

# Recipe Goulash

An easy dish to replicate at home but do try to use Hungarian paprika, which lends the dish its characteristic warmth and bittersweet taste. Chop the meat and vegetables to the same approximate sizes for even cooking.

## INGREDIENTS

500g (1lb) stewing or braising beef, cubed

1 tbs vegetable oil

2 medium onions, diced

2 cloves garlic, minced

3 tbs Hungarian paprika

1 tsp caraway seeds, ground

Pinch of cayenne pepper

3 medium carrots, cubed

400g (14oz) potatoes, cubed

2–3 cups (500–750mL) of water

## METHOD

1. Heat the oil in a heavy-based casserole pot. Add the onions and cook until soft and golden.

2. Add the beef and stir until the meat is no longer pink and any liquid has evaporated.

3. Add the garlic and spices and fry for a few minutes to coat the beef with the paprika. Add enough water to just cover the meat. Bring to a boil.

4. When the soup has boiled, add the potatoes and carrots. Turn down to a simmer for at least an hour or until the beef is tender and the potatoes and carrots are cooked.

5. Season the soup with salt and more caraway as required.

6. Serve with crusty bread or fresh egg noodles.

SERVES 4

# * Groundnut Soup *

### GHANA

**A creamy, nutty, spicy, comforting full-meal-in-a-bowl; groundnut soup is your lip-smacking passport to West Africa.**

## What is it?

A rich soup traditionally made with roasted groundnuts (peanuts) although peanut butter is more commonly used these days. It's simmered slowly along with ginger, garlic, tomato and chicken to create a quintessential Sunday lunch dish that's spicy but not painfully so. It's most commonly served with *omo tuo* (balls of sticky pudding rice), *fufu* (pounded cassava) or a side of grilled plantain.

## Origin

According to legend, the first versions of groundnut soup appeared in West Africa in the 1600s after Spanish and Portuguese colonists brought groundnuts to the continent from South America. The nuts were seen as an ideal thickener for soups or stews at a time when milk and dairy products were difficult to obtain.

Its influence has spread far and wide. African-Americans often serve groundnut soup (or peanut butter soup as they call it) during Kwanzaa – the week-long holiday between December 26 and January 1, that honours African culture and traditions – as a way of celebrating the modest nut's important ties to their African roots.

## Tasting

You're not looking for a bowl of liquid peanut butter; the best groundnut soup is an exercise in subtle nuttiness – deep, rich and enhanced by the zing of Scotch bonnet chillies and an aromatic, tomatoey base. The texture should be silky smooth, robust and satisfying without descending into sauce-like thickness.

Then there's the serious business of mopping up. Some prefer the dense stickiness of *omo tuo*; others a doughy glob of *fufu*. Both are a perfect vehicle for soaking up the creamy goodness. Chicken pieces should be firm, grab-holdable and on the bone – all the better for dunking and slurping.

And forget about cutlery – have a wash in the finger bowl and go: getting stuck in with your hands is all part of the experience (eat with your right hand please!). After all, shouldn't the end of a good meal be punctuated by the licking of the fingers?

## Finding it

Groundnut soup is served everywhere in Ghana, from the humblest of home kitchens to the chicest of Accra hangouts, but it's best enjoyed on a Sunday in a local restaurant; Accra's Country Kitchen is a good bet where a portion costs about 12 Ghana cedis (US$5.70).

* TIPS * If at all possible, hunt down the old-school version: the tang of freshly roasted groundnuts infuses the soup with a charred loveliness that's difficult to imitate.

* By Nana Luckham *

# Recipe Groundnut Soup

## INGREDIENTS

1 whole chicken, jointed, preferably free range and corn fed

2 medium onions

1 large, very ripe tomato

1 Scotch bonnet chilli pepper

Pinch cayenne pepper

3cm (1in) piece of ginger, peeled and grated

3 tbs peanut butter

1 small glass of water

Salt to taste

Additional water

## METHOD

1. Put the chicken pieces in a large pot, cast iron if possible.

2. Chop one of the onions and scatter over the chicken along with a pinch of salt.

3. Put the pan on the lowest heat, cover and cook very gently for 15 minutes.

4. Don't chop the remaining onion, the tomato or the Scotch bonnet chilli pepper but keep them whole and add to the pot with the cayenne pepper and grated ginger, then simmer for 10 more minutes.

5. Meanwhile put the peanut butter in a blender along with the glass of water and whizz to a smooth paste.

6. Pour the peanut paste into the pot and simmer for 10 minutes.

7. Remove the tomato, onion and Scotch bonnet chilli pepper from the pan. Put in the blender and puree to a smooth paste.

8. Pour back into the pot, add enough water to just cover the chicken and simmer for 30 minutes. Serve with *omo tuo* (rice balls) or *fufu* (pounded cassava).

# * Hong Shao Niu Rou Mian *

## TAIWAN

**Though Taiwan has earned its place on the Asian culinary must-visit map, Taiwanese dishes aren't known for incendiary spiciness. This blistering Taiwanese classic may change that.**

## What is it?
Big chunks of tender beef floating in a savoury, spicy broth rich with flavours found only in the Far East. Slow-cooking is the key to the beef's tenderness and spices are the key to its flavour. The experience is rounded off with fresh and crunchy bok choy and melt-in-your mouth noodles.

## Origin
You'll find dishes called 'beef noodle soup' throughout Asia, but Taiwan has made this dish its own by localising the ingredients and spicing it up several notches. Beef consumption wasn't big here before 1949 so it's likely the dish was brought to the island by mainlanders fleeing China's civil war. Spicy stewed-beef noodle soup has existed in China since the Tang Dynasty (AD 618-906). It was popularised by members of the Hui, a Chinese Muslim ethnic group known for making amazing hand-pulled noodles.

## Finding it
Tao-Yuan-Street Beef Noodle Shop (15 Taoyuan St, Zhongzheng District, Taipei) is famous for its good *hong shao niu rou mian*. A bowl goes for US$3.

## Tasting
So readily available is this dish in Taiwan that most take its complexity for granted; but as any chef will attest, making good spicy beef noodle soup is complex and time consuming. Is it worth it? Yes!

The secret of this dish lies in the process of heating and cooling, allowing the broth to concentrate a very diverse list of ingredients into a unified, spicy – and uniquely Taiwanese – flavour. Good spicy beef noodle soup tempts the tongue without burning it, the anise and five spice offering a rich, savoury counterpoint to the fiery Sichuanese chillies. The beef is both infused with flavour and tender enough to pull apart with chopsticks. It is often served with a small bowl of chilli-infused dark vinegar mixed with soy sauce.

**\* CURE FOR THE COMMON COLD? \*** If you are in Taiwan during a cold snap you may find that stalls selling spicy beef noodles have standing room only. The Taiwanese consider this dish prophylactic against colds, flu and other cold-weather ailments. Star anise is considered to be a traditional remedy and is often prescribed for rheumatism, colds and influenza.

**\* By Joshua Samuel Brown \***

# Recipe Hong Shao Niu Rou Mian

## INGREDIENTS

1 kg (2lb) beef chuck roast, cut into 4 chunks

1 tsp Chinese five spice powder

3 tbs canola oil

8 garlic cloves, chopped finely

2cm (1in) chunk of fresh ginger, sliced

5 spring onions (scallions), cut crosswise

4 dried star anise

2–4 tbs Sichuan peppercorns

3–4 red chillies, split lengthwise

¼ cup (60mL) chilli bean sauce

¼ cup (60mL) rice wine

6 tbs light soy sauce

2 tbs dark soy sauce

10 cups water

1 bok choy cut into large chunks

500g (1lb) thick Chinese egg noodles

## METHOD

1. Season beef with salt.

2. In a saucepan, heat oil and sear beef on both sides.

3. Add all remaining soup ingredients (except for noodles and bok-choy).

4. Bring to a boil, skimming fat from the top as necessary.

5. Lower heat and simmer for about two hours.

6. Take soup off heat; uncover pot, allowing broth to concentrate.

7. When broth has cooled, remove the meat and set aside.

8. Strain the broth into another pot, discarding solids before reheating over medium heat.

9. Cut the meat into half-inch thick pieces before returning it to broth. Add bok-choy.

10. Cook noodles in fresh pot of water until desired texture. Strain and place in individual bowls.

11. Add broth, meat and bok choy to bowls with noodles.

SERVES 6

# * Hot Chicken *

## NASHVILLE, TENNESSEE, USA

**In Nashville, 'hot' chicken doesn't refer to temperature, it refers to the near-atomic spice level of this chilli-battered fried delight, served up at hole-in-the-wall restaurants throughout Music City.**

## What is it?

Though the exact recipes are closely guarded secrets, hot chicken essentially consists of chicken quarters, brined, deep-fried to a shattering crisp in a cast-iron pan and then basted with a hot chilli glaze. It's served over slices of white bread to sop up the grease, and topped with a smattering of pickle chips.

## Origin

Fried chicken is beloved across the American South. Its origins lie with the Scottish immigrants who settled much of the region, bringing with them their taste for fried food. Later, slave cooks on Southern plantations added their own spices. The 'hot' twist comes from North Nashville's beloved Prince's Hot Chicken restaurant. Supposedly, the original owner's girlfriend fried him up a piece of secretly pepper-doused chicken as revenge for cheating. He loved it so much he opened a restaurant specialising in the mouth-burning stuff!

## Finding it

Prince's Hot Chicken is the original, and still by far the best (chicken quarter US$5).

## Tasting

Sampling hot chicken requires patience. The best of the dozen or so Nashville establishments specialising in the dish use cast-iron pans to fry their chicken, which takes significantly longer than using a deep fryer. Most are simple joints, tucked away in strip malls or between pawn shops in down-at-the-heels parts of town. Order a white-meat breast quarter, or – the local preference – a dark-meat thigh quarter, and choose from mild, medium, hot or extra hot. Newbies should not be embarrassed to go for mild – believe us, it will be more humiliating to spit a bite of extra hot across the table when you discover you can't take the nuclear heat. The crispy skin is orange with chilli, dripping salty, flavoursome juice from the brined meat. If the heat level is getting to you, order extra slices of cottony white bread to cool down your tongue.

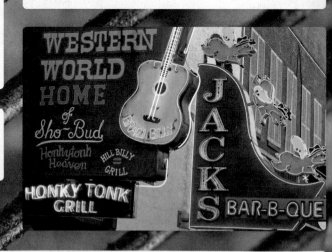

**\* VARIATIONS \*** Hot fish is a mild white fish, often catfish or whiting, fried in the same spicy batter as hot chicken.

\* By Emily Matchar \*

# Recipe Hot Chicken

## INGREDIENTS

2L cold water

250mL hot sauce (such as Tabasco)

150g (5oz) plus 1 tsp salt

100g (3½oz) plus ½ tsp sugar

1.6–1.8kg (3½–4lb) whole chicken, quartered

2.8L peanut oil

1 tbs cayenne pepper

½ tsp paprika

¼ tsp garlic powder

250g (9oz) flour

Black pepper to taste

## METHOD

1.  In a large bowl, stir the cold water, hot sauce, 150g salt and 100g sugar until the salt and sugar dissolve.
2.  Add the chicken to the brine and refrigerate, covered, for 30 minutes.
3.  Preheat oven to 95°C (200°F).
4.  Heat three tablespoons of peanut oil in a small saucepan over medium heat, and add cayenne, paprika, garlic powder, ½ tsp salt and remaining sugar. Cook for 30 seconds then transfer to a small bowl and set aside.
5.  Remove chicken from refrigerator and pour off brine.
6.  In a large bowl, combine flour, remaining salt and black pepper to taste.
7.  Dredge chicken pieces in the flour mixture then shake off excess. Repeat this process, then transfer chicken to a wire rack.
8.  In a large Dutch oven over medium-high heat, heat the remaining oil to 175°C (350°F).
9.  Fry chicken, two pieces at a time, at 150°C (300°F) to 160°C (325°F) until skin is golden brown (about 30 minutes). White meat must register 70°C (160°F) and dark meat 80°C (175°F).
10. Drain chicken on wire rack and keep warm in preheated oven while cooking the remaining chicken pieces.
11. Stir spicy oil mixture to recombine and brush over both sides of the chicken.
12. Serve chicken on sliced white bread with sliced pickles.

SERVES 4

# * Jamaican Jerk *

## CARIBBEAN

**This is a delicious, surprisingly easy-to-recreate dish from the Caribbean. The melange of allspice, cloves, cinnamon, nutmeg and thyme will evoke tropical breezes wherever you are.**

## What is it?

Jerk is a broad term, referring to both a spice mix and method of cooking. For cooking and eating pleasure, you need know only the following: unless your marinade is complex, spicy and tasty – containing at least half of the spices suggested and something from the capsicum pepper family – it's only barbecue. And if you're not turning frequently over a hot flame, you're not jerking it.

## Origin

Like many Caribbean dishes, Jamaican jerk traces its roots back to West Africa, where meats were spiced with a variety of tasty, tongue-numbing spices prior to cooking. There are two prevailing theories on the origin of the term jerk – one says it comes from the Spanish word *charqui*, meaning dried meat. Most Jamaicans, however, insist the term jerk comes from the cooking method, which calls for regular turning (or jerking, in Jamaica).

## Tasting

Good jerk should be simultaneously spicy and sweet, paradoxically simple and complex. The meat, marinated for at least four hours, is tender enough to cut with a spoon. And the flavour is complex; the sweetness of molasses brings out the fiery habanero peppers (the hottest of the capsicum peppers and not for the faint of heart) without covering them up, while the hodge-podge of other Caribbean spices adds a veritable bouquet of flavours not found in a typical barbecue dish. But making jerk is more art than science, and a true jerk chef cooks as much from intuition as any set recipe. When making your own, put on some reggae music and set your inner-child free. When cooking, turn and baste frequently to keep the meat from drying out. Leftover marinade can be boiled (to sterilise it) and used for dipping sauce.

## Finding it

Jambel's Jerk Pit on Ambergris serves some of the best jerk in Belize; their buffet is rightly famous. Expect to pay around BZ$20 (US$10).

**\* VARIATIONS \* Though chicken is the most popular jerk dish, nearly any protein that can be seasoned and jerked on a grill can be called jerk. In Belize, you'll find jerk shrimp, fish, conch, even lobster. And jerk goat is popular from Kingston to Brooklyn. Vegetarian? Freezing your tofu in the marinade will make it tough enough to stand up to any grill.**

* By Joshua Samuel Brown *

# Recipe Jamaican Jerk

## INGREDIENTS

1 tbs ground allspice

1 tbs dried thyme

½ tsp cayenne pepper

½ tsp freshly ground black pepper

½ tsp ground sage

¾ tsp ground nutmeg

¾ tsp ground cinnamon

2 tbs garlic powder

1 tbs molasses

¼ cup olive oil

¼ cup soy sauce

¾ cup apple cider vinegar

½ cup orange juice

2 habanero peppers, finely chopped

3 green onions – finely chopped

2–3kg (4–6¼lb) chicken breasts

## METHOD

1. Create marinade by combining the ingredients above then marinate your chicken overnight.

2. Cook on grill over medium-high flame, turning and basting frequently.

SERVES 4

# * Jambalaya *

### LOUISIANA, USA

**Iconic enough to inspire a classic country song (Hank Williams' 'Jambalaya (On the Bayou)'), *jambalaya* is the original fusion cuisine, a rice and meat concoction with a thousand possible variations.**

## What is it?

*Jambalaya* is essentially Spanish paella with French and New World twists – rice mixed with chicken, Andouille sausage, garlic, celery and capsicum (bell pepper), and various types of seafood. In the Cajun bayou lands, *jambalaya* might contain anything from alligator to turtle to *nutria* (a type of native rodent). The kick comes from a dash of Louisiana hot sauce or cayenne pepper.

## Origins

The word *jambalaya* is said to combine the French word for ham (*jambon*) with the French *a la* (meaning 'with') and *ya*, a West African word for rice, though this may be apocryphal. Born in Cajun Country Louisiana, it was likely an attempt to make paella without saffron. Local cooks substituted tomatoes for colour and flavour, and the dish became popular among frugal home cooks looking to make a hearty meal with whatever odds and ends were in the house.

## Tasting

*Jambalaya* is best known as a home-cooked dish, a staple of family Sunday lunches or church picnics. And everyone's *grandmère* makes the best version, mais oui! Non-natives can seek *jambalaya* at the more casual – some might say divey – pubs and late-night haunts of New Orleans. Order a steaming bowl of whatever's on special that night – gamey rabbit, salty-savoury sausage, sweet crayfish – and chow down, shaking more vinegary Louisiana hot sauce on to taste. Each bite holds dozens of flavors – the freshness of rice, the meaty chew of Andouille, the sting of garlic, the brininess of shrimp. Cool your sizzling taste buds with a chilled Abita ale, brewed just 30 miles away from NoLa.

## Where to find it

Cheap, local and open late, Coop's Place in New Orleans' French Quarter is the place to go for a cool brew and a hot bowl of *jambalaya* (US$6).

* **VARIATIONS** * *Gumbo*, another Cajun specialty, contains similar ingredients to *jambalaya*, but the rice is cooked separately. *Étouffée*, rice smothered with a spiced seafood stew, is also similar.

* By Emily Matchar *

# Recipe **Jambalaya**

## INGREDIENTS

2 tsp olive oil

2 boneless chicken breasts, chopped into 2.5cm (1in) pieces

250g (9oz) Andouille sausage, sliced

1 onion, diced

1 capsicum (bell pepper), diced

1 stick celery, diced

2 cloves garlic, chopped

½–1 tsp cayenne pepper

½ tsp onion powder

400g (14oz) white rice

1L chicken stock

3 bay leaves

2 tsp Worcestershire sauce

1 tsp hot sauce (such as Tabasco)

Salt and pepper to taste

## METHOD

1. In a large saucepan, heat oil over medium-high heat. Saute chicken and Andouille sausage until lightly browned.

2. Add onion, capsicum, celery, garlic, cayenne, onion powder and salt and pepper.

3. Cook, stirring, until onions are soft and translucent, about five minutes.

4. Add rice, chicken stock and bay leaves. Bring to the boil, then reduce heat, cover and simmer for 20 minutes.

5. Stir in Worcestershire sauce and hot sauce and serve.

SERVES 6

# * Jollof Rice *

WEST AFRICA

**No social function is complete without jollof rice, the poster food for West Africa, a delectable one-pot meal of fragrant, chilli-spiked rice.**

## What is it?

The region's version of paella or risotto, jollof is made by simmering long-grain rice with tomatoes, chilli, onion, stock and, depending on who you speak to, any number of meats or vegetables. Like the American dishes it influenced (it's at the root of *jambalaya* and *gumbo*), jollof has endless variations, but the colour remains the same: a joyful bright umber.

## Origin

Rumour has it that jollof rice was first cooked up by members of the Wolof tribe in Senegal (Wolof/jollof, get it?), whose empire covered wide swaths of western Africa from the 14th through to the 19th centuries. In some areas, including Gambia, jollof rice is known as *benachin*, which literally translates as 'one pot'. Whether you add okra, plantain or fish comes down to fiercely held regional preferences.

## Tasting

Good jollof rice isn't going to make you cry chilli-induced tears. It's much more subtle than that – a gentle burn of tomatoes, onions, hot pepper and perfectly al dente rice (this isn't a risotto or a rice pudding), that builds up slowly enough to warm the tastebuds without blowing your head off with intense spice heat. The best jollof is cooked outdoors in vast iron cauldrons over wood fires, infusing the rice with a delicate smokiness and leaving crunchy scrapings at the bottom of the pan.

Eat it shoulder to shoulder in a street-side 'chop bar' (local cafe, often in a shack) to add to the authenticity. Come late morning for lunch or dusk before the evening rush, when the food is fresh, the company warm and the radio blaring.

## Finding it

Chop bars, street stalls, fancy restaurants, wedding receptions: it's more surprising to find a place that doesn't serve jollof than one that does. Try the much-loved Katawodieso roadside cafe in Labone, Accra where you can fill up for 7 Ghana cedis (US$3.20).

* VARIATIONS * The authenticity of jollof is a subject of fierce debate – every country in West Africa has its own version and recipes differ from household to household. While Nigerians favour a 'pure' version, with little in the way of added vegetables or meats, others would think a bowl of jollof without meat or seafood incomplete.

* By Nana Luckham *

# Recipe Jollof Rice

To get the right texture make sure to use long-grain, preferably basmati rice, and don't overdo it on the liquid or you'll end up with a pile of mush.

## INGREDIENTS

1 tbs olive or vegetable oil

1 large onion, finely diced

6 large tomatoes, skinned and diced

1 red pepper, finely chopped

1 Scotch bonnet chilli, finely chopped

1 clove garlic

1 tsp curry powder

2 tbs tomato puree

¼ tsp cayenne pepper or chilli powder

225g (8oz) long-grain or basmati rice

1 vegetable or chicken stock cube

Salt and freshly ground black pepper

## METHOD

1.  Heat the oil in a large pan and cook the onion over a gentle heat until soft.

2.  Stir in the tomatoes, red pepper, Scotch bonnet chilli, garlic, curry powder and tomato puree, then season with salt, freshly ground black pepper and the cayenne pepper and fry for 15 minutes or until you have a thick pulp.

3.  Add the rice and fry in the tomato mixture for one or two minutes until well coated.

4.  Dissolve the stock cube in 500mL (2 cups) of water and add the stock to the pan.

5.  Bring to the boil then turn to a low heat and simmer, covered, for 20–30 minutes until all the stock is absorbed and the rice is cooked al dente.

6.  Serve with fried plantains or alongside grilled meat or fish.

# * Kak'ik *

## GUATEMALA

**This ancestral turkey soup boiled up by the Maya of Guatemala's highlands is as faithful to pre-Hispanic Latin American cuisine as it gets, with a startling red hue evoking the blood of ancient sacrificial rites.**

## What is it?

Amalgamate roasted endemic chillies, tomatoes, red peppers and the gooseberry-like tomatillo fruit along with garlic, onions and coriander (cilantro) into a broth invigorated by fiery annatto seed paste and boil with a ritually prepared turkey: preparation today is exactly as it was at the zenith of the Mayan Empire.

## Origin

*Kak'ik* is the dish time forgot: fascinatingly, it's unchanged from when the Q'eqchi' Maya, Guatemala's largest ethnic group, were cooking it a millennia back. Several ingredients, like the tomatillos and the *guaque/pasilla* chillies, herald from the Mexican part of Mayan civilisation, but *kak'ik* concocted in the proud home of the dish (Alta Verapaz's capital, Cobán) utilises miniscule-but-distinctive smoky *chiles cobaneros* (Cobán chillies). This limits the outlets serving true *kak'ik* to a select bunch around this highland city. The 'ik' suffix in Mayan means spicy. *Kak'ik* was granted intangible cultural heritage status by Guatemala's Ministry of Culture and Sports in 2007.

## Tasting

Don't visit the fanciest restaurants to experience *kak'ik*: it's the rudimentary back-street kitchens and street-side stalls, manned (actually, usually womanned) by the Maya, which offer the very best.

Better yet, sample it in a family home. Preparation, as eye-catching as the finished dish, begins hours before *kak'ik* arrives on the table, with the traditional killing, smoking, boiling and plucking of the turkey. Then there's the assembly of the vibrantly coloured vegetables: the reds (peppers, tomatoes), the greens (tomatillos) and a spectrum from vermillion through mahogany for the chillies. Cobbled together, the resulting broth should be russet red-orange, achieved by slow roasting until ingredients are caramelised and slightly blackened, and by adding annatto seed paste.

*Kak'ik* is as hot as its colour suggests. The 'ik' (spiciness) hits you in a four-flanked attack of the three chillies followed by the nutty pepperiness of the annatto seeds. The soup's other distinctive note is the citrus tang of the tomatillos. A *kak'ik* broth is smooth and velvety, with the turkey leg falling off your spoon in softened tomato and chilli-infused morsels.

## Finding it

Try El Peñascal, Avenida 5ta, 2-61 zona 1, in Cobán for Q60 (US$8). In less glam eateries *kak'ik* will cost as little as Q25 (US$3.25).

**\* TIPS \* *Kak'ik* typically comes served with a mint and coriander garnish, a side of rice and one of Guatemala's seemingly limitless tamale varieties (connoisseur cooks favour white tamales).**

* By Luke Waterson *

# Recipe Kak'ik

## INGREDIENTS

7 tomatoes, whole

225g (8oz) tomatillos, whole

3 medium red peppers

1 onion, roughly chopped

1 *guaque* chilli

1 *pasilla* chilli

6 Cobán chillies

6 cloves garlic

1 tbs annatto paste

1 bunch spring onion stalks

1 bunch coriander (cilantro), chopped

1.5kg (3½lb) turkey legs (approx 3)

4 cups (1L) chicken stock

Handful of mint leaves, chopped

Salt and pepper

## METHOD

1. To make the red sauce: under a hot grill place the tomatoes, tomatillos, red peppers, onion, four garlic cloves, *guaque*, *pasillo* and Cobán chillies. Remove the chillies and cook the vegetables until brown and beginning to char.

2. Blend the browned vegetables and the chillies, thinning the mixture if necessary with a little chicken stock (¼ cup). Add annatto seed paste and blend again. Strain and set to one side.

3. Put the turkey legs in a pot with enough chicken stock to cover each leg. Add one teaspoon of salt and two garlic cloves.

4. Cover and cook for about 1 hour on a low-medium heat until the turkey is tender.

5. Add the spring onions and half the coriander to the pot after 30 minutes.

6. When the turkey is cooked, remove the spring onions and add the red sauce. Stir well.

7. Add the rest of the chopped coriander and bring slowly to the boil. Reduce heat to medium low, and cook for another 30 minutes.

8. Season as desired with salt and pepper. Add mint to garnish.

SERVES 6

# * Kashgar Lamb Kebabs *

KASHGAR, XINJIANG, CHINA

**A tangy take on the traditional kebab, these are the quintessential Central Asian street snack: sizzling lamb crusted with chilli and pepper, cooked over coals.**

## What is it?

Once as popular with the cameleers of the Silk Road as they are with the modern denizens of urban China, Kashgar kebabs are a spicy Central Asian take on skewered lamb. The Turkic-speaking Uyghurs of Kashgar coat their kebabs in peppers, chilli flakes and cumin. Having migrated across China, they have taken these piquant portions to appreciative punters from Shanghai to Sichuan, who know them as *yangrou chuan* (lamb meat kebabs).

## Origin

The primordial kebab originated in the eastern Mediterranean millennia ago. The ancient Greeks skewered meats and cooked them over coals, apparently due to a shortage of firewood. Legend has it that Persian soldiers did the same, grilling meat on their swords over open fires, a tradition they carried east and introduced to the Turkic peoples of Central Asia.

## Tasting

Prepare for a sensory surround-sound experience. Waiting among expectant customers, you will notice the sound and scent of the kebab stall first: the aroma of the blue smoke rising from the grill, the sizzle of muttony fat dropping on charcoal embers. Stepping up to take your turn, you'll find your hunger mounting and your patience waning for the moment when you'll pull the chunks of spicy lamb off with your teeth. The exterior of each morsel is crisp and crusted with salt and chilli flakes: a sharp peppery rebuke. But chewing into the meat releases the pungency of moist lamb, an almost sweet rejoinder to counteract the fire. The flavour of the meat is at its height when piping hot; to eat it at any temperature other than its searing zenith would be to lessen the experience, so don't hold back.

## Finding it

Try Altun Orda, in Kashgar, for slap-up spiced lamb skewers with *laghman* (pulled noodles) and greens (¥40; about US$6.50). Alternatively, try any street stall in Kashgar or night market throughout Xinjiang (about US$0.50 per skewer).

**\* VARIATIONS \* The Muslim Uyghurs of Xinjiang traditionally use lamb or mutton for their kebabs, but elsewhere in China you may encounter chicken, beef, pork, and seafood skewers as well. In the Uyghur neighbourhoods of Yarkand, pigeon kebabs are also popular.**

By Will Gourlay

# Recipe Kashgar Lamb Kebabs

## YOU'LL NEED

Produces about 12 kebabs

500g (1lb) lamb or mutton (cut into 2cm/1in chunks)

1 tbs sunflower oil

3 tbs ground chilli flakes

3 tbs ground cumin

3 tbs ground black pepper

Sea salt

Skewers (wooden or metal; if using wooden skewers soak in water first so they don't burn on the grill)

## METHOD

1. Remove the lamb from the refrigerator; these kebabs cook best if the meat is at room temperature prior to cooking. Heat the barbecue or grill.

2. In a bowl, mix the sunflower oil, chilli flakes, cumin, salt and pepper. The mix will be quite gritty.

3. Place chunks of lamb onto skewers – five or six pieces per skewer.

4. While barbecue or grill is heating up, brush each skewer with the oil and spice mix, ensuring all are well lubricated with oil and coated with the spice mix.

5. Place each skewer onto the grill, turning only once and brushing with extra oil and spice mix if desired. The kebabs are ready after about two minutes on each side, or when the exterior of the meat is golden-brown with a slight crust of spice.

6. Serve the kebabs with flatbread or rice, and garnish with extra chilli flakes or salt to taste.

MAKES 12 KEBABS

# * Katsu Curry *

## JAPAN

**As one of their country's most popular dishes, the Japanese turn to *katsu* curry when in search of a quick and easy meal, soothing comfort food, or even a hangover cure.**

## WHAT IS IT?

*Katsu* curry is a complete meal of fried breaded pork cutlet doused with lashings of a thick, semi-sweet and rich curry sauce over a bed of boiled rice with a side of shredded raw cabbage. It is second only to ramen as Japan's favourite lunch and dinner staple, with specialist curry houses dotted around the country.

## TASTING

It might seem like a bit of a production line, buying a meal ticket from a vending machine and queueing up for seats at one of Japan's curry houses, which are likely to serve only one type of *katsu* curry and have their own cult following. Crisp and juicy deep-fried pork cutlets served with gooey, mildly sweet but still pungent curry, plain rice to soak up the sauce and balance the crunch, and surprisingly delicious raw shredded cabbage to refresh the palate, make for an immensely satisfying meal. Despite its richness, the Japanese like to enjoy *katsu* curry just as much in the summer as winter, believing spicy foods to be good for stimulating the appetite, served hot and fresh from the deep-fryer and enjoyed with an ice-cold beer or soft drink.

## ORIGIN

*Katsu* curry is a prime example of the Japanese penchant for adopting foreign ideas and techniques in the kitchen, known in local parlance as *yoshoku*. There is no doubt as to *katsu* curry's Western origins, from the use of pork (Japanese Buddhist society originally favoured vegetarian dishes), curry powder (from the British), and the flour and water paste known as roux in France, which gives the sauce its characteristic thickness and sheen, making it distinct from Indian or East Asia-style curries. The invention of instant curry mixes in cube or packet form in the 1930s has led to its popularity as an everyday food.

## FINDING IT

Go Go Curry is one of Japan's most popular curry house chains – expect all types of *katsu* curry and plenty of free cabbage. From ¥550 (US$5) for a small basic curry.

* VARIATIONS * Each curry house in Japan will have their own spin on the katsu curry, from the addition of *tonkatsu* sauce as a topping, fruit chutneys or chilli powder to further sweeten or spice up the curry sauce, to whoppers with deep fried prawns, eggs and sausages included on top of the pork cutlet.

* By Johanna Ashby *

# RECIPE Katsu Curry

Most Japanese home cooks happily rely on widely available instant curry mixes but this recipe is just as easy to make.

## INGREDIENTS

### Curry Sauce

1 tsp cumin seeds, ground

1 tsp coriander seeds, ground

1 tsp fennel seeds, ground

1 tsp turmeric, ground

1 tbs curry powder

1 medium onion, diced

1 tbs vegetable oil

1 tbs honey

2 tbs soy sauce

1 tbs rice flour or plain flour dissolved in 2 tbs of water

### Pork Cutlet

4 pieces pork loin (approx 500g/1lb)

250g (9oz) Japanese panko or ordinary breadcrumbs

1 large egg, beaten

Plain flour for dusting

Oil for frying

### To Serve

Plain boiled rice

Finely shredded cabbage

## METHOD

1. Prepare the pork cutlet by flattening each piece with the back of a knife or a rolling pin to tenderise the pork. Dust each piece with flour, dip in the beaten egg then coat with the breadcrumbs. Refrigerate for at least half an hour.

2. To make the curry sauce, dry fry the spices and curry powder in a saucepan for a few minutes to release their aromas then add the oil, onion, honey and soy sauce and cook for a few minutes until the onions have softened.

3. Add the flour mixture and cook until the sauce has thickened. Set aside.

4. To cook the pork cutlets, fry them in a pan with oil over medium heat, being careful not to overcrowd the pan. Cook both sides of each cutlet until the crumbs are golden. Drain the cooked cutlets on a wire rack.

5. Serve the pork cutlets with plain boiled rice, topped with the curry sauce and garnished with the shredded cabbage.

SERVES 4

# * Kimchi Jjigae *

### KOREA

**The dish for those who like their *kimchi* not just spicy hot, but bubbling hot too. This fiery stew features the country's most famous ingredient, with a little extra zing.**

## What is it?

*Kimchi jjigae* is simple to prepare, provided you have some old or leftover *kimchi* to hand. Boiled along with scallions, onion, garlic and *gochujang* (red pepper paste), the dish is an ideal winter warmer – that is, once you've added your chosen protein. Pork and tofu are favourites, though some cooks use tinned tuna.

## Tasting

Like many of the country's stews, *kimchi jjigae* is served literally boiling hot, the broth still bubbling when it reaches your table. It's traditionally a communal dish, eaten from one shared pot in the centre of the table, and while you'll often find it surrounded by the numerous *banchan* (side dishes) ubiquitous in Korean cuisine, it can also be ordered as a main meal with a simple side of rice at inexpensive lunchtime eateries.

Stewed *kimchi* retains a touch of crunch and lends a complex flavour to the broth – you'll taste not only the ingredients added to the pot but also everything used to make the *kimchi* itself in waves of spice-laden flavour. To lessen the heat, add a little rice as you eat, or if you need some total respite keep a stash of plain rice aside to chomp on between slurps.

## Origin

Despite being built to last, even *kimchi* can pass its best, but that doesn't mean it's ready for retirement. *Kimchi jjigae* was designed with recycling in mind using leftover *kimchi*. The stew is ideal on crisp, cold days and is being prescribed (non-medically of course) to clear up colds. Despite its heat – both of the temperature and spice varieties – you'll find it on menus nationwide even in the steamiest summer months.

## Finding it

Close to Seoul's Palaces, Gwanghwamun Jip is a hole-in-the-wall specialising in *kimchi jjigae* at KRW 5000 (US$4.50).

**\* TIPS \*** Soups and stews are often eaten from a communal pot in Korea, so don't be surprised if your dining mates dip their spoons straight into the *jjigae*. The dish is known as a sinus-clearer, but blowing your nose at the table is a Korean cultural no-no – excuse yourself if the stew gives you the sniffles.

* By Lucy Corne *

# Recipe **Kimchi Jjigae**

## INGREDIENTS

1 tbs sesame oil

300g (11oz) pork, preferably pork rashers or pork belly, chopped

Approx 2 cups of *kimchi* – the older and funkier the better

Half an onion, sliced

3 cloves garlic, crushed

2 tbs *gochujang* (hot pepper paste)

3 cups (750mL) hot water

200g (7oz) tofu, chopped

¼ cup scallions (spring onions), chopped

## METHOD

1. Heat a deep saucepan and add the sesame oil, heating briefly.

2. Add the pork and fry until lightly browned and any fat is slightly crispy.

3. Add the *kimchi* and cook for two minutes, stirring occasionally.

4. Add the sliced onion, crushed or minced garlic and two generous dollops of *gochujang* (more if your spice threshold is higher!)

5. Add two cups of water, plus any juices from the *kimchi* and bring to the boil.

6. Partially remove the lid and reduce the heat, simmering for 20-30 minutes. Add more water if the broth begins to evaporate or is too pungent for your tastes.

7. Add the chopped tofu and simmer for a further 10 minutes.

8. Sprinkle on the chopped scallions just before you remove the stew from the heat, and stir.

9. Serve the stew with steamed rice on the side – and keep a handkerchief handy!

SERVES 4

# * Klobasa *

## CENTRAL EUROPE

**Served with a beer, *klobasa's* hearty mix of smoked pork, chilli heat and paprika sweetness is hard to beat – especially when you crank up the fire with two zesty condiments.**

## What is it?

Spicy pork sausage – smoked and laced with paprika and chilli – served with robust dark bread, zingy mustard and finely grated horseradish. Either prop up a late-night sausage stand, or order *klobasa* in a bustling Slovenian, Czech or Slovak pub. Either way, a glass of *pivo* (beer) is virtually mandatory.

## Tasting

Don't expect fine dining. More than likely you'll be served by a gruff barman who is more interested in the ice hockey or football playing on the big screen TV. If you're ordering *klobasa* in the early hours of the morning from a sausage stand, the proprietor will also be juggling a few servings of fried cheese. But after one too many drinks on a big night out, a grilled smoked sausage will be just what you need. There's plenty of heat in the sausage itself – and the sweetish hit of paprika – but the addition of mustard and fresh horseradish take the culinary punch to another level. To balance it out, you'll also need a slice of caraway-seed infused rye bread.

## Origin

*Klobasa's* beginnings are shrouded by the mists of history, but in Slovenia the story goes that the spicy treat first became popular during the times of the Austro-Hungarian empire at the beginning of the 19th century. Reputedly it was first crafted in the Gorenjska region of what is now modern Slovenia, from where butchers in the town of Trzin supplied markets in Vienna and across the empire.

## Finding It

Match *klobasa* with regional Czech microbrews at Prague's Pivovarský Klub. A half-litre of beer and a spicy sausage with bread is around 135 Czech koruna (US$7).

**\* VARIATIONS \* Robust *klobasa*-style sausage is popular across Central Europe and the Balkans. In Poland, the name morphs to *kielbasa* and there are official government guidelines of sizes and what meats can be used. In Hungary, spins on *kolbász* include extra-spicy *kolbász lecsókolbás*, and in Serbia and Montenegro *kobasica* is spiced with black pepper and paprika.**

**\* By Brett Atkinson \***

# Recipe **Klobasa**

## INGREDIENTS

2.5kg (5lb) ground pork

4 cloves crushed garlic

1 medium onion, finely chopped

1 cup (250mL) white wine

1 tbs ground black pepper

1 tsp caraway seeds

2 tsp salt

4 tsp paprika

1 tsp chilli powder

Sausage casings

## METHOD

1.  Mix the ground pork together with all the other ingredients. Cover and place in a refrigerator overnight for the flavours to meld.

2.  Mix by hand again and fry a small sample to ensure the flavour and seasonings are acceptable.

3.  Carefully fill the sausage casings with the meat mixture to remove any pockets of air.

4.  Twist into uniform lengths of about 20cm (8in) long.

5.  The fresh sausages can then fried, roasted, or slowly smoked for around 48 hours.

MAKES ABOUT 20 SAUSAGES

# * Kothu Roti *

## SRI LANKA

**The fiery jumble of roti and curry known as *kothu* roti is not only popular street food, but its creation is also a spectacle in itself when cooked in Sri Lanka's atmospheric roadside stalls.**

## WHAT IS IT?

*Gothamba* roti, a type of fried flatbread, is chopped and mixed with a meat or vegetable stew spiced with Sri Lankan Jaffna curry along with plenty of dried chillies and crunchy vegetables. The result is a rich and fragrant stir-fry packing plenty of punch and more than enough protein and carbohydrates to satisfy the hungriest bellies.

## ORIGIN

*Kothu* roti is a truly indigenous dish, said to be the brainchild of Sri Lanka's peasant population as cheap, fast and filling food. It remains unclear exactly which region produced the first *kothu* roti but it is agreed to have been a recent creation from the 1970s. The name literally translates to 'chopped roti' and the main seasoning of Jaffna curry is a Sri Lankan blend comprising over ten different spices, including cinnamon, which is a defining feature of Sri Lankan curry dishes.

## TASTING

Street entertainment doesn't get better than at Sri Lankan roadsides where *kothu* roti is made. Think saliva-inducing aromas of curry and roti sizzling on a smoking hot flat griddle combined with a melodic cacophony of clanking oversized metal dough scrapers that shred and mix the roti with a spicy meat gravy. Each street vendor has their own signature 'tune' of clashing yet rhythmic scrapers as they hit the metal griddle. What might sound like heavy, stodgy fare with bread, curry, egg and vegetables seasoned with chillies and the local richly roasted Jaffna curry powder is in fact a feast for the senses – golden yellow, aromatic, and a melange of explosively hot and addictive savoury flavours. Despite its humble beginnings, the dish is now considered a Sri Lankan staple, including as a midnight 'snack' for clubbing types.

## FINDING IT

*Kothu* roti is never far away in Sri Lanka with most road-side stalls in Colombo serving this popular dish. Just follow your nose and ears!

* **VARIATIONS** * Home cooked versions generally use chicken curry for the gravy but mutton curry would be the traditionalist's choice.

* By Johanna Ashby *

# Recipe Kothu Roti

The roti and the curry can be prepared a day in advance and assembled just before serving. Store-bought roti is an acceptable substitute if time is tight. Ensure the curry has plenty of gravy to be soaked up by roti.

## INGREDIENTS

### Roti

225g (8oz) self-raising flour

1 tsp salt

1 tbs vegetable oil

Approx 120mL water

Oil for brushing and frying

### Lamb Curry

500g (1lb) stewing lamb, diced

1 tbs vegetable oil

1 medium onion

3 garlic cloves, crushed

1 green chilli, chopped

1 tbs curry powder

½ tsp cumin seeds

1 tbs garam masala

### Kothu Roti

1 tbs vegetable oil

1 medium onion

½ tsp mustard seeds

½ tsp cumin seeds

Handful of curry leaves

1 green chilli, chopped

2 eggs, beaten

1. To make the roti dough, mix all the ingredients together (apart from the extra oil) until the mixture starts to come away from the sides of the bowl. Turn out the mixture and knead until the dough is soft. Add a little flour or water as required to get a smooth, but not sticky, dough. Rest the dough for half an hour.

2. Divide the dough into six balls and with a rolling pin, roll out each to a thickness of about 2mm (¹⁄₁₆ in). Take one flat piece and brush a little oil on the bottom third and fold it towards the middle. Do the same with the top third. Turn the piece a quarter of the way clockwise and repeat with the bottom and top thirds. Do this with the rest of the rotis. Heat oil in a pan and flatten each roti with a rolling pin. Fry each piece on one side until the top side puffs up and the bottom side is blistered. Turn over until similarly puffed and blistered. Repeat with the rest of the rotis.

3. Heat the oil in a pan and fry the onion, garlic and chilli until the onions are soft but not brown. Brown the lamb in the pan. Add the spices and cook for about three minutes. Cover with water and simmer until the lamb is tender (at least an hour).

4. To make the kothu roti, heat the oil in a pan and fry the onion, mustard seeds, cumin seeds, curry leaves and chilli for a few minutes. Set the mixture to one side of the pan and scramble the eggs. Add the roti and the lamb curry and stir. Serve at once.

SERVES 6

# \* Lahmacun \*

## TURKEY

**A rolled-up, crunchy pizza crust bursting with the sweet tang of minced lamb and the zest of fiery chilli flakes, *lahmacun* is Turkey's oh-so-addictive street snack.**

## What is it?

*Lahmacun* are the diminutive, spicier cousins of Turkey's well-loved *pides* (pizzas). These small rounds of dough are topped with a peppery minced-meat mixture and cooked in a wood-fired oven. Sprinkled with chilli flakes and rolled, they provide fuel for everyone from bazaar porters to students.

## Tasting

With a thin, light crust, *lahmacun* are pulled from the oven, sprinkled with chilli flakes (often a distinctive, dark variety known as *isot*, from the city of Urfa in Turkey's southeast), and served rolled up in a paper bag. Your first bite will be mostly thin crust, crisp and flaky, with a hint of the delights within to fire your appetite. As you reach the moist, aromatic meat mixture, you'll notice a hint of tomato-salsa sweetness, offset by smouldering chilli and tart lemon juice. The sweet-meaty-spicy combo will tempt you back for more. There's no shame in that: most punters buy a stack and proceed through them, liberally strewing each successive one with more chilli as their palates blaze.

## Finding it

*Lahmacun* are produced across Turkey, but the spiciest varieties are found in the bazaars of the southeast, particularly Diyarbakir, Mardin and Urfa. Expect to pay around 3TL (US$1.50).

## Origin

In days long gone, the Byzantine Greeks sprinkled their flatbreads with olive oil and herbs. Known as *pita*, these were the precursors of the modern pizza. It is not known whether the Turkish nomads who conquered Byzantine territory adopted the idea from the Greeks, or whether Turkish pizzas are a modern adaptation of the Italian dish. Nonetheless, the doughy discs you encounter in Turkey are distinctive and delicious. The word *lahmacun* comes from the Arabic *lahm biajin* (literally 'meat and dough'), only adding to the culinary conundrum, but perhaps illustrating that this is a true fusion of culinary traditions.

**\* VARIATIONS \* An equivalent, known as *manakish*, is served in Syria and Lebanon. *Manakish* may be spread with *zaatar* and olive oil as a breakfast favourite. They may also be served plain with chilli flakes as a piquant side dish to main meals.**

\* By Will Gourlay \*

# Recipe Lahmacun

## INGREDIENTS

### Crust

600g (1lb 5oz) plain flour

300mL water

50mL olive oil

Instant yeast

Salt (sprinkle)

### Topping

2 large, ripe tomatoes

1 large, ripe red capsicum

1 large onion

1 bunch of parsley

250g (9oz) ground lamb or beef

1 tbs tomato salsa or sugo

50mL olive oil

Red paprika powder

Ground cumin

Ground black pepper

Salt (to taste)

Red chilli flakes (to taste)

Lemon segments

## METHOD

1.  Combine all the crust ingredients in a bowl to create a dough. Knead thoroughly and leave it to rise for at least an hour.

2.  Tear off balls of dough, about enough to fill your palm. On a board dusted with flour, roll out the dough thinly with a rolling pin to form the *lahmacun* bases. Ideally each base should be about 20cm (8in) in diameter and 2–3mm (⅛in) thick.

3.  Place tomatoes, red capsicum, onion and parsley in a food processor and blend to reach the consistency of a thin sauce.

4.  Place this mixture in a mixing bowl with minced meat, salsa, olive oil, paprika, cumin, pepper and salt. Manually mix until all ingredients are integrated. The mix should be slightly moist.

5.  Ladle a portion of the topping onto each base, spreading evenly.

6.  Place the discs into a pizza oven or standard kitchen oven (preheated to around 220°C/430°F) for between five and eight minutes (until base is just crisp and topping is sizzling).

7.  Sprinkle *lahmacun* with chilli flakes and/or a squeeze of lemon juice as desired.

# * Laksa Lemak *

INDONESIA, MALAYSIA, SINGAPORE

**A rich soup of seafood, coconut, and rice noodles, spiked with the complex spices of the region. It's Southeast Asia in a bowl.**

## What is it?

You could say laksa is just a spicy noodle soup, but you wouldn't have any friends left in Southeast Asia. Here, laksa is a point of pride. Every neighbourhood has its own take, each one is uniquely delicious. Some are fish-based and sour with tamarind, others are creamy with coconut. All pack plenty of heat.

## Origin

How each version of laksa came to be has been lost in time. Its name may come from the Malay word for a mint-like herb, the Hokkien word for 'dirty', or the Cantonese word for 'spicy sand', or it may have roots in an ancient Persian dish. What is known is that an immigrant named Janggut from China's Fujian Province put Singapore's Katong neighbourhood on the culinary map in the 1940s with his version – a coconut-based broth with noodles cut short so beachgoers could slurp it up with a spoon.

## Finding it

In Penang, head to Pasay Ayer Itam Laksa (11500 Air Itam), a small stand serving bowls for 3RM (US$1) nonstop. In Singapore, all the cooks in the Katong neighborhood have a story about Janggut. A large laksa at 328 Katong Laksa (51 East Coast Road) is S$7 (US$5.50).

## Tasting

At hawker centres and roadside food carts throughout the region, you'll find vendors slinging laksa that falls in two main schools – *lemak*, a coconut-based curry soup, and *asam*, a sour tamarind, fish-based soup. A bowl of *lemak* is like a reassuring hug followed by a pinch on the cheek; it's creamy and smooth with a lingering spice kick. Vendors heap in plenty of fried beancurd, fish cake, shrimp and cockles. A bowl of *asam*, on the other hand, is a slap on the butt; it's pungent and bracing, and the chillies bite back. Sometimes you have to look to the soft, round rice noodles or the garnish of fresh mint, onion, and ginger flower to cool things down. But of course, in all cases, it's the pinch and the slap that keep you coming back for more.

* TIPS * Laksa should be slurped with just the help of a spoon. Dip into a little *sambal belacan* (chilli and shrimp paste) to take it from spicy to inferno, and if you're still hungry, add a side of *otak-otak* (fish cake wrapped in a banana leaf) and wash it all down with iced *calamansi* (citrus juice).

* By Tienlon Ho *

# Recipe Laksa Lemak (Katong style)

## INGREDIENTS

12 dried, red chillies, soaked to soften, coarsely chopped

16 shallots, minced

7 candlenuts, or use macadamias or cashews

Medium knob fresh galangal, minced

Small knob fresh ginger, minced

3 stalks lemongrass, just the tender parts, sliced

1 tbs coriander seeds, toasted and ground

Small knob fresh turmeric, peeled

Salt

250mL (1 cup) vegetable oil

60g (2oz) dried shrimp, soaked to soften, ground

750mL (3 cups) water

750mL (3 cups) coconut milk, kept separated (not stirred)

4 tbs laksa leaves, minced

Fish stock, or water, as needed

275g (10oz) dried, round, rice noodles, soaked to soften

2 fishcakes, sliced

275g (10oz) shrimps, peeled and deveined

1kg (2lb) fresh cockles

Salt to taste

Sugar to taste

4 slices dry, firm tofu

100g (4oz) bean sprouts

### Garnish

Sambal belacan

Extra chilli, chopped

Laksa leaves, coarsely chopped

## METHOD

1. Combine the chillies, shallots, candlenuts, galangal, ginger, lemongrass, coriander seeds, turmeric and salt in a mortar and pestle and pound into *rempah* (a smooth paste). Or use a food processor, adding a few drops of oil as needed.

2. Heat 250mL oil in a large pan and add the *rempah*. Stir continuously over a low heat until fragrant, about 30 minutes.

3. Add the dried shrimp powder stirring for about five minutes, then add water and simmer for another 30 minutes.

4. Add half the thick coconut milk, a teaspoon at a time, stirring continuously.

5. Stir in the laksa leaves.

6. Add the thin coconut milk a teaspoon at a time, stirring continuously.

7. Add the rest of the thick coconut milk as before and simmer at medium heat for another 30 minutes. The broth should be thick but still soupy. Add fish stock or water to thin, as needed.

8. Add the fishcakes, shrimp, and cockles to the broth, simmer until the cockles open and the shrimps are cooked, about three minutes. Season with more salt and sugar, as needed.

9. In a separate pot, cook the rice noodles according to the package instructions, then drain.

10. Fry slices of the tofu in vegetable oil until golden, about two minutes, season with salt. Set aside.

11. To serve, divide noodles and bean sprouts among four large bowls. Fill each with the broth, then top with even portions of fishcakes, cockles, shrimps and tofu.

12. Garnish with laksa leaf, chilli, and a spoonful of *sambal*.

SERVES 4

# * Larb *

## LAOS/NORTHERN THAILAND

**Minced meat, shards of crisp red shallot, lime juice, herbs, roasted rice powder and dried chillies... *larb* can be fresh and fragrant, skipping across the tongue, or seriously, pungently powerful.**

## What is it?

The national dish of Laos (it's also popular in the north of Thailand), *larb* is a spicy mince salad. There are dozens of different styles, from versions with pounded raw buffalo meat and offal to cooked chicken and pork. But the dressing is always spicy and rich with red chilli powder, while mint and coriander provide aromatic relief. It's all bound together with a good sprinkling of crunchy roasted rice powder.

## Origin

As ever, arguments rage as to *larb*'s roots. Some say it originated in Laos, others that it has the same roots as steak tartare – simply raw meat and onions – and was spread with Haw merchants from the southwest of China into northern Thailand. It's known, though, as a dish of northeast Thailand and Laos, although regional variations abound.

## Tasting

This is a dish that can be ethereally delicate (albeit with a proper chilli punch), or viscerally carnivorous (buffalo hide, spleen, heart and liver can be a little testing when raw). As ever, balance is everything. The meat (cooked or uncooked) is finely minced or ground, and cooked (or bathed) in a dressing made of meat broth with dried red chilli powder. Optional lime juice adds citrus zing. In the Laotian version, shallots and garlic are blackened over an open flame first, to give that distinctive charred tang. Various herbs play their usual fragrant role, and the addition of roasted, ground glutinous rice powder at the end not only adds crunch, but a nutty depth too.

## Finding it

In Vientiane and Luang Prabang you'll find street stalls selling *larb* everywhere. Look for the stall with a constant flow of punters, and don't be afraid to customise.

**\* VARIATIONS \* There are versions of *larb* made with raw buffalo tripe and dried water buffalo skin; others use chicken and pork. Some are sharp with lime (especially in Thailand), others, in Laos, fragrant with star anise, cloves and cinnamon. You'll never find two dishes the same. But start with the cooked chicken or pork versions. You might find some alien leaves served alongside, plus sticky rice and the usual bowl of fresh chillies. Wash it down with a cool Beerlao.**

* By Tom Parker-Bowles *

# Recipe Larb Gai

Chicken is the classic choice for this Thai dish, but pork/beef or even firm tofu would certainly suffice.

## INGREDIENTS

1 tbs peanut/olive oil

500g (1lb) minced chicken

2 kaffir lime leaves, sliced

3–4 dried red chillies

½ red onion, thinly sliced

2 spring onions, finely chopped

¼ cup (60mL) chicken stock

1 tbs cornflour

2–3 tbs fish sauce (to taste)

1 tsp sugar

Juice of 1 lime

Cos lettuce

¼ cup fresh mint leaves, chopped

Handful of fresh basil, ripped into pieces

4 tbs uncooked sticky rice or 3–4 tbs chopped cashews

## METHOD

1. Heat the oil in a large wok over high heat.

2. Add the chicken mince and stir for 1 minute, until brown.

3. Add the dried chilli, kaffir lime leaves, sliced onion and spring onions and fry for 2 minutes.

4. In a jug, mix together the stock, cornflour, fish sauce, sugar and lime juice then pour into the chicken mixture.

5. Reduce the heat to medium-high and cook for 3–4 minutes.

6. If using the sticky rice, put it in a dry frying pan and stir over medium-high heat for 6–8 minutes.

7. When rice makes a 'popping' sound, transfer it to a pestle and mortar and grind to a coarse powder.

8. Transfer the warm chicken to a big serving bowl, pour over the ground rice/chopped cashews and accompany with cos lettuce leaves, fresh mint, basil and – if you can take it – extra chilli!

SERVES 4

# * Larb Moo *

NORTHEASTERN THAILAND & LAOS

**A simple salad packed with fiery, fresh flavours, *larb moo* wows you with superb minced pork and its combination of herbs and chillies give it a killer kick.**

## What is it?

Combining minced pork with mint, coriander and toasted rice, *larb moo* is a classic Thai or Lao dish that is easy to make and readily available all year round. It is created by parboiling the pork and then dousing it in a smorgasbord of zinging seasonings that provide that famous freshness. The dish can be an appetiser, but it is usually one of several sharing plates that everyone can sample.

## Origin

Laos claims *larb moo* as its national dish. That hasn't stopped its neighbours in northeastern Thailand from taking it, transforming it and laying claim to their own version of *larb*. The Lao variety tends to omit any limes and fish sauce, opting instead for dried spices and chillies. For a truly authentic taste, *larb* is sometimes made using raw pork. Because of a significant Lao population in the US, it's relatively easy to find there.

## Tasting

Eating *larb moo* is an experience. You can opt for the fork-and-spoon method favoured by most Thais, but you can also be creative. Grab a lettuce leaf (some will arrive with the dish) and pile a spoonful of *larb moo* onto it. Wrap the leaf into a small ball, pop it in your mouth and wait a second. The fusion of crunchy lettuce, spicy pork and fresh herbs all simultaneously competing for your attention is unforgettable.

Chances are you'll be savouring this moment in a local Thai or Lao restaurant. That means you'll probably get to see the family matriarch mashing, bashing and mixing your *larb* into shape in the fiery, open kitchen. It will be accompanied by sticky rice contained in a small bamboo holder. Work the rice into a ball with your right hand, dip it into the *larb* and you'll be eating it just like the locals. If your *larb* is too spicy, munch on the cucumber that accompanies the dish to cool things down.

## Finding it

Lahb Ubon, based in Sri Racha, eastern Thailand, sells several varieties of *larb* – all delicious for around US$2.

---

**\* VARIATIONS \* Although *larb* is usually eaten with minced pork, there are numerous other ways that it can be served. Popular alternatives include duck, chicken or beef – our personal favourite is *larb* salmon.**

* By Mark Beales *

# Recipe Larb Moo

## INGREDIENTS

350g (12oz) minced pork

1 cup (250mL) water

3 tbs spring onions, chopped

2 tbs coriander leaves, chopped

2 tbs mint leaves, chopped

3 tbs lime juice

2 tbs fish sauce

1 tbs ground roasted rice

1 tbs chilli powder

1 tbs sugar

## METHOD

1.  Boil water then add the pork and cook for two minutes.

2.  Once cooked, remove the pork and drain off the water.

3.  Place the pork in a mixing bowl and combine with the spring onions, coriander leaves and most of the mint.

4.  Keep mixing and season with the lime juice, fish sauce, sugar, ground roasted rice and chilli powder.

5.  Garnish with leftover mint.

6.  Serve with cucumber and sticky (or steamed) rice.

SERVES 2

# * Machbous *

## ARABIAN GULF

**The epic journeys of Gulf Arabs – across the seas in ancient times, and more recently from poverty to wealth – sizzle through this rice dish in which spicy prawns from the Gulf's waters take centre stage.**

## What is it?

*Machbous* is a slightly spicy stew made with fish, meat, chicken or, our favourite, prawns. The prawns, locally sourced along the Gulf Coast, are cooked in garlic, before being mixed with a riot of spices in the form of *baharat* – one of the Middle East's most widely used spice mixtures. Although added at the end, *machbous* wouldn't be *machbous* (its name translates roughly as spicy rice) without basmati, making this dish a little like a Middle Eastern risotto.

## Origin

For centuries, long before Marco Polo introduced spices to European larders, Arab seafarers carried on their ships the spices of the Indian Ocean and beyond. Thus spices from India, Zanzibar and elsewhere made their way to the fishing communities along the Arabian shoreline of the Gulf. That other essential ingredient of *machbous*, prawns, was once a plentiful food of the poor that played second fiddle to meat in prestige and local favour. As rising incomes from oil transformed Arabian society into one of the richest places on earth, prawns were similarly transformed (like oysters in Western countries) into a delicacy of some status.

## Tasting

*Machbous* bursts with flavour thanks to the cocktail of ingredients that runs through the dish. The spice mix of *baharat* that bequeaths flavour to *machbous* is at once a mildly spicy and aromatic whole and the heady sum of its parts: there's a hint of Thailand in the cardamom; echoes of India in the cumin; and the fragrance of Zanzibar in the cloves. *Baharat*'s secret is to infuse the entire dish with flavour without overwhelming the underlying taste of the prawns – that taste is ultimately what lingers on the palate. And the use of basmati rice is deliberate: its aromatic characteristics and hard grains make it perfect for the long, slow cooking that Arab Gulf chefs prefer. This is a dish that must be eaten close to the sea, perhaps at a family barbecue along the Gulf shoreline or at a fish restaurant along a city corniche as the fierce heat drains from the day.

## Finding it

*Machbous* is a staple anywhere along the coast, from Kuwait to the United Arab Emirates. Try the Palace Café in Dubai, where you can expect to pay 65 dirham (US$17.70).

**\* TIPS \* Gulf Arabs love to choose their own prawns. Do the same and try a restaurant that displays its seafood in a glass cabinet out front – if it's not fresh, the restaurant will be empty.**

**\* By Anthony Ham \***

# Recipe Machbous

Unlike many dishes from far-flung places, *machbous* is quite easy to produce in your home kitchen. If you decide to cook on a lower heat and take longer than we suggest below, you'll be following the lead of many a Gulf Arab chef.

## INGREDIENTS

1kg (2lb) uncooked prawns

3 tbs ghee

3 cloves garlic, finely chopped

2 small onions, chopped

2 tbs *baharat* (see recipe, below)

1–2 tsp turmeric

2 cups (500mL) tomatoes, peeled and chopped

1 tbs salt

Ground black pepper

2 tbs chopped parsley

1 tbs chopped coriander leaves

2–3 cups (500–750mL) water

2–3 cups basmati rice

### For the baharat

These quantities will make enough for a number of servings

1 cup (14 tbs) black peppercorns

½ cup (7 tbs) coriander seeds

½ cup (7 tbs) cassia bark (available in speciality food stores and multicultural grocery stores)

½ cup (7 tbs) cloves

⅔ cup (9 tbs) cumin seeds

8 whole nutmegs (or ½ cup, 7 tbs, ground nutmeg)

1 cup ground paprika

SERVES 4

## METHOD

1. To make the *baharat*, grind all of the *baharat* ingredients (except the nutmeg and paprika) into a powder, then grate in the nutmeg and add the paprika. Store in an airtight container.
2. Shell and devein the prawns.
3. Heat one tablespoon of the ghee along with the garlic in a large pot. Add the prawns and cook over a moderate heat until the prawns stiffen and take on a pink colour. Remove the prawns and set aside.
4. In the same pan, gently fry the onion in the remaining ghee until transparent, then stir in the *baharat* and turmeric. Fry for one minute.
5. Add the tomatoes, salt, pepper and remaining herbs to the mixture, bring to the boil and add the water. Cover and allow to boil over a moderate heat for five minutes.
6. Stir the rice into the sauce and bring to the boil again. Cover and cook for 10 minutes, turning the heat down low.
7. Return the prawns to the pan and stir them into the rice.
8. Cover and simmer over a low heat for 20 minutes, stirring around the 10-minute mark.
9. Stir once more, remove from the heat, cover and set aside to rest for five minutes. Serve with flatbread and salad.

# * Mao Xue Wang *

## SICHUAN, CHINA

**Literally 'fur blood extravaganza', this is a dish for demons –
blood curd, entrails, eel and other delectable fare swirl in a simmering
broth laced with chillies and Sichuan peppercorns.**

## What is it?

A lip-tingling stew featuring blood curd ('*xue wang*' in the local dialect), yellow eel, pork and an embarrassment of other ingredients including tripe, pig's heart and intestines, black fungus, and bean sprouts, sitting in an oil-laced broth of pork bones, dried chillies and Sichuan peppercorns. Once a street snack, this hearty and fiery dish is now available at almost all eateries specialising in Sichuan cuisine.

## Origin

Many years ago, in the ancient town of Ciqikou in Chongqing, a young woman invented a stew to help her father-in-law, a butcher, make the best of the offal from the day's slaughter. She boiled up a cauldron of broth using a pig's head and bones and some peas, then added offal, spices and, on a whim, blood curd. The last, she discovered, became tender and tofu-like with prolonged cooking. The resulting stew was so delicious, it sold like hot cakes.

## Tasting

*Mao xue wang* is one of the hottest dishes in China's hottest cuisine. First up you'll surprise your palate by the fast heat and fruitiness of the dried red peppers and the slow tongue-numbing quality (*ma-la* in Putonghua) of the Sichuan peppercorns which lends depth to the heat. Venture further and a feast of textures awaits — silky (blood curd), chewy (heart), gelatinous (sea cucumber), firm (eel), crunchy (black fungus, bean sprouts), rubbery (cuttlefish), stringy (tripe), spongy (cooked tofu)... You'll find the mild flavours of the ingredients offer some respite from the heat, cooling your lips and tongue just enough that they can wrap themselves around the next titillating piece.

## Finding it

Shunfeng 123 (3rd fl, West Bldg, Dabuhui Shopping Centre, Jiefangbei) in Chongqing, Sichuan whips up a mean *mao xue wang* for ¥20 (US$3.20).

**\* VARIATIONS \*** Most places use curd made with duck blood, though you may find a few using pig's blood. The other ingredients also vary slightly from restaurant to restaurant with some featuring spam, sea cucumber, tofu, quails' eggs, lettuce or cuttlefish. Modern versions of the dish tend to tone down the offal selection.

* By Piera Chen *

# Recipe Mao Xue Wang

## INGREDIENTS

3 tbs oil

1½ tbs Sichuan peppercorns

2 tbs crushed dried chillies

½ cup garlic, minced

20 cumin seeds

1 Chinese star anise

50g (2oz) Sichuan broad-bean-chilli paste

750mL (3 cups) pork or chicken stock, plus extra if needed

4 slices ginger

150g (5oz) leek, cut into 3cm pieces

200g (7oz) honeycomb beef tripe, cut into 1½cm slices

250g (9oz) blood curd, cut into 1cm slices

1 yellow eel or any white fish, meat only, cut into 1½cm slices

300g (11oz) bean sprouts

2 handfuls soaked black fungus

1 tbs Chinese yellow wine

1 tbs light soy sauce

2 tsp Chinese black vinegar

1 handful coriander leaves, roughly chopped

Salt to taste

## METHOD

1. Add the oil to a pan and when it's hot enough, fry the Sichuan peppercorns, crushed dried chillies, cumin seeds and Chinese star anise for a few seconds until fragrant.

2. Add the minced garlic and Sichuan broad-bean-chilli paste and saute for another few seconds.

3. Pour 750mL of stock into the pan. Throw in the ginger, leek, tripe and blood curd. Bring to a boil then let it simmer on a low heat for 45 minutes. Check the level of stock every 15 minutes and make sure none of the ingredients are sticking to the bottom of the pan. Add more stock if necessary.

4. Add the eel, bean sprouts, black fungus, wine, soy sauce and vinegar and let simmer for another 10 minutes.

5. Taste and add salt if necessary.

6. Sprinkle on the coriander and serve.

SERVES 3

# * Mapo Doufu *

## SICHUAN, CHINA

**Silky bean curd swimming in a chilli-black-bean sauce that glows a fiery red sums up Sichuan cuisine in one bowl — feisty, comforting and tongue-numbingly good.**

## What is it?

This traditional Sichuan staple is a sumptuous mix of soft bean curd, beef and *suanmiao* (tender sprouts of a wild leek) cooked in lots of oil with fermented black beans, *lajiaojiang* (chilli paste), soy sauce and heaps of dried chillies. A dusting of ground *huajiao* (Sichuan pepper) leaves a tingle on the tongue not unlike licking a battery – a delicious one, at least.

## Origin

*Mapo doufu* means 'pockmarked old lady's bean curd', (*ma* means pockmarked, *po* means elder lady). In late 19th-century Chengdu, Chen Mapo ran an eatery on a route travelled by porters who worked up a hunger carrying heavy goods. As one story goes, a labourer moving rapeseed oil asked Chen Mapo to fry up lunch in exchange for some of his haul. She tossed together what she had to hand, topped it with infused chilli oil, and her namesake dish was born.

## Tasting

Known for its distinctive *ma-la* (numbing and hot) flavour, Sichuan cuisine (called Chuan) is distinguished by spicy, oil-based sauces and *huajiao* and dried chillies. In a dish of *mapo doufu*, that combination is utterly transfixing – it quickens the pulse, dilates the pupils, and drops you into a euphoric stupor. In proper *mapo doufu*, tender bean curd luxuriates with slivers of beef in a generous pool of dayglo-red sauce – a salty, spicy, numbing stew of sorts that's over-the-top good. Whether in an open-air street stall or a fancy restaurant, it is best accompanied with a plate of simple, stir-fried greens – and maybe some rice to temper the heat.

## Finding it

Chen Mapo Dofu, a chain in Sichuan's capital of Chengdu, has ties to the 19th-century original. The oldest branch (197 Xi Yulong Jie), serves a much-loved version for ¥16 (US$2).

**\* VARIATIONS \* Chinese emigrants have carried *mapo doufu* across the globe, adapting it to local tastes often to the point where Chen Mapo wouldn't recognise her dish. In Japan, *mabo* tofu is more of a sweet curry. In Korea *gochujang* (fermented chilli paste), lends an intense kick. In America the dish is often made without meat, but with extra vegetables, a sweet-and-sour sauce and with less tingle (import laws demand *huajiao* arrives pre-cooked).**

* By Tienlon Ho *

# Recipe Mapo Doufu

## INGREDIENTS

2 tsp plus 1 tbs *huajiao*

1 tsp cornflour

2 tsp water

2 tbs Shaoxing wine

1 tbs soy sauce

¼ cup (60mL) chicken stock

680g (1½lb) medium-firm bean curd, cut in 1-inch cubes

¼ cup (60mL) vegetable oil

110g (¼lb) beef, thinly sliced

3 garlic cloves, diced

Small knob fresh ginger, peeled and diced

2 tbs fermented broad-bean-chilli sauce

¼ cup (60mL) chilli-sesame oil

3 *suanmiao*, or you can substitute spring onions, tender parts only, bias sliced

## METHOD

1. Toast 2 tsp of *huajiao* in a wok over a medium-high heat, stirring continuously, for 30 seconds. Transfer to a mortar and pestle. Let it cool, then grind finely.

2. Whisk together the cornflour and water. Then add the wine, soy sauce and stock.

3. Cover the bean curd in water in a saucepan, bring to the boil and boil for about five minutes. Drain.

4. Pour the oil into the wok set over a medium heat. Add 1 tbs *huajiao*. Cook for 30 seconds, stirring continuously until you see a thin wisp of smoke. Remove the peppercorns, retaining the oil.

5. Turn the heat to medium-high. Add the beef. Stir-fry for about 30 seconds.

6. Add the garlic and ginger. Stir-fry for another 30 seconds.

7. Add broad-bean-chilli sauce. Stir fry for another 30 seconds.

8. Pour in cornflour mixture. Bring to a boil, stirring constantly.

9. Carefully add the bean curd and chilli oil. Bring to the boil and then immediately turn off the heat. Transfer to a serving bowl.

10. Top with a dusting of the ground *huajiao* and *suanmiao*.

# * Mirchi ka Pakoda *

## INDIA & PAKISTAN

**Forget chilli poppers or Padrón peppers –
India's *mirchi ka pakoda* (whole chillies in batter)
take spiciness to a whole new level.**

## What is it?

A whole green chilli, dipped in lentil-flour batter and deep-fried. Cooks who prepare these fiery fritters take the philosophical stance that a chilli is a vegetable, rather than a spice, and therefore a prime candidate to be fried up as a light snack, alongside more commonplace vegetables such as potatoes, onions and eggplants.

## Origin

The translation of *pakoda* is mundane – it means 'cooked lumps' – but the dish is as ancient as the Indian hills. Many trace the origins of the *pakoda* to Uttar Pradesh, famed for its fusion of Hindu and Muslim cooking ideas, but the word is Sanskrit, placing the *pakoda* on a far older calendar. The Sanskrit language was spoken as early as 2000 BC, so this could well be one of the world's first fritters.

## Tasting

For new arrivals in India, *pakoda* seem like a safe bet. Battered vegetables. Sounds risk-free. Nothing too spicy there. Even your first few bites of these friendly-looking brown parcels will probably be reassuringly mild. And it's at this point, after you have been lulled into a false sense of security by chickpeas, onion, spinach, potato and eggplant, that *mirchi ka pakoda* chooses to strike. Just another nut-brown morsel on the outside, this scorching snack conceals a whole green chilli, seeds and all. Fast cooking in hot oil preserves the heat, so what goes into your mouth is only slightly less explosive than what went into the batter in the first place. Seek out delicious regional variations: in Gujarat, the *mirchi ka pakoda* are first stuffed with a mix of spiced tamarind and mango powder; in Rajasthan, the chillies are laced with spiced potatoes.

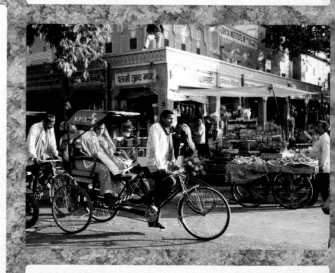

## Finding it

*Pakoda* are served anywhere and everywhere in India – identify *mirchi ka pakoda* by the chilli stalk sticking out from the batter (a portion will set you back around US$0.50).

**\* TIPS \* *Pakoda* are the perfect snack for travelling on Indian trains – cheap, portable and available on every station platform. However, when sampling *mirchi ka pakoda*, be sure to have a cup of *masala chai* (sweet milky tea) to hand to douse the flames.**

* By Joe Bindloss *

# Recipe Mirchi ka Pakoda

## INGREDIENTS

### Tamarind paste stuffing

6 tbs tamarind pulp

1 tsp palm sugar

¼ tsp ground cumin

½ tsp salt

### Pakoda

10–15 large green chillies, with stems

60g (2oz) gram (chickpea) flour

1½ tbs rice flour

¼ tsp baking powder

¼ tsp salt

½ tsp ground chilli

½ tsp ground turmeric

½ tsp whole cumin seeds

A little cold water

Vegetable oil for deep frying

## METHOD

1.  Mix the tamarind pulp, palm sugar, ground cumin and salt into a thick paste.

2.  Using a small knife, make a cut in the side of each chilli pepper, and press in a teaspoon of the tamarind paste stuffing.

3.  Combine the gram flour, rice flour, baking powder, salt, ground chilli, turmeric and cumin seeds and mix into a thick batter with a little cold water.

4.  Holding the stem, dip each chilli into the batter until it is thickly coated, then pour a teaspoon of batter over the chilli and drop quickly into the hot oil.

5.  Deep-fry the chilli pakoda in small batches for two to three minutes until golden brown, then remove from the oil and drain.

6.  Serve with lime chutney, chopped onions and coriander leaves.

SERVES 4 AS A SNACK

# * Mole *

## OAXACA, MEXICO

**Crafted from a diverse and surprising array of ingredients, this richly satisfying and spicy sauce celebrates the history and heart of the Mexican nation.**

## What is it?

Blending a variety of herbs, spices, chillies and sometimes also integrating dark chocolate, *mole* (pronounced 'mol-eh') is the quintessential slow-cooked Mexican sauce. Recipes now vary across Mexico but, with seven different *moles* to its name, Oaxaca is regarded as the dish's heartland. *Moles* are usually served with poultry or fish.

## Origin

While Oaxaca is world famous for its septet of *moles*, the state of Puebla is reckoned to be the dish's original birthplace. During the early days of the Spanish colonial period, nuns at the Convent of Santa Rosa improvised the dish from meagre ingredients when an archbishop dropped by for an unscheduled visit. All they had were an old turkey and a few spices, chillies, nuts and chocolate, so they crafted a sauce from scratch and the archbishop loved it. An alternative story says a Puebla monk inadvertently invented the dish after dropping his spice tray into a cooking pot.

## Finding It

Only open for lunch, try Restaurante Tlamanalli in the weaving village of Teotitlán Del Valle, around 25km (15 miles) northwest of Oaxaca. *Mole* dishes cost around 120 Mexican pesos (US$9).

## Tasting

Blending the culinary influences of Mexico's original indigenous inhabitants and the Spanish conquistadores, *mole* is a truly *mestizo* (mixed) dish, and widely popular across the country. Styles may vary, but the bitter-chocolate infused *mole poblano* is the one to surprise and occasionally confuse Western taste buds. With ingredients including up to 30 different spices – and often up to 10 different chillies – the concoction is rich, unctuous and slightly disorienting with its blend of savoury and bittersweet. It's an acquired taste for some diners, but without doubt one of Mexico's most iconic dishes.

**\* TIPS \*** Local markets are scattered around Oaxaca and stalls sell breakfast plates of *mole negro* with cinnamon-infused chocolate, along with exotic snacks like fried grasshoppers and smoked worms. Oaxaca is also good for travellers keen to learn the secrets of Mexican cuisine, with cookery schools including La Casa de los Sabores and La Cocina Oaxaqueña.

* By Brett Atkinson *

# Recipe Mole Poblano

## INGREDIENTS

3 large chicken breasts

1 small onion, finely chopped

1L water

35g (1.5oz) dark cooking chocolate

1 tbs sugar

Salt

Freshly ground black pepper

### Chilli Paste

8 dried ancho chillies, stems and seeds removed

2 poblano chillies, roasted then peeled and seeds removed

Around 80mL stock from cooking chicken

### Mole Sauce

60mL cooking oil

35g (1.5oz) almonds

35g (1.5oz) pecans

35g (1.5oz) hazelnuts

35g (1.5oz) sesame seeds

35g (1.5oz) raisins

½ tsp star anise seeds

½ tsp cumin seeds

½ tsp black peppercorns

3 cloves

1 stick cinnamon

6 cloves garlic, peeled and chopped

1 medium onion, sliced

Around 900mL stock from cooking chicken

## METHOD

1. Boil the water in a pan and add the chicken breasts and chopped onion, skimming any fat or grease from the top as they cook.

2. When the chicken has been lightly poached, remove it from the water and strain the stock to remove the onions. Set aside the stock and chicken and refrigerate both.

3. For the chilli paste, open the ancho chillies so they are flat and toast in a hot pan for a few seconds on either side. Soak in hot water for around 30 minutes so they are very soft. Drain them and then puree in a blender with the roasted poblano chillies and around 80mL of the chicken stock. Season with salt and set aside.

4. For the *mole*, heat around 15mL of oil in a pan over a medium heat and lightly toast the almonds, hazelnuts, pecans and sesame seeds for around three minutes. When toasted, transfer the nuts and seeds to a blender (don't blend yet).

5. In the same pan, add the raisins and toast them for around a minute until they puff up and become plump. Add the star anise and cumin seeds, peppercorns, cloves and cinnamon stick and cook for around a minute until the combination becomes fragrant. Add these ingredients to the nuts and seeds in the blender.

6. Add around 15mL more of oil to the pan, brown the garlic and onions for around 10 minutes and add to the blender.

7. Add around 250mL of chicken stock and blend all ingredients to a smooth paste.

8. In another large pan, heat the remaining 30mL of oil over a medium heat and combine the *mole* paste, the chilli paste, the chocolate and sugar, and the remaining chicken broth.

9. Season with salt and pepper, and simmer on low heat for about an hour.

10. Add the poached chicken breasts to the mole sauce and stir through until warm. Serve with white rice.

SERVES 3

# * Mosterdsoep *

## THE NETHERLANDS

**It's a condiment, it's a soup, it's a taste sensation: mustard soup warms the cockles (and tongue) like only a steaming serving of spice-spiked chowder can.**

## What is it?

A rich, thick, creamy broth with the nostril-tingling tang of mustard, this hearty soup is central heating in a bowl. It might include cream or soft cheese (or both), chillies or chives, vegetable or chicken stock – but always the finest, whole-grain Dutch mustard.

## Tasting

The wind blows chill along the canal as weak, winter sunlight glints off the ice. Shivering, you spot a likely looking brown café and duck inside; the cosy atmosphere and dark wood panelling, chatter and chinking of beer glasses envelop you in a warm hug of *gezelligheid*. There's one thing on your mind, and you want it in your belly: hot *mosterdsoep*. You have time for only a reviving sip or two of *jenever* (Dutch gin) before a steaming bowl appears, flecks of green chives floating on its golden surface. Liberally sprinkling *spekjes* (crispy bacon bits), you gingerly sip a spoonful, savouring the creamy, smooth richness. A tickle teases your nostrils as the heat of the mustard sneaks up on you. It's a strange sensation, and weirdly addictive – you can't tell if it hurts or excites. Best try another mouthful to be sure...

## Origin

Mustard as a condiment harks back to Roman times, when seeds were ground and blended with young wine ('must') for a fiery flavour, hence the Latin *mustum ardens* – 'burning must' – that's reputedly the origin of the English word mustard. The tongue-tickler has been made in the Netherlands since at least 1457 in Doesburg.

## Finding it

Café Restaurant Goudkantoor ('Gold Office', www.goudkantoor.nl) on Waagplein, Groningen is in a fabulous 17th-century building. It serves creamy mustard soup for €5.30 (US$6.50).

---

**\* VARIATIONS \*** In the Netherlands, regional pride is as fiery as mustard itself. Is it best in Zaan, north of Amsterdam? Or Doesburg, near Arnhem, where arguably the country's oldest mustard factory still grinds and blends? We'd head for Groningen, where dried sausage might be substituted for *spekjes*.

* By Paul Bloomfield *

# Recipe Mosterdsoep

For extra richness, cream cheese (*smeerkaas*) can be added to the mixture before final heating. Finely chopped chillies add extra potency – if you feel it's needed!

## INGREDIENTS

1 medium-sized onion, finely chopped

50g (2oz) butter

50g (2oz) sifted flour

1L stock (chicken or vegetable)

1 tbs grainy mustard (ideally from Groningen)

1 tbs smooth mustard

½ tsp mustard seeds

100mL (3½ fl oz) cream (or crème fraîche)

Salt and pepper

### Garnish

Freshly chopped chives

Bacon (150g/5oz), fried in crispy bits

## METHOD

1. In a saucepan, slowly fry the onion in the butter.
2. Stir in the flour to form a paste.
3. Gradually add the stock, stirring constantly to remove lumps and create a smooth liquid.
4. Add the mustards and mustard seeds.
5. Simmer on a low heat for a few minutes, adding the cream just before serving.
6. Season to taste.
7. Ladle into bowls, scatter over the chopped chives and bacon bits and serve with crusty rolls or bread.

SERVES 4

# * Nachos *

## NORTHERN MEXICO & SOUTHWESTERN USA

**Is there a more perfect bar food than a fresh plate of nachos? An addictive combination of crispy, gooey and spicy, they're hearty enough to stand up to a *cervesa* or two, and are perfect for sharing.**

## What is it?

Your classic Tex-Mex restaurant nachos are a plate of tortilla chips smothered in melted cheese, salsa and a range of toppings from pickled jalapeños to beans, guacamole and minced beef. A cheap, popular variety of nachos sold at convenience stores, ballparks and movie theatres involves something known as '*nacho cheese*' – a hot, creamy, slightly spicy processed-cheese topping poured over the chips.

## Origin

Ignacio Anaya, called 'Nacho' (a common nickname for Ignacio) by his friends, was the maître d' of a restaurant in the Mexican border town of Piedras Negras, which was popular with the wives of American military officers stationed in nearby Eagle Pass, Texas, during World War II. One day, when the restaurant's cook was away from the kitchen, the quick-thinking Nacho served the hungry ladies a plate of tortilla chips covered in melted cheese with pickled jalapeños. He called the item 'Nacho's special', and the beloved snack was born.

## Tasting

Though invented in Mexico, it's the US that is up to its ears in nachos – every mid-range chain in the country has its own 'fully-loaded' nachos creaking under the weight of beef mince and sour cream and every ballpark serves buckets of tortilla chips drowned in neon-orange cheese product. These are definitely good, but for our money, the best kind of nachos are the pared-down version found at classier Tex-Mex joints: fresh hot tortilla chips smothered with real cheddar cheese, a thin layer of refried beans, a handful of pickled jalapeños and a healthy dollop of guacamole and house-made pico de gallo salsa.

## Finding it

Tex-Mex capital San Antonio, Texas, is nacho heaven. Try the River Walk district, where at least a dozen eateries serve their own version (US$8 per serve).

**\* VARIATIONS \* Nachos beg for improvisation. Look for chipotle-smoked-chicken–topped nachos in Texas, barbecue-pulled-pork nachos in Memphis, Chinese-influenced nachos using fried wonton crackers at Asian-fusion restaurants, and much more.**

* By Emily Matchar *

# Recipe Nachos

## INGREDIENTS

500g (1lb) tortilla chips

230g (8oz) cheddar cheese, grated

100g (3½oz) pickled jalapeños

## METHOD

1. Cover a baking tray with tortilla chips and sprinkle liberally with the grated cheese.

2. Top with pickled jalapeños.

3. Bake at 175°C (350°F) for 10 to 15 minutes or until the cheese is melted.

4. Serve with sour cream, salsa and Mexican hot sauce (such as Valentina).

SERVES 4 AS A SNACK

# * Nasi Lemak *

## MALAYSIA & SINGAPORE

**The fragrance of this classic breakfast-until-brunch dish of steamed coconut rice wafts from waking households across the Malay Peninsula. Teamed with a savoury sambal (chilli sauce), it's an ideal yin-and-yang start to the day.**

## What is it?

*Nasi lemak* is rice cooked in coconut milk that is flavoured with pandanus palm leaves. It's accompanied by sambal of dried anchovies and tongue-tingling fresh red chillies pounded with garlic and onions, then garnished with hardboiled egg, cucumber, peanuts and small crispy fried fish. The takeaway version (*bungkus*) comes as a small pyramid wrapped in banana leaf.

## Origin

In its *bungkus* form, the dish probably developed as the ideal portable breakfast for rural folk working from dawn in the fields. But a more creative origin story comes from Melaka in Malaysia; it tells of a young girl who accidentally spilled coconut milk into cooking rice. When her mother asked about the different flavour the girl, thinking she would be scolded, said '*nasi le, mak*' – it's just rice, mother – and the phrase stuck!

## Tasting

Unwrapping a green pyramid of *nasi lemak* is a ritual to savour, with its contrasts of smooth rice, piquant sambal and the crunch of raw cucumber and crispy fish. Part of the pleasure is discovering exactly what's inside. Each cook has their own favourite version of sambal (*pedas* is seriously spicy, with the accent on chilli; *manis* is made spicy-sweet with the distinctive and delicious addition of palm sugar) and combination of garnish (omelette instead of hardboiled egg; fried chicken wing instead of fish). It's the perfect picnic food: fresh, readily available and served in biodegradable packaging. Traditionally *nasi lemak* is eaten with the fingers – the rice is slightly sticky and malleable – but most *bungkus* come with plastic spoons. Or sit and eat from a heaped plate under the whirring fans at a food market and admire the coordinated movements of the stallholders in their tiny kitchens.

## Finding it

In Singapore, head to the hawker stalls at Changi Village Food Centre, and expect to pay around S$2–3 (US$2).

**\* VARIATIONS \* *Nasi lemak's* Malay origins have been adopted and adapted by the Indian and Chinese communities of Malaysia and Singapore. Indian-style, it comes with fish, lamb or chicken curry on the side; the Chinese version adds pork luncheon meat.**

* By Virginia Jealous *

# Recipe Nasi Lemak

## INGREDIENTS

### Coconut rice

2 cups rice

A knot of pandan leaves, if available

2 cups (250mL) coconut milk

2 cups (250mL) water

Salt

### Tamarind water

1 cup (250mL) water

2 tsp tamarind pulp

### Anchovy sambal

1 cup dried anchovies (*ikan bilis*), if available

1 tsp shrimp paste (*belacan*)

4 shallots or 2 small onions

1 clove garlic

5–10 dried chillies

½ red onion, thinly sliced

1 tbs sugar

Salt to taste

Peanut oil or similar

## METHOD

### Coconut Rice

1. Rinse the rice. Cook the ingredients together in a rice cooker or bring to the boil in a pan, cover and simmer for 12 minutes or so. Turn off and leave covered for 15 minutes.

### Tamarind Water

2. Soak tamarind in the water, squeezing from time to time. Strain after 15 minutes and discard pulp.

### Anchovy Sambal

3. Rinse and drain the anchovies; fry until light brown and put aside.

4. Grind the shrimp paste, shallots, garlic and deseeded chillies in a pestle and mortar, or whizz in a food processor.

5. Heat the peanut oil and fry the spice paste. While stirring, add the onion slices, anchovies, tamarind water, sugar and salt.

6. Simmer for around 15 minutes, until the sauce thickens.

7. Serve *nasi lemak* with sambal on the side. Garnish with quartered hardboiled eggs, crisp fried fish, fried salted peanuts and cucumber slices.

SERVES 4

# * 'Nduja *

CALABRIA, ITALY

**In Calabria, the sunbaked toe of the Italian boot, pigs roam almost wild, grazing on chestnuts, marjoram and spearmint. 'Nduja, a spreadable salami, is formed from the alchemy of their fragrant meat and fiercely hot Calabrese peppers.**

## What is it?

This soft spread is created by chopping cheap cuts of pork into a fine paste. This is mixed with salt and the local crimson *peperoncino* (peppers). Stuffed into natural sausage skins and tied with hemp string, it's then cured and left to dry. When the salami is ready it's eaten either spread on local artisanal bread, or mixed into sauces to give them some oomph.

## Origin

Created as a way to use up a pig's more humble parts, 'nduja has become a Calabrian speciality. The Spanish imported chilli peppers to Italy in the 16th century, but it's possible 'nduja ('an-DO-yah') developed from the French 'andouille', a coarse, spicy smoked-pork and garlic sausage, as the pronunciation is similar. But this incarnation – with its extraordinary marriage between taste and heat – was born in Spilinga, in Calabria's deep south.

## Tasting

The salami paste is deep, dark, chilli red. Try it thickly spread on a chunk of locally made bread. A bite starts with the blowtorch blast of the infamous Calabrese peppers, which then slowly subsides, allowing the powerful, creamy flavour of the pork to foreground. The complex, punchy taste also enhances multiple Calabrese dishes, such as pasta with *'nduja* and *fagioli* (beans).

To outsiders, Calabria has an air of mystery, infamous for its local mafia (the 'Ndrangheta) and wild countryside strewn with higgledy-piggledy towns. The best place to try 'nduja is here, somewhere near Spilinga, where it was invented. Warm your cockles with it in autumn or winter (in the baking summer sun it could make you overheat), at a rustic neighbourhood trattoria, or as part of a shepherd-worthy picnic overlooking wooded landscapes.

## Finding it

To try the best 'nduja, head to Vibo Valentia on 8 May, when the town celebrates this spiciest of salamis with a spreadable-salami-themed festival.

**\* TIPS \* When eating 'nduja, spread some creamy ricotta onto the bread as well to tame the fierce heat; a deliciously hot and cool combination. 'Nduja is said to be an aphrodisiac, or at the very least, good for the heart. Whichever it is, have a hanky handy to dab at your watering eyes.**

* By Abigail Blasi *

# Recipe Pasta Pommodoro e 'Nduja

## INGREDIENTS

1 tbs olive oil

1 small onion, chopped

*'Nduja* to taste

400g (14oz) good-quality tinned Italian tomatoes

480g (1lb) dried pasta

Grated *ricotta salata* (salted ricotta)

## METHOD

1. Heat the oil in a saucepan and gently cook the onions until caramelised. While they are cooking, put on a pot of salted water to boil for the pasta.

2. When the onions have softened and have a golden colour, add the *'nduja* to them and let the salami paste melt over the gentle heat. The more you add, the punchier the sauce, so add as much as you feel it needs.

3. Once all the salami fat has melted, mix in the tomatoes, and continue cooking the sauce as you cook the pasta, which you'll now add to the boiling water.

4. Cook the pasta until al dente (still has some bite), drain and mix in the sauce.

5. Serve, topping with a sprinkling of ricotta *salata*.

SERVES 4

# * Ostras Picantes *

## GUINEA-BISSAU

**Nothing brings out Guinea-Bissau's charms more than eating *ostras picantes* (spicy oysters) as the sun goes down. Saltwater oysters from mangrove-fringed islands are bathed in a loose lime sauce spiked with hot pepper.**

## What is it?

Mangrove and ocean oysters casually barbecued in their shells on naked, burning charcoal. When the heat has worked its magic, the shells crack open and the woody flesh is dunked into bowls of sweet, citrusy fire.

## Tasting

Often used as an aperitif ahead of a night out dancing, the oysters are grilled in their shells in a loose pyramid pile that's flung directly onto burning charcoal. They're ready when they pop open, giving off super-heated steam. Diners grab a small colourful cloth and a short blunt knife, prising out the briny beasts and dunking them into the thin spicy sauce – made from fresh local lime, salt, bouillon cube and lots of cut chilli pepper, all bound together using a mortar. The resulting taste combines the crisp flavour of lime with memories of hot summer days on the beach, wrapped up with hints of roasted timber and fire. Eating *ostras picantes* in Guinea-Bissau feels like night-swimming in cool ocean while fireworks light up the jungle beyond.

## Origin

The spice may have gone out of Portugal's political relationship with its former colony Guinea-Bissau, but the recipes are still going strong. *Ostras picantes* is the marriage of Portugal's culinary traditions and the sizzle of a small seafaring nation. Oysters are easy to come by in Guinea-Bissau and unlike in other parts of the world, here they've never lost their working-class roots. The season generally runs from December to July, after which oysters are best avoided due to the heavy rains.

## Finding it

Make tracks for fishing spot Quinhamel, two hours by shared taxi outside the capital Bissau. You can buy grilled oysters by the roadside or sit down to *ostras picantes* (around US$8) at Mar Azul, which has a pool and overnight accommodation

* SERVE WITH BEER AND FRIENDS * In Guinea-Bissau, this dish is more than just a recipe – it's an early-evening ritual. On special occasions friends gather in gardens and on terraces, sharing the preparation and cloaking the citrusy oysters in ice cold beer.

* By Kate Thomas *

# Recipe Ostras Picantes

## YOU'LL NEED

### Oysters

8–15 small- to medium-sized oysters per person

### Grilling

Charcoal barbecue/grill with coals

### Sauce

10 large, fresh, squeezed limes

Handful of diced hot chilli peppers

¼ of a bouillon cube

Pinch of salt

## METHOD

1. Remove grill pan from barbecue and throw the oysters, in their shells, onto the naked burning coals.

2. In a grinder or mortar, pound the diced chilli peppers together with the salt and bouillon cube until it forms a fine damp powder.

3. Add the juice of the fresh limes and mix well.

4. Remove the oysters from the coals when they crack open, releasing hot steam.

5. Serve the oysters in a large communal bowl, with a small bowl of sauce served separately.

6. Each diner receives a blunt knife and colourful tea towel to prise open the oysters.

7. Dip and enjoy.

SERVES 6

# * Palm Butter *

## LIBERIA

**Rich, buttery and infused with everything from hot pepper and nutty oil to tropical sunshine and sweat, palm butter tastes as if it has all of Liberia locked inside it.**

## What is it?

This thick golden sauce is made by softening and pounding the nuts that grow high on palm trees. Fish or chicken (sometimes both) is added, along with garlic, onions and a generous handful of Liberian hot peppers.

## Origin

Made almost exclusively from local ingredients, palm butter has been filling bellies in Liberia for centuries. Some claim it was originally a speciality of the Kru ethnic group, from the balmy south-eastern corner of the country.

## Tasting

Liberian comfort food at its best, palm butter's rich fiery taste easily rivals that of the Indian curry. Bowls of the stuff make daily specials boards all over the country, and you'll find it on the menu everywhere from upscale restaurants to the simplest of rural 'chop bars'. Local joints tend to up the fire factor; useful if you need to sweat out a fever but beware – it can be served hot enough to hurt. In Liberian homes, preparation often takes hours, beginning with boiling, then grinding the palm nuts with a four-foot tall pestle to extract the buttery oil and jungle flavour. Then blindingly hot spice (known as 'pepe check') is thrown into the mix, along with salt, garlic, onions, water and locally-sourced palm oil. The resulting thick sauce, complete with chicken or fish, is poured over rice or thinned with water to make a soup that's typically served with *fufu* (a sticky West African staple made from cassava).

## Finding it

In Monrovia, Evelyn's on Broad Street serves hot bowls of medium-spiced palm butter with rice (US$8) or *fufu*. Sweet Lips on the corner of Carey and Gurley Streets does a hotter, simpler version.

**\* CULTURAL REFERENCES \* Palm butter has been written about, sung about, even danced about. A variation on the dish makes a cameo appearance in Hollywood blockbuster *Blood Diamond*. And in the 1940s, Monrovia's famous Greenwood Singers penned popular lyrics sympathising with a man whose wife didn't know how to make palm butter. *'Chicken is nice'*, they harmonised, *'with palm butter and rice'*.**

* By Kate Thomas *

# Recipe Palm Butter

## INGREDIENTS

4 handfuls of palm nuts

1 onion

1 clove garlic

1 lemon

3 cups (750mL) water

Handful of hot chilli peppers

1 large cleaned fish or half a chicken

600g (1lb 5oz) rice

## METHOD

1. Add palm nuts to a saucepan filled with boiling water and boil for about 15 minutes until the nuts are semi-soft.

2. In a blender (or with a mortar and pestle) pound the chilli peppers, garlic and onion.

3. Parboil chopped fish, or chicken, with the blended pepper, garlic and onion mixture in water. Vegetables such as mushroom, zucchini, tomato or aubergine (eggplant) can also be added.

4. Next pound the softened palm nuts in a blender (or with a mortar and pestle) until they form a pulp.

5. Add water and press the pulp through a strainer into a saucepan. Discard the fibers and kernels that are left in the strainer.

5. The remaining pulp should contain the oil and fruit of the palm nuts, as well as the water.

6. Heat the pulp, adding extra water where necessary.

7. Add the fish, or chicken, to the heated palm butter and boil until the mixture is the consistency of Indian curry sauce.

8. Cook the rice and serve the palm butter over it.

SERVES 4

# Papas a la Huancaína

## PERU

**This classic Peruvian version of cheese-topped tubers delivers you to the heart of the Andes with a soulful marriage of two indigenous ingredients: potatoes and the *ají amarillo* pepper.**

## What is it?

Thick slices of boiled potatoes blanketed in a creamy, *ají* chilli pepper-spiked cheese sauce and adorned with hard-boiled eggs and olives, this dish is an Andean staple. Served cold or at room temperature as a starter or salad, *papas a la huancaína* are ubiquitous in Peruvian restaurants and available at street stalls.

## Tasting

Sauntering amid the bustle of Huancayo's Feria Dominical Sunday market high in the Andes, taking in the array of colourful weavings and handicrafts, you're feeling peckish, and stop for a plate of *papas*. That first forkful of cheese-topped potato soothes your palate as the delicate, velvety sauce envelopes the potato and dissolves on your tongue – there's no hard work involved here. Give yourself a moment to detect the unique fruit and grassiness of the Peruvian *ají* pepper, which shines through the sauce before it kicks your tongue on the way down. Add a bit of olive, egg and lettuce for your second bite and you'll get a well-choreographed dance of sweet, salty, smooth and crunchy. Take a sip of *chicha de jora* (corn beer) and repeat.

## Origin

Folklore has it that *papas a la huancaína*, practically a national dish, was invented by a woman from Huancayo, a city in the agriculture-rich Mantaro valley and the final stop for a train route from Lima that is now the second highest railway in the world. While the railroad was being built in the late 19th century, women generated income by bringing workers food to eat. There was stiff competition, as many of them sold potatoes! One market-savvy *señora* from Huancayo doctored hers with a unique sauce and the potatoes quickly became a favourite. (Of course, some say that's hogwash and the dish was actually invented in Chosica, a suburb of Lima.)

## Finding it

*Papas* are commonly found at street stalls and in restaurants. A reliable option in Lima or Huancayo is Huancahuasi (S6 or US$2.17).

---

**\* TIPS \*** *Huancaína* sauce is not reserved for potatoes only. The creamy, delicate topping is as versatile as it is addictive and frequently shows up with chicken, fish or pasta. It's also used as a dip.

---

\* By Caroline Veldhuis \*

# Recipe Papas a la Huancaína

## INGREDIENTS

6 potatoes

Lettuce

2–3 *ají amarillo* peppers

225g (½lb) queso fresco, or farmer's cheese, crumbled (a reduced salt feta, mild goat's cheese or ricotta *salata* can be substituted)

2–3 cup (500–750mL) evaporated milk

2 tbs vegetable oil

4 saltine crackers

3 eggs, hardboiled

¼ cup (a handful) whole black Spanish olives

## METHOD

1. Scrub, boil and peel potatoes. Allow them to cool and cut in thick slices lengthwise. Arrange on serving plate(s) on top of a few lettuce leaves.

2. Wash and cut the peppers, stripping out the ribs and most of the seeds. Cut into large pieces and saute gently for a few minutes until they begin to soften.

3. Put the peppers, cheese, evaporated milk, oil and saltines into a blender and blend until you have a fairly thick sauce. Add extra evaporated milk if the mixture is too thick or saltines if it's too runny. Season with a dash of salt and pepper.

4. Pour the sauce over the potatoes. Cut eggs in half and arrange on the plate, along with a few olives.

SERVES 4 AS A STARTER

# * Pasta all'Arrabbiata *

## ITALY

**Literally translating as 'angry pasta', *pasta all'arrabbiata* is all hot and bothered because of its sauce, a spicy mix of tomatoes, garlic and hot chilli flakes.**

## What is it?

This Italian classic is pasta – usually spaghetti or penne – tossed in a simple sauce of tomato and garlic cooked in olive oil and spiced with dried hot red chilli flakes (though some cooks use fresh chillies). A sprinkling of good grated pecorino romano is optional.

## Origin

Italians have been cooking pasta for nearly a millennium. It was likely brought to Sicily by Arab traders (not, as popular legend has it, imported by Marco Polo from China!) *Pasta all'arrabbiata* is especially associated with the lusty, earthy cuisine of Rome, though you can find it nationwide.

## Tasting

Look for *pasta all'arrabbiata* in Rome's neighbourhood *trattoria*, where rustic dishes are accompanied by a carafe or two of house Chianti. The beauty of the dish is in its simplicity: al dente pasta in a light, bright sauce of garlicky tomatoes, studded with tongue-numbing dried red chilli flakes. A hearty plateful will keep you full for hours. *Pasta all'arrabbiata* is also a popular home-cooked meal, the kind of thing your nonna throws together in 20 minutes on a Monday evening. If you're lucky enough to befriend a few locals, perhaps you'll also be lucky enough to be invited to supper – they'll supply the pasta, you bring the vino.

## Finding it

Rome's once-working-class Trastevere neighbourhood is now a nightlife hotspot, dotted with *trattoria* feeding huge plates of pasta to hungry partygoers. Expect to pay around €8 (US$10).

**\* VARIATIONS \* Anything can be made *all'arrabbiata* – 'angry-style' – not just pasta. Look for chicken, lamb, gnocchi and even pizza, all with the same spicy, garlicky tomato sauce. Similar to *pasta all'arrabbiata*, *pasta amatriciana* features a tomato-and-chilli based sauce, with the tasty addition of *guanciale* – salt-cured pork jowl.**

* By Emily Matchar *

# Recipe Pasta all'Arrabbiata

## INGREDIENTS

500g (1lb) dry pasta (penne or spaghetti)

400g (14oz) tinned tomatoes, drained

1 medium onion, chopped

2 cloves garlic, minced

60mL olive oil

½ tsp red chilli flakes

100g (3½oz) pecorino cheese, grated

Salt to taste

## METHOD

1. Over medium heat, saute onion and garlic in half of the oil until golden.

2. Add the tomatoes and chilli and bring to a simmer.

3. Meanwhile, cook pasta to al dente and drain.

4. Stir the remaining oil into the tomato mixture and pour over the pasta.

5. Serve with freshly grated cheese.

SERVES 4

# * Pepperpot *

## GUYANA

**Guyana's national dish, this zesty meat stew gets its dark colour from cassareep – syrup derived from cassava root – and its fiery kick from Caribbean chillies.**

## What is it?

A highly spiced meat stew containing anything from pork, goat, beef or lamb, pepperpot is a beloved special-occasion dish in the South American nation of Guyana. While spices vary from cook to cook, clove and cinnamon are common flavourings, and Scotch bonnet or wiri wiri chillies typically provide the heat. But the non-negotiable ingredient for true Guyanese pepperpot is the cassareep, made by boiling down the juices of an old cassava root until it resembles molasses.

## Origin

Pepperpot is an Amerindian dish, originally invented by Guyanese natives as a way to preserve meat without refrigeration. The cassareep acts as a preservative, allowing cooks to leave the pepperpot on the back of the stove for days (or, in legendary stories, years), reheating and adding more cassareep at mealtimes. Traditionally, pepperpot is made in a special pot (also called a pepper pot) that retains and imparts flavour from one stew to the next. According to myth, never double dip a spoon in the pepper pot or the whole batch will spoil!

## Tasting

In Guyana, pepperpot is best known as a Christmas dish, its rich, spicy scent perfuming the house on Christmas Eve and into Christmas morning. Extended families gather round the pot for servings of the glossy brown stew, the meat so tender it's falling off the bone. Sop up the juices with a slice of soft homemade plait bread, a braided loaf that resembles Jewish challah. The spice of the chilli warms the back of your throat as you gobble spoonful after spoonful, savouring the deep, complex flavour. If you're not lucky enough to be invited to Guyanese Christmas, a handful of restaurants in the nation's capital of Georgetown serve the labour-intensive dish.

## Finding it

The Dutch Bottle Café in Georgetown, Guyana offers pepperpot (US$10) and other local specialties.

* VARIATIONS * Philadelphia pepper pot, which usually contains tripe and lacks cassareep, is a variation that's been kicking around the US since the Revolutionary War, likely brought north by West Indian slaves.

* By Emily Matchar *

# Recipe **Pepperpot**

## INGREDIENTS

1kg (2lb) stewing beef, cubed

1kg (2lb) ox tail, goat or mutton, cubed

250mL (1 cup) cassareep (available in West Indian specialty stores or ordered online)

2 red peppers

2.5cm (1in) piece dried orange or lemon peel

2.5cm (1in) piece of cinnamon stick

3 cloves

60g (2oz) sugar

Salt to taste

## METHOD

1. Place meat in a large pot, adding enough water to cover. Bring to the boil, skim, then reduce heat to medium-low and simmer for one hour. Add other ingredients, simmering until the meat is tender, up to three hours. Serve with bread.

SERVES 8

# * Pica Pau *

## PORTUGAL

**What's that? *Pica pau* means fried WOODPECKER?! Thankfully, this dish of peppery Portuguese meat-magic might have a somewhat misleading name, but ordering it is certainly no mistake.**

## What is it?

*Pica pau* is one of many *petiscos* – a Portuguese equivalent to tapas. Eaten as a starter, or to be shared among friends, this dish comprises slices of pork loin (or beef steak) fried up and served in a rich, thick, beery, zingy gravy that's loaded with pickles.

## Tasting

You can find *pica pau* on fancy menus, where avant-garde chefs reinvent traditional cuisine. But really, there's no need. Find a spit-n-sawdust *tasca*, with FC Porto vs Sporting Lisbon blaring on the corner TV and a bloke drinking *ginjinha* (cherry brandy) at the bar, and you're good to go. Order a large *pica pau* and chilled beers for all your friends and get ready to peck; essential tools are a toothpick to spear the meat, fresh bread to soak up the gravy and a stack of serviettes for the mess. A connoisseur might be looking for the right balance of olive oil, pickles and acidity, and a spiciness to make your lips tingle but not enflame. Hungry football fans won't care a fudge for such subtleties – this is comfort food after all. To them, the tender pork, oozy sauce, cold beer, banter and beautiful game are a match made in heaven.

## Origin

Though *pica pau* translates as woodpecker, no crimson-quiffed Woodies were harmed in the making of this dish. The moniker merely relates to how it's typically eaten, pecked at with toothpicks. The sauce that smothers the strips of meat may date to the 1960s, when returning emigrant Daniel da Silva tried to adapt French food for the Portuguese palate (see the *Francesinha*, below). Whatever its provenance, its no-fuss piquant heartiness is now a local staple.

## Finding it

Tasca da Esquina (www.tascadaesquina.com), Rua Domingos Sequeira, Lisbon, offers a modern twist on *petiscos*, including *pica pau*; expect to pay around €20 ($26) a head.

**\* VARIATIONS \* A *Francesinha* (meaning 'Frenchie') is some sort of meat – such as fresh sausage, steak or roasted pork – dripping in a thick tomato-beer sauce and ensconced in bread. Essentially, this is *pica pau* in sandwich form. It's most popular in Porto, where it's usually eaten with French fries and cold beer.**

**\* By Sarah Baxter \***

# Recipe Pica Pau

Not all recipes contain chillies – the spiciness levels are up to you. Be warned: if you use Portuguese *piri-piri* chillies, these are hot, hot, hot!

## INGREDIENTS

500g (1lb) pork loin

Olive oil

2 tbs of butter

½ onion, sliced

4 garlic cloves, sliced

Salt and pepper to taste

Paprika and chillies to taste

500mL (2 cups) beer (or white wine)

Sliced pickles

## METHOD

1. Cut the meat into thin strips; season with salt and pepper.

2. Heat the oil and butter; saute the onions and garlic until soft.

3. Add the paprika, chillies, salt, pepper and meat; simmer for 10 minutes.

4. Add the beer; bring to boil then simmer for 45 minutes.

5. Stir in the pickles.

6. Serve with bread for dipping.

SERVES 4

# * Pickled Herring in Mustard Sauce *

## NORWAY

**Herrings for breakfast? Norwegians adore the humble herring, served in vinegar and mustard, so much so that many can't wait until lunchtime for their first fix of the day.**

## Origin

Before oil was discovered in Norwegian waters in the 1960s, Norway was one of the poorest countries in Europe; rich in fish and little else. The Atlantic's vast schools of herring were so abundant that the silvery fish became a Norwegian staple, even among the poor. Affections for the humble herring, now rehabilitated as a delicacy and far less abundant, have never waned. In fact, it's more popular than ever – not least because it reminds Norwegians just how far they've come in a short space of time.

## Tasting

Let's face it, pickled fish with mustard is an acquired taste – especially at breakfast. And yet, many find themselves returning to try this punchy pungent favourite again and again, drawn to its tangy strangeness and to the cold, smooth texture of raw, white fish soaked in a zesty mustard and vinegar coating. Find it at the hotel breakfast bar or, as the locals do, in one of the open sandwiches that Scandinavians love to feast on. Served atop a wedge of bread, you'll most appreciate it sitting by a Norwegian fishing harbour as seabirds whirl and squawk overhead. Here by the water, you'll be surrounded by the invigorating pong of fish fresh off the boats and of boat traffic coming and going, as it has along Norway's Atlantic coast for centuries.

## What is it?

Small, plump slices of raw, pickled herring bathed in mustard and vinegar are the most common version of this dish. It's a snack, a side dish and a recurring theme at Norwegian hotel breakfast buffets.

## Finding it

There is no better place to try this dish than the stalls at Bergen's famous fish market along the Torget waterfront in the town centre. Expect to pay Nkr50 (US$8.50) for a small serving or Nkr100 (US$17) for a good-sized take-home pack.

* VARIATIONS * Norwegians also serve up raw herrings pickled with onions, or paired with tomato instead of mustard sauce. In these versions, as with the pickled herring in mustard sauce, the fish is invariably served cold. Alternatively, the herrings are grilled and served warm in a mustard sauce, but this version lacks the piquancy of its pickled cousin and is more likely to hit the dinner table than the breakfast bar.

* By Anthony Ham *

# Recipe Pickled Herring in Mustard Sauce

This dish works best if you allow ample time for the fish to soak and marinate – preferably 48 hours. If you can buy the herrings already pickled you'll save yourself a lot of time.

## INGREDIENTS

### Pickling liquid

3 cups (750mL) water

1 cup (250mL) vinegar

2 tbs sugar

1 diced carrot

1 chopped red onion

½ a leek (white part only)

1 bay leaf

3 black peppercorns

3 white peppercorns

8 preserved herring fillets

### Mustard sauce

1 tbs sweet (Bavarian) mustard

1 tsp of Dijon mustard

2 tsp sugar

1–2 tbs distilled white vinegar

Pinch of salt

Pinch of freshly ground white peppercorns

¾ cup (10 tbs) canola oil

½ cup (7 tbs) chopped dill

## METHOD

1. To make the brine, combine all ingredients for pickling in a saucepan and bring to the boil. Stir every now and then until sugar is completely dissolved. Remove from the heat, cover and set aside.

2. Submerge and soak the herring fillets in cold water overnight to remove the saltiness from the fish.

3. Remove the fillets from the water and pat dry with paper towel. Arrange in a shallow baking dish, cover with the pickling brine and refrigerate overnight.

4. To make the mustard sauce, combine the mustards, sugar, vinegar, dill, salt and pepper in a food processor. Drizzle canola oil into the mix in a slow, steady stream until the sauce is thick. Leave in the fridge overnight.

5. The next day, remove the herring from the brine and cut into slices, then serve with the mustard sauce.

SERVES 4 (AS AN ENTRÉE OR APPETISER)

# * Pig Trotter Curry *

## HIMALAYAN FOOTHILLS (NEPAL, DARJEELING & SIKKIM, INDIA)

**Rare in restaurants but popular in Himalayan homes, this spicy meat dish, known as *khutta ko achaar*, is rooted in Nepali tradition. It's common around festival times and is a meal around which to make merry.**

## What Is It?

The core ingredient is, of course, pigs' trotters – aka their feet. Although recipes vary from home to home, the trotters are typically stewed with vegetables such as onion and tomato, and heavily seasoned; don't stint on the garlic paste, red chilli powder or fresh green chilli peppers to set the taste buds ablaze. The fiery result is enjoyed throughout the year and at any time of day, but usually dinner.

## Origin

It's virtually impossible to pin down how long this curry has been adding zing to Himalayan kitchens. After all, the original curries – a catch-all term for the perplexing array of Asian stews given punch by an amazing mix of spices – are thousands of years old. The use of pigs' trotters as the base element probably stems from age-old rural practices that put to use every part of a slaughtered animal.

## Tasting

The curried-trotter eating experience unfolds in distinct stages. First, the smell is unmistakable – meaty, spicy and aromatic, but not overpowering like dishes from northern India. Once the eating has begun, the stewy piquancy of ginger and garlic flavours emerge foremost. Then as you chew into the tender meat, you'll get a hit of the juicy pork tang, heightened by the thick gravy of tongue-coating fat and bone marrow typical of a trotter. The last blast is enduring chilli, relieved only by the rice or roti accompaniment or a medicinal dose of local raksi (sinus-clearing alcohol). This sensory adventure usually takes place in the high-spirited company of a family for whom the trotters are a treat, as is the occasion to share it with a special guest.

## Finding It

Despite their ubiquity, curried trotters are not normally served in restaurants. You'll have to get invited to someone's home!

**\* VARIATIONS \* There is no one indisputable recipe. Every Nepali household has a special way of currying pig trotters and everyone passionately believes that his or her own mum makes the best one around.**

* By Ethan Gelber *

# Recipe Pig Trotter Curry

## INGREDIENTS

1–2 pig trotters (1–1½kg/2–3lb)

3 onions, chopped

½ tsp cumin powder

½ tsp turmeric powder

2 tbs ginger garlic paste (or crush 15 garlic cloves and 25–50g/1–2oz ginger)

½ tsp red chilli powder (mostly for colour, so any red chilli powder will do, like Kashmiri mirch or Degi mirch)

30 green chilli peppers (for a very spicy curry), halved or diced

3 tomatoes, chopped

2 tbs black mustard seeds, ground (optional)

2 tbs lime juice

2–3 tbs mustard oil (vegetable oil can be used too)

Salt

## METHOD

1. Chop the trotters into pieces, large or small according to taste.
2. Stir-fry the chopped trotters in a wok or pan until the meat is slightly brown on all sides.
3. In a separate pan, heat the mustard oil. Do not use too much oil, as pork fat will later add to the liquid.
4. Add the chopped onions to the oil and fry until golden brown.
5. Add the cumin powder, turmeric powder and ginger garlic paste, and fry until it starts sticking to the pan.
6. Add the red chilli powder and green chillies, salt to taste and fry for about 30 seconds. Note that 30 green chillies will make a very spicy curry; reduce the number of chillies to moderate the strength of the curry.
7. Add the chopped tomatoes and cook for about two minutes.
8. Add the stir-fried trotters to the spices and mix together.
9. Transfer the ingredients to a pressure cooker and cook for around 20 minutes (five or six whistles).
10. While this cooks, roast the ground black mustard seeds in a separate pan.
11. Once the trotters are ready, add the roasted black mustard seeds and the lime juice, then return to the heat for two minutes.
12. Serve the curried trotters hot or at room temperature.

SERVES 8

# * Pimientos de Padrón *

## PADRÓN, GALICIA, SPAIN

**Nine times out of 10, you'll simply get sweetness and crunch from this popular *tapa* (snack), but every so often you bite into a whole pepper only to be met with a mouthful of fire.**

## What is it?

Known as Russian roulette peppers, *pimientos de Padrón* are the star of a simple and enduringly popular dish found on tapas menus nationwide. Fried whole and seasoned with nothing more than a sprinkle of salt, the small, green peppers are famous for their unpredictability on the spice-o-meter. A simple Galician saying sums up what to expect: '*Os pementos de Padrón – uns pican e outros non*' (Padrón peppers – some are hot and some are not).

## Origin

The diminutive peppers made their way to Spain in the late 16th century, imported as seeds by Franciscan monks returning from Mexico. Theories abound on why some are spicy while others lack zing. Some say it's the soil in the valleys around Padrón, where the peppers are cultivated, others put it down to southern Galicia's weather. Most agree that timing is crucial, with peppers picked earlier in the season packing less punch than those harvested in the later summer months.

## Finding it

As well as serving them traditional-style, A Casa Dos Martinez in Padrón features the peppers in a range of other dishes. Dishes start at €5 (US$6.50).

## Tasting

Simply showcasing a trio of quality ingredients, *pimientos de Padrón* epitomise authentic, unpretentious Spanish cooking. It's a classic tapa, and a rare vegetarian addition to the table, usually ordered alongside portions of potatoes, meat, seafood and salad. The sweetness of the slightly browned peppers provides a perfect contrast with the crunch of a coating of rock salt, while the drizzle of pepper-infused oil left on the plate just begs to be soaked up with fresh bread. But the true allure of the dish is their unpredictability. Some fear that rogue fiery flavour, others hope for it, but despite theories and old wives' tales, no one can really tell which peppers will sting until they shove the whole thing, seeds and all, into their mouth.

**\* CELEBRATING THE SPICE \*** Each year, on the first Saturday in August, peppers take centre stage in Herbón, a district of Padrón, for the annual Pepper Festival (Fiesta del Pimiento). After a church mass dedicated to the ingredient, tractors arrive to distribute some 2000kg of free peppers to gastronomes looking for the ultimate lucky dip.

* By Lucy Corne *

# Recipe Pimientos de Padrón

## INGREDIENTS

500g (1lb) fresh Padrón peppers, whole

Approx 1 cup (250mL) virgin olive oil

Coarse salt to season

## METHOD

1. Thoroughly rinse the peppers and pat dry with kitchen towel.

2. Heat the oil in a frying pan over a medium heat. You can alter the amount of oil used to suit your tastes but don't be too sparing, the dish is ideally prepared with plenty of oil.

3. Add the peppers to the frying pan in batches, frying for two to three minutes on each side.

4. Turn the peppers when they just begin to brown and start to shrivel a little.

5. Once browned all over, place the cooked peppers onto a piece of kitchen towel to drain some of the oil.

6. Transfer to a clean plate and sprinkle with coarse salt.

7. Serve as one of a number of tapas dishes. The peppers can also be served as a side dish for a main meal.

SERVES 4

# * Piri-piri Chicken *

## MOZAMBIQUE

**Flame-grilled chicken marinated in east Africa's most famous blend of chilli and spices is served oceanside with a cold beer. The simple things in life are often the best.**

## What is it?

After carefully marinating in chillies, ginger, garlic, lemon juice, paprika, salt and pepper, chicken is barbecued until the skin is crispy and slightly charred. A more innocuous version of *piri-piri* chicken may be available at global fast-food restaurants, but it's no comparison to hot off the grill on a beach in Mozambique.

## Tasting

Sunday afternoon at the beach is a great family tradition in Maputo, Mozambique's capital city. *Futebol* (soccer) games with scores of players on each side swarm up and down the sand, and there's a steady stream of frosty bottles of local 2M (*'Doshem'*) lager being retrieved from ice-boxes. In the distance, Maputo's mini-Manhattan emerges from the heat haze and the beach's essential aroma is chicken being grilled with spicy *piri-piri* sauce. If the friendly locals don't ask you to join their barbecues, seek out the busiest of the *piri-piri* stalls punctuating the beach and dive in. Look forward to a smoky flavour combination of chilli heat and citrusy zing, underpinned by expertly grilled chicken with a slightly charred and caramelised skin.

## Origin

*Piri-piri* sauce is one of the world's original fusion concoctions. Reputedly the first chillies to reach Europe were brought back from the New World by Columbus, then Portuguese navigators exported them to colonies in Africa including Angola and Mozambique. In Africa, the fiery bird's-eye chillies were dubbed *pili-pili*, Swahili for 'pepper-pepper', and subsequently cross-pollinated with local African chillies. Eventually, the chillies were transported back to Europe and Portugal, retaining their African name.

## Finding it

Head to Maputo's Costa do Sol and score grilled *piri-piri* chicken from simple beachfront shacks. Expect to pay around 120,000 New Meticals (US$4).

**\* VARIATIONS \*** *Piri-piri* sauce is also a great accompaniment to local Mozambican seafood. In Portuguese colonial times, Maputo was known as Lourenço Marques and plump 'LM Prawns' were renowned across Africa. Echoes of Mozambique's colonial heritage still linger at Maputo's grand Hotel Polana, especially on Saturday nights for the weekly seafood barbecue buffet.

**\* By Brett Atkinson \***

# Recipe Piri-piri Chicken

## INGREDIENTS

1 tbs olive oil

4–8 bird's-eye chillies, depending on how hot you want the dish

4 cloves garlic, roughly chopped

½ cup (125mL) lemon juice

1 tbs paprika

1 tsp sea salt

1½ tsp chopped fresh ginger

½ tsp pepper

4 chicken legs

## METHOD

1.  To make the marinade, combine the olive oil, chillies, ginger, garlic, lemon juice, paprika, salt and pepper in a food processor. Rub the chicken with roughly half the marinade and refrigerate for around three hours.

2.  After marinating, grill the chicken on a barbecue at medium heat, basting regularly with the remaining marinade until the skin is slightly charred and the juices run clear.

3.  Serve with rice or fried potatoes and a fresh green salad.

SERVES 4

# * Rasam *

## SOUTH INDIA

**Revered for its comforting and healing properties, the endlessly versatile *rasam* is South India's 'hot and sour' soup, infused with the exotic herbs and spices so abundant in this region.**

## What is it?

A tangy spice broth flavoured with simple, sun-kissed ingredients such as tomatoes, black pepper and tamarind, every South Indian mother has her own *rasam*. The aromatic elixir is crafted by toasting, grinding and simmering spices in water. Traditionally poured over rice to form a meal's second course – following the thicker *sambar* and preceding yoghurt or cheese curd – *rasam* eventually became a soup in its own right.

## Origin

As early as AD 1700, South Indians were witnessed drinking peppered water, the Tamil *milagu rasam*, as a digestif and were later seen by British colonialists pouring this and other spice infusions over their rice as flavouring agents. Traditionally cooked in an *eeya chombu* – a lead vessel believed to enhance the flavour – *rasam* continually reinvents itself with headline ingredients such as tomato, pineapple, garlic or lemon. It is known as the thicker *saar* in Karnataka, or *chaaru* in Andhra Pradesh. Lauded for its Ayurvedic properties, *rasam* stokes *agni* (fire) and remedies sore throats, colds and coughs. With South Indian expats citing it as an antidote to homesickness, it's little wonder the soup is regarded as a cure for all that ails.

## Tasting

A steaming, aromatic bowl of *rasam* is a wondrous thing for your senses. Amid the pungent smells and cacophony of sweltering Chennai's teeming streets, it will ground you – the intensity of freshly ground peppercorns and tangy tamarind demand attention and tingle your sinuses. Slurping is encouraged – *rasam* is even ladled into cupped hands at festivities such as weddings – but let a mouthful linger for a moment while this deceptively simple broth dazzles your tastebuds. Tamarind's bright sourness coupled with a dragonlike burst of heat from pepper and chilli never fail to cheer and enliven.

## Finding it

*Rasam* is available at virtually all South Indian eateries and costs about 50 rupees (US$0.80). Try it at Hotel Saravanaa Bhavan in Chennai.

* VARIATIONS * The British colonialists in Madras (often referred to as 'Mulls' by their countrymen) wanted to develop a heartier soup out of the ubiquitous *milagu tannir*. The addition of meat stock, additional spices and coconut resulted in the thicker, Anglo–Indian concoction that veered into North India and beyond, known and loved as *mulligatawny*.

* By Caroline Veldhuis *

# Recipe Tomato Rasam

## INGREDIENTS

1 tsp black peppercorns

1 tsp cumin seeds

2 large plum tomatoes

3 cups (750mL) hot water

1 ½ tsp salt

2 heaped tbs tamarind paste

3 tbs ghee or canola oil

¼ tsp black mustard seeds

¼ tsp fenugreek seeds

2 medium-sized dried red chilli

2 tbs brown sugar

Handful of fresh coriander leaves

## METHOD

1.  Using a coffee grinder, or pestle and mortar, grind pepper-corns and cumin seeds until fine, set aside.

2.  Wash and chop tomatoes and puree with a few tablespoons of water in a food processor, set aside.

3.  Pour hot water into a soup pot and add tamarind paste, bring to the boil, reduce heat to simmering and add tomatoes, salt and ground spices. Cook for about 10 minutes.

4.  In a heavy saucepan, heat oil over a medium heat and drop in the mustard seeds until they begin to crackle. Break up the chilli into two or three pieces and add along with the fenu-greek seeds. Cook until the seeds release their aromas (one to two minutes).

5.  Add the oil and spices to the soup mixture, as well as the brown sugar. Taste and season with more salt or sugar as required.

6.  Ladle soup into bowls and top with torn coriander leaves.

SERVES 4

# * Ras el Hanout *

## MOROCCO

**Slow-cooked, buttery lamb literally melts off the bone, thanks to hours of tenderising in a tagine steaming with aromatic *ras el hanout*, Morocco's secret spice mix!**

## What is it?

*Ras el hanout* is the key to the mystery behind every authentic Moroccan tagine. While the ingredients and quantities vary (often carefully guarded secrets among families and spice merchants), the complex blend can feature up to 50 different spices.

## Origin

The Arabic term *'ras el hanout'* translates as 'head of the shop', an assurance that it's the best your *attar* (spice master) in the souk (open-air market) has to offer. There are also rumours that it dates back to biblical times, 'ras', being the title for an Ethiopian king. Intriguingly, there are tales of *attars* customising their *ras el hanout* with hashish for very special clients!

## Tasting

Imagine wandering the labyrinths of Marrakesh with every sense on red alert: the cacophony of buzzy bartering, blaring Arabic music, vibrant kaftan colours, dodging donkeys and snake charmers. The heady aroma of molten lamb penetrates the incense-laden undertow and you veer in the direction of a quiet rooftop for your first taste of authentic tagine. As the terracotta lid is lifted by your host, revel in the steamy, aromatic anticipation. The first nugget of lamb falls apart on your tongue, unctuous with *ras el hanout*'s layers of sweet, spicy, warmth, depth. Take a sip of mint tea or perhaps fresh pomegranate juice, tear off some *khobz* (bread) and dive in again. And again.

## Finding it

Al Fassia in Marrakesh offers authentic lamb tagines (€11.50/US$15.25).

**\* VARIATIONS \*** If seafood floats your boat, *Le Saveur du Poisson* in Tangier doesn't even bother opening if the catch of the day isn't fresh enough.

* By Karyn Noble *

# Recipe Lamb Tagine

## INGREDIENTS

1 kg (2lb) boneless lamb shoulder, cut in chunks

2 onions, thinly sliced

1 tbs of fresh ginger, finely chopped

2 cinnamon sticks

800g (1lb 10oz) diced tomatoes

175g (6oz) dried apricots

3 bay leaves

3 tbs olive oil

1 pomegranate

Handful coriander leaves, chopped

Salt and pepper

2 tsp *ras el hanout*
(see below for 40g recipe)

### Ras El Hanout

½ tsp roasted cardamom seeds

½ tsp roasted fennel seeds

1 tbs roasted coriander seeds

1 tbs roasted cumin seeds

1 tsp cinnamon

1 tsp turmeric

1 tsp cayenne

2 tsp sweet paprika

1 tsp salt

½ tsp sugar

½ tsp allspice

2 whole cloves

¼ tsp ground nutmeg

## METHOD

1.  Heat the oil in a large, deep casserole dish (or tagine!). Add onions, saute until soft. Stir in the ginger, add the lamb in portions and fry until lightly coloured. Return all the meat to the pan.

2.  Blend/crush *ras el hanout* ingredients, add to lamb. Stir in cinnamon sticks and cook for 1 minute.

3.  Add tomatoes and 300mL water and bring to boil, stirring occasionally. Add bay leaves and other seasonings to taste, then cover and simmer for approx 1.5 hours.

4.  Stir in apricots and heat for 5 minutes.

5.  Serve sprinkled with coriander leaves and pomegranate seeds.

SERVES 4

# * Rendang Daging *

## MALAYSIA & INDONESIA

**Thailand can keep its green curry; in Malaysia and Indonesia,
*rendang daging* – dry beef curry with roasted coconut
and lime leaves – rules the roost.**

## What is it?

The Malay Straits' favourite curry, *rendang daging*
starts with the quintessential ingredients of
Southeast Asia – coconut, chilli, lime leaves, ginger,
galangal, garlic, turmeric and lemongrass – and
takes them on a magnificent journey. Hearty hunks
of beef are first simmered and then fried in a slowly
reducing blend of coconut milk and spices.

## Origin

*Rendang daging* was first conceived by the
Minangkabau people of West Sumatra, and its
ingredients and preparation are said to be a
metaphor for the philosophy of *musyawarah* –
consultation with elders – that binds Minangkabau
society together. The meat is taken to represent
the tribal elders, coconut milk represents teachers,
poets and writers, chilli represents the guidance
of Islam and the spice mix represents the ordinary
population, unified by mutual discussion.

## Tasting

The slow, labour-intensive preparation of *rendang
daging* gives this dense, dry curry remarkable
properties of preservation – the dish takes half a
day to prepare, but can safely be stored for days at
room temperature, even in tropical heat. However,
in the average Muslim canteen, the *rendang* sitting
on the counter was probably prepared the day
before, and left overnight to mature the complex
flavours. The first surprise when tasting *rendang*
is how different it is to Thai or Indian curries.
The use of roasted coconut gives *rendang* a rich,
smoky quality more common in Mexican cooking.
And while there's plenty of chilli to give the dish
some kick, in *rendang* the heat plays a supporting
role, allowing the aromatic herbs and spices –
lemongrass, lime leaves, garlic, galangal and ginger
– to shine through. Eat it with steamed rice parcels
and a big mug of *teh tarik* (Malay 'pulled' tea).

## Finding it

Our favourite place to sample *rendang daging*? The
*mamak* (Indian Muslim) canteens opposite Kuala
Lumpur's Central Market, where a plate will cost
around RM12 (US$3.70).

**\* THE SECRET INGREDIENT \* *Rendang daging* would be nothing without its secret
ingredient – *kerisik*, a dense paste made from coconut roasted in a dry pan and ground
in a mortar and pestle. Lending dishes sultry, smoky overtones, the resulting mix is less
like powder and more like cocoa butter – rich, oily and aromatic.**

* By Joe Bindloss *

# Recipe Rendang Daging

## INGREDIENTS

### Kerisik

50g (2oz) ground coconut

### Spice Paste

6 shallots

2.5cm (1in) piece of galangal

2.5cm (1in) piece of ginger

3 stalks of lemongrass, crushed

4–5 cloves garlic

10 dried chillies, soaked in warm water and de-seeded

### Curry

750g (1½lb) lean beef, cut into cubes

6 tbs kerisik

1 cup (250mL) coconut milk

1 cup (250mL) water

2 tsp tamarind juice

1 stalk lemongrass, cut into pieces and crushed

1 cinnamon stick

4 cloves

4 star anise

3 cardamom pods

6 kaffir lime leaves, finely chopped

1 tbs palm sugar

Salt to taste

## METHOD

### Kerisik

1.  Roast the ground coconut in a dry pan until it turns light brown, then blend in a spice mill or mortar and pestle to produce a thick, oily paste.

### Spice paste

2.  Grind the shallots and other spice ingredients in a blender or mortar and pestle to create a fine paste.

### Curry

3.  Heat oil in a pan and add the spice paste, cinnamon, cloves, star anise and cardamom and fry for a minute or so to release the aromas.

4.  Add the chopped beef and crushed lemongrass and stir-fry until the meat is browned.

5.  Add the coconut milk, tamarind juice and water and simmer until the meat is almost cooked.

6.  Add the kerisik, palm sugar, kaffir lime leaves and salt to taste, then cover the pan and cook on low heat for one to 1½ hours, until the meat is tender and the liquid has almost all been absorbed.

5.  Leave overnight to mature the flavours, then warm and serve with rice.

SERVES 4

# * Saliva Chicken *

## SICHUAN, CHINA

**'Made to make your mouth water' would be a better translation for this searing chicken salad from Sichuan.**

## What is it?

Poached chicken, steeped in a marinade of sesame oil, red chilli oil and lashings of Sichuan pepper. Served hot or cold, it's a favourite starter for people with fireproof tastebuds. Soy sauce, coriander, peanuts, rice wine and ginger add subtle flavours, but it's the heat of the chilli and Sichuan pepper that will be etched into your memory.

## Origin

Don't be put off by the English name – this is one of those 'lost in translation' moments. What the Chinese name is supposed to suggest is a dish so delicious that you cannot help but start salivating when you think about it – think 'mouth-watering' rather than 'from the chef's mouth'. In Sichuan, the dish is served as a starter to stimulate the tastebuds for the banquet ahead.

## Tasting

Despite its potent heat, saliva chicken is remarkably subtle by Sichuan standards. Instead of being an all-out assault on the senses, this is a spicy dish with a sensitive heart. Sure, your first bite will deliver the expected hammer-blow of chilli and Sichuan pepper, but behind the menacing-looking marinade, the creaminess of the poached chicken provides a cool, calm place to escape the fire. Each mouthful starts with an explosion but ends with blessed relief. You'll still leave with your lips burning at the end of the meal, but you'll also remember the more subtle flavours in the poached chicken – sesame, coriander and the delicate overtones of ginger and spring onion. Eat it at the start of a lavish banquet dinner to take full advantage of its saliva-stimulating qualities.

## Finding it

Saliva chicken is found everywhere in Sichuan, and most other places in China. A generous portion will cost around ¥15 (US$2.50).

* THE OTHER, OTHER PEPPER * Chilli is a relatively recent arrival in Asia; before this South American import stole the show, cooks added heat using fire-cracker-hot Sichuan pepper. Technically a seed pod, this western-Chinese spice has a heat that burns like black pepper, but that lingers on the palate like the hottest chilli. The Chinese even have a special term – *ma-la* – for this numbing warmth.

* By Joe Bindloss *

# Recipe Saliva Chicken

## YOU'LL NEED

### Poached Chicken

1 fresh chicken cut into quarters

Pinch of salt

2.5cm (1in) piece fresh ginger, peeled

2 spring onions, chopped

2 tbs sesame oil

### Marinade

2 tbs Sichuan peppercorns

1 clove garlic, minced

1 tbs ginger, minced

3 tbs regular soy sauce

3 tbs light soy sauce

2 tbs dark vinegar

1 tsp granulated sugar

2 tbs sesame oil

3 tbs chilli oil

40g (1–2oz) roasted peanuts

### Garnish

2 tbs sesame seeds

Handful of coriander leaves, chopped

## METHOD

1.  Rub the chicken with salt, then poach in boiling water in a covered pan with the ginger and spring onions for 20 to 25 minutes.

2.  Turn the chicken and poach for another 20 to 25 minutes, then cool in cold water and rub with sesame oil.

3.  Bone the chicken quarters and chop the chicken into bite-sized pieces.

4.  Mix the marinade ingredients together, pour over the chicken and leave to marinate for half an hour.

5.  Top the cooked chicken with the garnish and serve.

SERVES 4

# * Samak Harrah *

## LEBANON, SYRIA & JORDAN

**The countries of the Levant – Lebanon, Syria and Jordan – stand at the crossroads of numerous historical and culinary currents and this baked fish dish blends Mediterranean subtleties with an uncharacteristically fiery Arabian chilli climax.**

## What is it?

*Samak harrah* is a whole white fish that is fried and then baked in its own juices before a riot of spices are added in the final cooking. These include tahini, that staple of Lebanese hummus, and chilli powder, with pine nuts sprinkled over as a garnish to finish.

## Tasting

This dish celebrates an exotic cocktail of flavours from the spice-bearing traditions of the Arabs while also showing fidelity to that great tenet of Mediterranean cooking: take the freshest ingredients and interfere with them as little as possible. The result? A sophisticated balancing act in which the fish cleverly remains star of the show. Garlic and chilli pepper add the fire and bite, while coriander and lemon juice bathe the fish in freshness. To avoid the dish being pulled too far in either direction, tahini smoothes over their differences with a dense and reassuring texture. Syria may be off-limits but if you eat Levantine *samak harrah* in its natural setting in Jordan or Lebanon, your meal will almost certainly be accompanied by the mournful strains of an Arabic diva – Egypt's Umm Kulthum or Lebanon's Fairuz – in the background, punctuated by the *muezzin* call to prayer from a nearby mosque.

## Origin

Fish – grilled, baked or, less commonly, fried – has been the essence of eastern Mediterranean cooking for centuries. The fishing fleets of Lebanon and northern Syria, the descendants of the seafaring Phoenicians, long ago placed fish at the heart of the region's culinary traditions. The dish's spices were carried to Arabian ports by the spice-laden ships of traders returning to their home ports from southern India and Zanzibar, then transported across the deserts of Arabia by camel caravan to the Levant.

## Finding it

Try Bab al-Mina (www.babelmina.com) in Byblos, an ancient fishing port north of Beirut, which is renowned for the quality of its fish dishes. Expect to pay 25,000 Lebanese pounds (US$16).

**\* TIPS \* Eat the meal with *khoubz* (Arab flatbread) to soak up the sauce and follow it with the three customary doses of thick, Arabic coffee. It is widely considered impolite to refuse a host's offer of coffee and that extends right through to the third glass – after that, you're free to say no.**

* By Anthony Ham *

# Recipe Samak Harrah

This dish is easily prepared at home and we recommend asking your fishmonger to clean and scale the fish, which cuts back on your own preparation time.

## INGREDIENTS

1 whole white fish (such as snapper), around 2–2.5kg (4½–5½lb) in size (make sure the fish has been gutted)

Salt

½ cup (125mL) olive oil

5 cloves garlic

1 handful finely chopped coriander leaves

1 cup (250mL) tahini

½ cup (125mL) water

½ cup (125mL) lemon juice

½ tsp hot chilli pepper, to taste

2 tbs pine nuts

## METHOD

1. Pat the fish dry with paper towel or a tea towel, then open two cuts along each side of the fish. Sprinkle salt both inside and out, cover and leave in the fridge for up to two hours.

2. Pat the fish dry again, then heat the oil to a high temperature in a large frying pan and fry the fish for two to three minutes on each side, but do not cook through. Place the fish in a lightly oiled baking dish.

3. With a pestle and mortar, grind the garlic, one teaspoon of salt and the coriander until combined.

4. Remove most of the oil from the frying pan before heating again. Add the garlic-coriander mixture and fry until crisp but not burnt. Remove from the heat and allow to cool.

5. Combine the tahini with water while beating it to thicken the consistency. Fold in the lemon juice when thick, then stir in the garlic-coriander mixture and chilli pepper — how much you add of the latter depends entirely on personal preference.

6. Pour the combined mixture over the fish until it is covered and then bake for 30 to 35 minutes at 180ºC to 200ºC. Remove when fish is cooked through and sauce is simmering.

7. While the fish is in the oven, use a frying pan to gently fry the pine nuts with a little oil until lightly toasted.

8. Sprinkle the fish with the pine nuts and serve.

SERVES 4

# * Sambal Udang Petai *

## INDONESIA, MALAYSIA, SINGAPORE

**The fragrant chilli kick of sambal (chilli paste) fried with *udang* (prawns) and *petai* (stinky bean) is a familiar mainstay on many tables in Southeast Asia.**

## What is it?

Sambal, a spicy chilli paste, is wok-fried and serves as a base to which tamarind juice, fresh prawns and a strong-tasting, almond-shaped bean known as *petai* are added. The dish is generally eaten as one of several main course 'share' plates.

## Origin

*Sambal udang petai* is based on the ubiquitious sambal condiment, thought to have originated in Java where the word *sambel* evolved into the Bahasa word *sambal*. It was the Spanish who first brought chilli to the Indonesians, when they introduced the bird's-eye chilli in the 16th century. Migration and trade patterns later brought the cuisine – along with sambal – to other parts of Southeast Asia. Sambal is notably popular in countries with a sizable Malay population, including Malaysia, Singapore and Borneo. This dish is made using ingredients found locally – prawns from local fishermen and the *petai* bean from a tree indigenous to Southeast Asia.

## Finding it

Any self-respecting family-run stall or good restaurant in Indonesia, Malaysia or Singapore serves this up for around US$3–10 per dish.

## Tasting

The versatility of sambal means it's commonly used as a building-block ingredient when frying up vegetables, meat and seafood. However, this fiery chilli paste isn't the star of *sambal udang petai*. The *petai* bean, also know as the 'stink bean' or 'bitter bean', harvested from the pods of *parkia speciosa* trees, offsets but never overwhelms the spicy heat. Some say that *petai* tastes like strong shiitake mushroom with a bitter aftertaste. It has a nuttiness and crunch and its high amino acid content (akin to asparagus) means you'll face the same strange-smelling pee for the next day or two! When combined with the chilli and juicy sweetness of the prawns, this intoxicating, polarising dish will have you wondering whether you'll be able to find *petai* back home.

## * VARIATIONS *

This dish works perfectly well sans *petai* (we hear some people heaving a sigh of relief). In fact, that's how it's commonly served throughout Southeast Asia. The versatile sambal can be used to fry up squid, pork or chicken.

* By Shawn Low *

# **Recipe** Sambal Udang Petai

## INGREDIENTS

2 tbs tamarind water

½ cup (125mL) coconut milk

1 tsp sugar, to taste

200g (7oz) *petai*

2 kaffir lime lime leaves, shredded

1kg (2lb) small–medium prawns, shelled

Juice of 2 small limes

Salt, to taste

## Sambal

2 tbs dried shrimps

1 tbs *belacan* (shrimp paste)

10 shallots, chopped

5 cloves garlic, chopped

4 candlenuts, chopped

30 dry chillies, soaked in water for 10 minutes and drained, chopped

10 fresh chillies, sliced

4 stalks lemongrass, white portion only, sliced

1 small piece galangal or ginger, roughly 15g (½oz)

Tamarind juice (35g/1oz tamarind paste soaked in 1 cup/250mL hot water, strained; reserve some pulp)

**NOTE** If you can't find the ingredients for sambal, Asian grocers stock acceptable premade stuff. Look for one that doesn't use MSG.

## METHOD

1.  Begin by making the sambal. Dry-fry the dried shrimps until browned and fragrant. Set aside.

2.  Dry-fry the *belacan* and shallots until fragrant. Make sure your kitchen is well ventilated as the *belacan* smell can get very fishy. Set aside.

3.  In a mortar, add dried shrimps, shallots and *belacan* to the rest of the sambal ingredients and blend together with the tamarind juice and a little pulp to make a paste. You can also use a food processor for this.

4.  For the main dish, add oil to a wok or large pan, heat until shimmering and fry the sambal paste until fragrant. When you see oil coming out from the paste, it's ready.

5.  Add the tamarind water, coconut milk, sugar, *petai* and lime leaves. Cook on medium heat, stirring until the *petai* is slightly cooked (it will soften), approximately five to seven minutes.

6.  Add the prawns and stir through for another minute or two until they turn white. Add the lime juice and give it one last stir through.

7.  Serve with jasmine rice.

SERVES 4

# * Sambaro *

## TANZANIA

**Few African staples add zing to a meal quite like Tanzania's carrot *sambaro*, a dish in which the humble carrot swims in the flavours of the Indian Ocean spice trade.**

## What is it?

Carrot sambaro is a side dish served to accompany a main meal or family banquet. Most such dishes in East Africa are hearty and heavy rather than noticeably tasty, which is what makes this dish stand out. The carrots – parboiled then pan-simmered – are smothered in the piquancy of mustard seeds, green chilli and turmeric.

## Tasting

Never have carrots tasted this good! There is an intensity of flavours, each of which is discernible above the whole. Savour the subtle and familiar bite of garlic, the sharper edge of chilli and the aromatic pungency of mustard seeds. Then, to confound everything, you'll be hit by an undercurrent of sugar, giving the dish a moreish quality that makes the next bite irresistible. Tanzanians love to share meals with family and friends, so *sambaro* is invariably accompanied by much laughter and a cacophony of Swahili in crosscurrents of conversation as everyone talks at once. Whether that's against a backdrop of traffic noise in Dar es Salaam or the farmyard sounds of rural Tanzania, the effect is the same; one of everyone being equal and welcome as hungry hands dip into the communal pot.

## Origin

In the 1960s, newly independent Tanzania was ruled by Julius Nyerere – a president who made a virtue of agricultural self-sufficiency. Home-grown vegetables became a national obsession. At the same time, the spices grown on or imported into Zanzibar, one of the world's most important spice hubs in ancient times, are responsible for most of Tanzania's export earnings. Marry the two and you have carrot *sambaro*: both a symbol of Tanzania's culinary diversity and a key, unifying strand running through the country's gastronomic story.

## Finding it

*Sambaro* is street food and home-cooking. Try Tanzania's ubiquitous *hoteli* (small, informal restaurant stalls) or *mama lishe* (food stands where the 'mama' does the cooking). Expect to pay around 1000 Tanzanian shillings (US$0.60) for a serving, although it's often served as a garnish alongside a main dish.

* TIPS * Even if you're on an all-expenses paid safari, take the time to escape the confines of your lodge at least once and eat at a local restaurant. Not only will the foods be more authentically Tanzanian, you'll be eating alongside ordinary Tanzanians without the barriers that tend to exist behind the rarefied walls of Safari Africa.

* By Anthony Ham *

# Recipe Sambaro

This dish is pulled in two directions: one sweet, the other spicy. The latter's influence will depend on which type of mustard seeds you have to hand – black mustard seeds are strongest, white mustard seeds are milder, while the in between brown mustard seeds will give your dish a hint of Dijon mustard.

## INGREDIENTS

250g (9oz) carrots, finely chopped

1–2 tsp mustard seeds

½ tsp turmeric

2 cloves garlic, crushed or finely chopped

½–1 green chilli, seeded and finely chopped

1 tsp caster sugar (optional)

2 tbs lemon or lime juice

4 tbs oil

1 tbs salt

## METHOD

1. Bring to the boil a large pot of water and add the carrots. Boil until the carrots are almost cooked, but still firm. Remove the carrots from the water and set aside.

2. In a heavy pan, heat the oil and mustard seeds, stirring so that the oil coats the seeds, then add in the turmeric, garlic and chilli. Simmer gently for at least one minute.

3. Stir the carrot into the spice mixture until the carrots are coated in the spices, then add the salt and sugar. Cover and allow to simmer gently for five minutes.

4. Just as you're about to serve, splash the lime or lemon juice over the carrots.

SERVES 4

# * Samosas *

## INDIA

**Forget pasties and pies – the humble samosa takes the idea of a portable pastry and fills it with Indian spice.**

## What is it?

Triangular pockets of *maida* (wheat) flour dough are stuffed with a vegetarian mixture of spiced potatoes, onions, peas, coriander, green chillies and spices, and deep fried in vegetable oil until golden brown. They're best served hot with fresh mint, coriander or tamarind chutney, but they're just as tasty cold, making this the perfect portable snack for those epic Indian train rides.

## Origin

Samosas are known to have existed since at least the 10th century in Central Asia, where they were known as *samsas*, but thanks to flourishing trading routes, they were introduced to India somewhere between the 13th and 14th centuries. They were traditionally cooked around trading caravan campfires, and served hot the first night, with any leftovers munched cold on the next day's trek.

## Tasting

Finding a samosa in India is pretty much a case of following your nose; at the end of the aroma trail, you'll find the samosa *wallah* (vendor) hard at work, preparing his little pastry parcels of goodness and dropping them into a sputtering pan of oil. A few flips to cook both sides of the triangle to golden perfection, and the vendor will scoop out your piping-hot samosa and drop it onto a serving plate with a splodge of tangy chutney. Sinking your teeth into the warm, flaky pastry and savouring the blend of spices and the soft, yielding texture of the potato is one of the great pleasures of the subcontinent. The blend of spiced potato, coriander, peas and chillies is an inspired combination!

## Finding it

Samosa vendors are found near bus and train stations, on street corners and in every bazaar in India. One samosa costs around Rs10 (US$0.16).

**\* VARIATIONS \* Samosa fillings vary as you roam across the subcontinent. In parts of South India, the potato filling is replaced with fried cabbage, onions, carrots, peas and curry leaves. In Bangladesh, the samosa-like *shingara* is often stuffed with mince meat or beef liver. Pakistani samosa *wallahs* are also fond of meaty stuffings, and cooks like to add extra chilli to the mix. There are even sweet samosas, filled with dried fruit and nuts.**

**\* By Joe Bindloss \***

# Recipe Samosas

Making your own pastry for this traditional North Indian vegetarian version is easy and delivers a texture that you simply won't get from the shop-bought variety. You can cook samosas in a deep-fryer, but a heavy-bottomed saucepan will do just as well.

## INGREDIENTS

### Dough

1 cup plain flour

2 tsp semolina flour

¼ tsp salt

1 tbs vegetable or canola oil

¼ cup (60mL) lukewarm water

### Filling

2 tbs vegetable or canola oil

½ tsp cumin seeds

⅓ cup green peas

2 green chillies, seeded and chopped

½ tsp coriander seeds, ground

½ tsp garam masala

2 large potatoes, peeled, boiled and diced (not mashed)

1 tsp amchur (mango powder)

vegetable or canola oil for deep-frying

mango chutney to serve

## METHOD

1. To make the dough, combine all the ingredients in a mixing bowl.
2. Knead with your hands until the dough is soft, smooth and elastic. Set aside to rest for at least 20 minutes.
3. In a small saucepan, heat the oil and lightly fry the cumin seeds.
4. Add the green peas and cook for a couple of minutes.
5. Add the chillies, coriander seeds and garam masala and stir for another couple of minutes.
6. Add the potatoes and gently mix through (so as not to crush the potatoes) until coated in the spices.
7. Stir the amchur through the mixture and place in a bowl to cool.
8. When the dough has rested, knead it lightly and divide into 2 balls. Keep dividing each ball until you end up with 8 balls (or 16 if you are making mini-samosas).
9. Using a rolling pin, flatten out the first ball into a circular shape about a millimetre thick and cut the circle in half.
10. Hold one half flat in the palm of your left hand and lightly moisten the edges of the dough with water
11. Fold the semicircle in half and press the straight edges together to form a cone.
12. Stuff the cone with the filling and close the cone into a triangular shape by pinching and sealing the top edge. You should now have a triangle-shaped stuffed samosa.
13. Repeat with the rest of the dough.
14. If not using a deep-fryer, heat the oil in a saucepan and test for readiness by dropping in a tiny piece of dough. The oil is ready if it sizzles and comes up to the surface gradually.
15. Fry the samosas until golden, a few at a time. Do not overcrowd the pan.
16. Serve immediately with your favourite chutney.

MAKES 8 LARGE OR 16 MINI-SAMOSAS

# * Shakshouka *

## TUNISIA

**Served just piquant enough to wake you up, or sizzling with a spice that'll light a fire in your belly, *shakshouka* is a good reason to get out of bed in the morning.**

## What is it?

*Shakshouka* is a breakfast dish originating from Tunisia, but beloved as a wake-me-up throughout North Africa and the Middle East. Eggs poached in a spicy tomato stew are served simply or as base for a mouth-watering array of variations. Chillies – or harissa, a North African spiced chilli paste – provide the fire and paprika the smouldering sweetness that light up the tomato sauce. Cumin adds depth and that distinctive North African aroma. Common additions to the tomato stew are capsicum, spicy sausage and salty cheeses such as feta.

## Origin

Some food historians claim it was first introduced to North Africa by the Ottoman Turks, but *shakshouka* is commonly acknowledged as Tunisian in origin. It's certainly likely that in Israel, where the dish is enormously popular, *shakshouka* first arrived thanks to the immigration of Tunisian Jews in the mid-20th century. However, it's a simple and elegant concept that has arisen independently in far-flung parts of the world – it's remarkably similar to Mexican *huevos rancheros*.

## Tasting

Who needs coffee when spice can get the synapses firing in the morning? *Shakshouka* is a visual treat as well as a savoury one – try making it yourself to watch the eggs turn opaque and start googling up at you from the pan. But don't break the yolks! That's a pleasure to reserve for the eating: experience the gradual merging of tastes as the wholesome, rich yolk mixes with its spicy surrounds, cutting through the acidity while taking on all the pep of the chillies and paprika. Be sure to have some fresh, crusty bread on the side; use it to mix the colours, textures and delightful flavours of this warming, invigorating dish.

## Finding it

*Shakshouka* is easy to find in restaurants across Tunisia, but the truly famous spot for it is in Israel, at Dr Shakshuka (3 Beit Eshel, Tel Aviv).

---

**\* VARIATIONS \* In Tunisia, *shakshouka* is often made with *merguez*, a spicy sausage that's popular throughout North Africa. It's made from lamb or beef, and spiced with cumin and chilli or harissa, along with an array of other optional spices and flavours including fennel, garlic and sumac.**

**\* By Kate Whitfield \***

# Recipe **Shakshouka**

## INGREDIENTS

3 tbs olive oil

1 large onion, chopped

2 garlic cloves, minced

3 red capsicums, diced

1 red chilli, chopped

2 tsp caraway seeds

750g (1½lb) fresh tomatoes, peeled, seeded and chopped (tinned tomatoes can be substituted)

2–3 tsp paprika

1 tsp ground cumin

1 tsp sea salt

1–2 tbs harissa (optional)

4 large eggs

## METHOD

1. Add the oil to a medium-sized frying pan over medium-high heat. Saute the onion and garlic for about 5 minutes, until soft.

2. Add the capsicum, chilli and caraway seeds. Saute until the capsicum is tender (about five minutes).

3. Add the tomatoes, paprika, cumin, salt and harissa (if using). Bring to a boil then reduce the heat to medium-low and cook, stirring occasionally, for about 15 minutes.

4. Make shallow wells in the sauce for the eggs (you can use the back of a spoon). Carefully break the eggs in.

5. Cover the pan and cook the eggs over a low heat. For soft yolks, allow around five minutes. If you wish, you can swirl the sauce into the egg whites as they cook, being careful not to damage the yolks.

6. Serve with fresh crusty bread.

SERVES 4

# * Shawayuh *

YEMEN

**The very essence of Bedouin hospitality and steeped in Yemeni tradition, spicy grilled *shawayuh* meat evokes the charcoal smell of a remote campfire deep in the deserts of Arabia.**

## What is it?

*Shawayuh* is meat that has been sprinkled with *hawaij* (a spice mix incorporating peppercorns, caraway seeds, saffron, cardamom and turmeric) and then flame-licked over a charcoal grill. Meat can be a luxury in Yemen, the Arabian Peninsula's poorest country, but so special is this dish that the best available is always reserved for it. The genius of *shawayuh* is its adaptability: any meat you choose will sing sweet symphonies when introduced to the harmonious love affair between open-fire cooking and spices.

## Origin

This is a dish born in celebration. In more traditional times, the festivities might have been to mark a successful hunt, one that brought the rare treat of tender gazelle meat into the camp of semi-nomadic Bedouin. Or it might have been to seal a treaty between once-warring tribes, pacts sealed over a meal of baby camel eaten from a communal bowl. In modern Yemen, *shawayuh* remains the centrepiece of extended family gatherings and a reminder of Yemen's links to the epic Arabian past.

## Tasting

*Shawayuh* is the taste of the open fire as the meat's smoky flavour lingers on the tongue. The piquant *hawaij* seasoning enhances the experience in subtle ways, through a sharp bite from the peppercorn, a delicate hint of saffron and the aromatic suggestion of humid tropical coasts in the combination of cardamom and turmeric. It is a dish that tastes best when shared among family and community; individual portions may be cut and distributed, but tradition demands that the meat be placed in the centre of the table (or, better still, a picnic blanket alongside the open fire) and torn off in chunks by bare hands. Imagine a soundtrack of locals telling tall tales in guttural Arabic and the meal is complete. Satisfied finger licking is obligatory.

## Finding it

Look for *shawayuh* in restaurants in the old city of Sana'a, particularly around Hadda Street. Expect to pay at least 1000 Yemeni riyals (US$5).

**\* TIPS \*** Friday is the night when well-to-do Yemeni families are most likely to eat out in a restaurant and it's then that you'll see *shawayuh's* enduring power to bring people together. Better still, if you're invited into the home of a local family for the nightly feast that greets sunset during Ramadan (an otherwise difficult time to travel in Yemen), you've hit the jackpot.

* By Anthony Ham *

# Recipe Shawayuh

The only way to replicate the traditional way of cooking this dish is over the hot coals of a barbecue or an open fire. Although the dish can be cooked in other ways, you'll miss the charcoal smell and taste that permeate the meat and are the essence of the dish.

## INGREDIENTS

4 large grilling steaks or lamb chops

3 tsp *hawaij* (see below)

10 tbs olive oil

Salt, to taste

### Hawaij

5–6 tsp black peppercorns

2–3 tsp caraway seeds

1 tsp saffron threads

1 tsp cardamom seeds

2 tsp turmeric

## METHOD

1. To make the *hawaij* mix, grind the peppercorns, caraway seeds, saffron threads and cardamom seeds until blended together. Then stir in the turmeric and store in a sealed jar.

2. Coat the meat all over with the *hawaij* mix and set aside for 30 minutes.

3. When your coals are red hot, very lightly coat the meat in the oil and position over the fire. Once seared, turn the meat over and repeat on the other side. When evenly seared, move the meat to a cooler part of the fire and leave until cooked to your preference. You may need to apply light brushes of oil throughout the cooking.

4. Season with salt and serve.

SERVES 4

# * Sichuan Crescent Dumplings *

## SICHUAN, CHINA

**Prepare for a kick in the tastebuds. Here the traditional, crescent-shaped darlings of the dim sum world have been given a Sichuan makeover – a soaking in a chilli oil and Sichuan pepper sauce.**

## What is it?

Sichuan crescent dumplings are dough wrappers filled with a dumpling combination of minced pork, coriander, spring onions, garlic chives, ginger and garlic. They are poached briefly before being soaked in a concoction of chilli and sesame oils, and soy and hoisin sauces. Dumplings are typically eaten for breakfast and brunch in China, but Sichuan crescent dumplings are on Sichuan menus at any time of day.

## Origin

Known as *jiao zi* in Mandarin, traditional crescent dumplings play a big role in Lunar New Year festivities in northern China. Preparing the dish is something of a ritual, with family members all taking part, kneading and rolling, mixing and filling, pinching the wrappers, and, finally, plunging them into boiling water. In Sichuan, they pared down the mince but compensated with the tongue-titillating addition of chilli and Sichuan sauce. It is said that a peddler named Zhong Xiesen was responsible for this so-called *zhong jiao zi* Sichuan version over a century ago, and his descendants are still trading the street snack in the Sichuan capital of Chengdu today.

## Tasting

Dumplings are the Chinese taste sensation bar none. So it's fair to say the Sichuan tradition of adding to this delicate little palate pleaser deserves the lowest of bows indeed. With chopsticks in hand, grasp the slippery sucker before it escapes the bowl. If it's not already red hot with sauce, swipe the dish, attracting some fresh coriander to the mouthful in the process. If your chopstick skills are up to it, bite the dumpling in half, noting the chopped garlic chives amid the minced pork – a sign of freshness and quality. Or pop the whole lot in to your mouth for a flavour pop and stand by for the chilli to heat your insides and the tingling Sichuan pepper to numb your tongue. Now, wipe that chilli sauce from your cheek and dive in for number two.

## Finding it

Try *Long Chao Shou* restaurant at Chunxi Lu and Songxin Qiao, Huaihua, Beilu 9, Chengdu. Expect to pay ¥28 (US$4.50) for the SIchuan snack set.

* TIPS * Dumplings were originally a street snack, sold inexpensively in bite-size portions to be eaten fast-food style, steaming hot and doused in sauce. In Sichuan restaurants today, three to four dumplings are served per person, or per table, nestled together in small bowls. When you make dumplings at home, you should follow suit.

* By Penny Watson *

# Recipe Sichuan Crescent Dumplings

## INGREDIENTS

### Dumplings

1 garlic clove

5cm (2in) piece fresh ginger

3 spring onions

Salt

White pepper

2 garlic chives

½ cup bean sprouts

½ cup fresh coriander leaves

500g (1lb) minced fatty pork

1 tbs Shaoxing rice wine

30 wonton wrappers (found in Chinese supermarkets)

### Sauce

1 tbs sesame oil

1 tbs chilli oil

1 tbs light soy sauce

1 tbs hoisin sauce

2–3 tsp hot chilli sauce (depending on your capacity for spice)

4 garlic cloves

3cm (1in) piece fresh ginger

4 spring onions (green and white parts)

1 tsp ground Sichuan peppercorns

3 tbs chicken stock

1 tsp sugar

## METHOD

1. In a mortar, pound the garlic, ginger, spring onions, salt and pepper. Transfer to a large mixing bowl, preferably metal.

2. Finely slice the garlic chives, bean sprouts and three quarters of the coriander. Add to the mixing bowl.

3. Add the pork and rice wine to the bowl and mix all ingredients together with your hands.

4. When the herbs are evenly distributed through the mixture, throw small handfuls of the meat mixture repeatedly against the side of the bowl. (This will bind the mixture together and should negate the need for egg or flour).

5. Thaw wonton wrappers (if frozen) and keep covered with a damp cloth to prevent drying out.

6. With your finger, lightly wet the edges of the wonton wrapper with water.

7. Place a rounded teaspoon of the mixture in the centre and fold the sides up. The water should help stick the edges together. Seal by pinching the edges in two or three places. There should be no holes in the seam.

8. Cover with damp cloth and refrigerate.

9. Combine all the sauce ingredients in a small saucepan and heat gently, without allowing it to boil.

10. When you're ready to eat, bring a large pot of lightly salted water to boil.

11. With a slotted spoon or similar, gently add eight to ten dumplings to the water making sure to not overcrowd the pot.

12. When they float to the surface, reduce heat and simmer for four minutes.

13. Ladle them out and transfer three or four into small serving bowls.

14. Spoon sauce over dumplings and garnish with remaining coriander. Serve straight away.

15. Uncooked dumplings can be stored in freezer.

# * Singapore Noodles *

CHINA (HONG KONG), UK, US, CANADA, AUSTRALIA
(EVERYWHERE BUT SINGAPORE!)

**A tantalising blend of subtle curry and oriental flavours
and a surf and turf combination of pork and prawns make Singapore
noodles a winning fusion of East and West.**

## WHAT IS IT?

Thin rice noodles are wok-fried and flavoured with fragrant curry, garnished with generous lashings of *char siu* pork, prawns, chicken, green capsicum, chilli and bean sprouts. The complete one-dish meal is a lunch and dinner favourite of fusion lovers everywhere it seems but its namesake country. In Hong Kong, Singapore noodles are also enjoyed as a hearty breakfast dish.

## ORIGIN

Singapore noodles' elusive history remains a mystery, not helped by the fact that the dish itself is not found in Singapore. Theories abound, but a common belief is that the dish was an invention of the Cantonese chefs who hoped to reflect multicultural influences in their cuisine by combining a Cantonese stir fry with a British-style curry. Given its popularity in countries like the UK and the US, a more likely beginning involves an attempt by Western chefs to replicate the fusion flavours of Singapore-style noodles such as *char kway teow* (originally from the Swatow province in China) and *mee goreng* (Indian/Malay origins).

## TASTING

A complete meal in itself, nothing beats Singapore noodles when craving a savoury, protein-laden, moreish treat. The dish is an explosion of flavours and textures – smoky curry provides plenty of oomph to soft chicken and crunchy prawns, balanced by the sweet *char siu* and crispy vegetables. Golden-hued noodles, green capsicum, and deep-red pork also make for a veritable feast for the eyes. This cheap and filling dish is found everywhere from street food stalls to teahouses, restaurants and everything in between, not to mention a cinch to cook at home. Variations include the addition of cabbage, mushrooms or sesame oil.

## FINDING IT

Explore gourmet delights at low-key neighbourhood Tin Hau (Hong Kong), including an authentic version of Singapore noodles at Cantonese specialist, Kin's Kitchen (approx US$7).

* **TIPS** * **Don't ask for this dish in Singapore lest you are prepared for a puzzled or even withering response from the locals!**

* By Johanna Ashby *

# Recipe Singapore Noodles

Have all your ingredients prepared and ready to go in the wok for fast cooking. Feel free to use more or less chilli according to taste.

## INGREDIENTS

300g (11oz) dried rice noodles

2 tsp madras (hot) curry powder

1 tsp ground turmeric

3 tbs light soy sauce

2 tbs rice wine or sherry

125mL chicken stock or water

3 medium eggs, beaten

150g (5oz) medium raw prawns

100g (3½oz) chicken breast, sliced into strips

100g (3½oz) *char siu* pork, sliced thinly

1 clove garlic, crushed

2cm (1in) piece of ginger, grated

1 medium red chilli, chopped

4 spring onions, chopped

1 small green capsicum, sliced thinly

150g (5oz) bean sprouts

Vegetable oil for stir-frying

Chopped spring onions, coriander leavse and lime wedges for garnish

## METHOD

1. Soak the noodles in boiling water for a few minutes until soft, then drain the water and set aside.

2. Make the sauce by combining the curry powder, turmeric, soy sauce, rice wine and chicken stock in a small bowl.

3. Put a teaspoon of oil in a wok on medium-high heat, scramble the eggs then take them out of the wok and set aside.

4. Add a little more oil. Sear, but do not cook, the prawns and set aside.

5. Add a little more oil if necessary, cook the chicken and set aside.

6. Put a tablespoon of oil in the wok, then quickly fry the garlic, ginger, chilli and spring onions for a few minutes.

7. Add the sauce and the capsicum until the sauce is simmering.

8. Toss in the noodles, stirring thoroughly to coat the noodles in the sauce.

9. Put the prawns, chicken and egg back into the wok and add the pork and bean sprouts. Stir-fry for a few minutes.

10. Garnish with the spring onions and coriander. Serve immediately with lime wedges.

SERVES 6

# * Som Tam *

## THAILAND & LAOS

**Think green papaya salad is nothing to be scared of? Think again. To create *som tam*, papaya is pounded with raw bird's-eye chillies, creating a dressing that would strip the paint off a Boeing 747.**

## What is it?

*Som tam* translates to 'pounded sour' – an accurate description of the method of preparation, where shredded green papaya, lime juice, fish sauce, palm sugar, chilli and dried shrimp are beaten vigorously together in a mortar and pestle. The pounding is an essential part of the preparation, pushing chilli oil and acidic lime juice deep into the fibres of the papaya to add flavour and aid digestion.

## Origin

The prototype for *som tam* almost certainly came from Laos, but it was the Thais, more specifically the chefs serving generations of backpackers in Bangkok, who put the dish on the international menu. Even today, the version served in Bangkok is celebrated as the fieriest, thanks to the addition of an extra-generous handful of bird's-eye chillies.

## Tasting

Before you taste *som tam*, you get to enjoy the theatre of its preparation. First comes the shredding of the green papaya into a mound of semi-translucent strips. Then comes the pounding, as papaya, chilli, dried shrimp, lime juice, palm sugar and any supplementary ingredients are thrashed to within an inch of their lives in an earthenware mortar and pestle. Atomised chilli is already thick in the air when the dish is served, and the only option once you start eating is to keep on going, consuming every delicious mouthful before the awful reality of how much raw chilli you are eating starts to dawn. But what flavours! *Som tam* is at once tart, sour, sweet, salty, pungent and fresh. Eating is followed by a lengthy phase of panting and wishing there was something to take away the heat of all that chilli!

## Finding it

Seek out the best *som tam* on the banks of the Mekong River near Nong Khai, where vendors sell freshly pounded portions alongside river fish grilled on lemongrass spears for around 30B (US$1).

**\* VARIATIONS \* *Som tam* is a dish where anything goes. Alongside green papaya and lime, you may find peanuts, tomatoes, yard long beans, soft-shell crab, garlic, eggplant, shrimp paste or the curious-sounding hog plum, the fruit of a distant relative of the cashew-nut tree.**

* By Joe Bindloss *

# Recipe Som Tam

## INGREDIENTS

½ green papaya

3–4 cloves of garlic, crushed

4–5 raw bird's-eye chillies, crushed

3 tomatoes, cut into wedges

225g (8oz) bean sprouts

150g (5oz) yard long beans, chopped

40g (1–2oz) dried shrimp

40g (1–2oz) roasted peanuts, chopped

### Dressing

Juice from 1 lime

2–3 tbs fish sauce

2 tbs palm sugar

## METHOD

1.  Cut the green papaya in half, then remove the seeds and grate the flesh into thin strips.

2.  Add the green papaya to a large mortar and pestle with the garlic and chillies and pound to release the flavours.

3.  Add the chopped tomatoes, bean sprouts, yard long beans and dried shrimp, then top with the dressing ingredients.

4.  Mix roughly in the mortar and pestle. Top with chopped peanuts and serve.

SERVES 4 AS A SIDE DISH

# * Souse *

## CARIBBEAN ISLANDS

**What's the world's best hangover cure? A Caribbean native would name this cold spicy soup made from pickled pig parts. Don't knock it till you've tried it.**

## What is it?

Souse is a soup made from the 'leftover bits' of the pig – usually trotters, head and tail. The parts are boiled, cooled and served in a cold, briny broth full of cucumber and sliced chillies, seasoned with lime and black pepper. Its sour, spicy bite is famed as a pick-me-up for the hung-over or otherwise out-of-sorts.

## Origin

Souse has its origin with the West African slaves brought to the Caribbean to work the plantations of Barbados, Trinidad, Saint Kitts and other islands. It is inspired by English 'head cheese' – loose patés made of leftover meat bits – modified to the local climate to be a cold soup, rather than a solid. Slave cooks worked with what they had, which was often the parts of the pig thrown out by the masters.

## Tasting

Souse is a weekend treat throughout much of the Caribbean. You'll find it served for Saturday lunch, along with its traditional accompaniment – blood pudding. In some countries, the pudding is more like a sausage, savoury black blood flecked with soft rice. In others, such as Barbados, the pudding is made from sweet potatoes darkened to look like blood pudding, without any actual blood. On weekends, hung-over souse-lovers queue up outside the homes of popular souse-makers, waiting for their hit of cool, spicy, salty, porky broth. Line up with them, eat your souse standing up in the front yard, then return the bowl to the souse-maker. You'll also find a big tureen of souse at any Caribbean festival or dance party, right alongside the rum.

## Where to find it

Crop Over, Barbados' biggest festival, lasts nearly all summer and always includes plenty of souse (US$10 a bowl).

**\* VARIATIONS \*** In the American South, souse is gelled and served in a loaf. Also known as hog's head cheese, it comes in mild or spicy versions, both with the same vinegary kick as the Caribbean broth. It's typically served on crackers or as a sandwich filling.

* By Emily Matchar *

# Recipe Souse

## INGREDIENTS

500g (1lb) ham hocks

½ medium red onion, thinly sliced

Juice of 4 limes

1 Scotch bonnet chilli (or 2 jalapeño chillies), thinly sliced

1 tsp salt

2 cloves garlic, crushed

1 cucumber, thinly sliced

Large handful coriander (cilantro), chopped

1L water

Black pepper to taste

## METHOD

1.  Wash ham hocks and place in a large pot with water (enough to cover the meat) and garlic.

2.  Bring to the boil, then reduce to a simmer and cook until tender – about two hours.

3.  Drain the meat and set aside to cool.

4.  Once cooled, shred the meat and toss with lime and black pepper.

5.  Add remaining ingredients and water, and allow to marinate for several hours.

6.  Serve cold.

SERVES 4

# * Thai Green Curry *

## THAILAND

**Along with *phat thai*, this is one of the quintessential Thai dishes. Sure, there are plenty of other Thai curries but perhaps none beats the green iteration for its comfort-food factor.**

## What is it?

Thai green curry is a blend of green chillies and spices cooked in coconut milk and coconut cream along with meat or seafood and vegetables. You'll find it in every Thai restaurant in the world, though you may have to look hard to find an authentic version – one that's spicy and zesty instead of creamy and sweet. Why not make your own?

## Origin

Each Southeast Asian country has its own variation of curry. Thailand has many of them – red, *panang*, *massaman*, yellow, sour and green. During the Ayutthaya period (AD 1351–1767), Siam opened its borders to trade. While merchants from China, Japan, France and Portugal travelled through, it's said to have been the Indians and Moors who added milk and/or cream to the local spice pastes of coriander, cumin, peppercorns, lemongrass, lime, garlic, shallots and dried shrimp. Through the years, the cream was replaced with coconut cream. The rest is (food) history.

## Tasting

Yes, the colour comes from the chillies! But along with zingy Thai green chillies, green curry paste is made from a bunch of other deliciously fresh ingredients: zesty lemongrass, kaffir lime leaves and strong liquorice-flavoured sweet Thai basil. During cooking, coconut cream and coconut milk are added to soften the spicy edge of the chilli, and fish sauce provides umami (savoury flavour). True gourmands will seek out a restaurant that serves this curry spicy, with an oily sheen on top – from oil that splits from the coconut cream. The versatility of this dish explains much of its universal popularity – it's just as tasty with seafood as it is with chicken or pork. Vegetarians can simply add more eggplant and tofu for a tasty, protein-filled meal. It's also one of the easiest curries to prepare. Served on fragrant, fluffy jasmine rice, this is truly a dish worth salivating over.

## Finding it

For around 160B (US$5) try the green curry at the homestyle Krua Apsorn Restaurant, Samsen Rd, Bangkok, also famous for its crab-meat dishes.

* TIPS * You could make your own paste but the ready-made stuff sold at Asian grocers is actually very good – go for the type in a vacuum-sealed pack inside a round plastic tub. You're probably used to serving your curry with jasmine rice, but consider pairing it with *khanom chin* (fermented, boiled rice noodles) or *roti* (flatbread) as they also do in Thailand.

* By Shawn Low *

# Recipe Thai Green Curry

## INGREDIENTS

2 cups (500mL) coconut milk

500g (1lb) sliced chicken, pork, sea-food, or tofu

100g (3½oz) eggplants

100g (3½oz) pea eggplants

2 tsp palm sugar

2 kaffir lime leaves

Fish sauce, to taste

3–5 red chillies, deseeded, finely sliced

1 cup fresh Thai sweet basil leaves

### Paste

20 Thai green chillies

2 tbs galangal, chopped

6 tbs lemongrass, white portion, scraped and chopped

2 kaffir lime leaves

4 pieces coriander root, chopped

1 tsp chopped red turmeric

4 shallots, chopped

4 garlic cloves, chopped

1 tsp shrimp paste

## METHOD

1. Pound the paste ingredients in a pestle and mortar until well mixed. Set aside.

2. Heat a large saucepan or wok and add the cream from the top of the coconut milk (don't shake the can before opening it).

3. Stir the cream. When it has split, add the curry paste and fry with the cream until it's fragrant. Add the remaining coconut milk.

4. Add your meat, seafood or tofu and bring the mixture to a boil. Simmer for five to 10 minutes.

5. Add the eggplants, pea eggplants, palm sugar and kaffir lime leaves to the curry and simmer for another two minutes, stirring occasionally.

6. Add fish sauce for saltiness and chillies for spice. Boil through and stir in the basil leaves for a minute more before serving with jasmine rice.

SERVES 4

# * Tikka Masala *

## UNITED KINGDOM

**Its roots might be in India but the heartland of this creamy curry lies further west. Tikka masala has become a national treasure, and an edible exemplification of multicultural Britain.**

## What is it?

It's the most popular curry in Britain, that's what, and practically the country's national dish, despite its clearly Indian provenance. Traditionally, tikka masala is chicken pieces (tikka means 'bits') marinated in yoghurt and spices, then baked in a tandoor oven and served with a creamy, tomatoey masala (mixed spice) sauce.

## Tasting

The classic curry-house experience is usually after a night on the town. First, you destroy a pile of poppadoms and a cold Indian beer. Then the tikka masala arrives – a vibrant-red vision, so bright it glows. It feels like cheating – amid the *phaals* and *vindaloos*, this is the soft option, a creamy treat rather than a fiery challenge. But, so what? You value your bowels and tastebuds, and would prefer your head not blown off, thanks very much. Plus, it looks so good: chunks of chicken enveloped in velvety sauce, pungent with ginger, garlic and spices. And, with rice and naans, it's ideal for soaking up the excesses of the night.

## Finding it

Shish Mahal (www.shishmahal.co.uk), Park Road, Glasgow, claims to be the inventor of chicken tikka masala. A serving here costs £9.95 (US$15).

## Origin

The roots of chicken tikka can be traced back to the Punjab, and the 16th-century court of Babur – a descendant of Genghis Khan. The ruler couldn't abide bones in his food, so his cooks pulled the meat into pieces to remove them. However, the masala magic wasn't added (allegedly) until the 1970s. Following a complaint from a diner about the dryness of his chicken, it's said that Ali Ahmed Aslam – owner of Glasgow's Shish Mahal restaurant – hastily knocked up a sauce using assorted spices and a tin of condensed tomato soup.

* VARIATIONS * Few masalas are made the same – different restaurants will use different combinations of the many spices or add more chilli for extra zing, though traditionally this is a mild dish. As masala is merely a sauce, it can be slathered on more than *murgh* (chicken) – try it on vegetables, king prawns and lamb, too.

* By Sarah Baxter *

# Recipe Tikka Masala

Marinade the chicken for several hours for the tastiest tikka.

## INGREDIENTS

2 chicken thighs per person, boned, skinned, diced

### Marinade

2 bunches of coriander leaves

120mL (4 fl oz) yoghurt

4 fresh green chillies

½ tsp salt

2.5cm (1in) fresh ginger

4 cloves garlic

### Masala sauce

1 cinnamon stick

2 cloves

3 red chillies, minced

Vegetable oil

1 onion, chopped

3 garlic cloves

2.5cm (1in) fresh ginger, grated

½ tsp ground ginger

½ tsp ground cumin

½ tsp ground coriander

½ tsp ground turmeric

½ tsp ground fenugreek

1 tsp hot chilli powder

1 tin (400g/14oz) chopped tomatoes

400mL (13 fl oz) water

120mL (4 fl oz) single cream

½ tsp sugar

½ tsp salt

## METHOD

1. Blend the marinade ingredients into a paste; pour over the chicken and leave for at least two hours.

2. Fry the cinnamon, cloves and minced chilli in oil; add the onion and fry until soft.

3. Blend the garlic and ginger to a paste and add to the onions.

4. Add the ground spices and chilli powder and cook for five minutes.

5. Stir in the tomatoes and water, and cook until reduced by half; then remove from the pan and blend to smooth paste.

6. Return to the pan; off the heat, add the cream, sugar and salt, stirring well before returning to heat.

7. Grill the chicken until cooked thoroughly, with a slight char.

8. Toss the cooked chicken in pan with sauce.

# * Tom Yam Gung *

## THAILAND

**Take prawns and stock, add one part lemongrass, one part lime and one part napalm and serve – Thailand's favourite soup is a chilli-laced masterpiece.**

## What is it?

Thailand's answer to bouillabaisse, *tom yam gung* blends fresh prawns, straw mushrooms, lemongrass, kaffir lime leaves, lime juice, fish sauce, galangal and chilli. The name translates to 'boiled hot and sour' and that's what this soup is – hot from the chilli, sour from the lime juice. Think of it as a fiery palate cleanser, to be sipped between curries and stirfries.

## Origin

Ubiquitous across the Malay Peninsula, *tom yam* is served everywhere from Thailand and Laos to Malaysia and Singapore. Prawns have been farmed in Thai creeks for centuries, so the dish may have its roots far from the sea, but liberal use of chilli dates *tom yam* to after the 17th century, when the first chillies were transported to Southeast Asia from South America by Portuguese seafarers.

## Tasting

Floating pools of red chilli oil provide the first warning that something fiery lurks beneath the surface of this seafood soup. Vapours of lemongrass, galangal and lime rise from the surface of your bowl, promising a visceral tour through the flavours of Southeast Asia. The first sensation as you sip from your spoon is the sharp tang of lime, but almost immediately, the chilli takes control. This is a dish to eat quickly, without pausing, in case the fire proves too powerful to quench. The main ingredients – prawns and mushrooms – are secondary to the complex blend of spices and seasonings. Each flavour takes its own moment to shine; some spoonfuls are dominated by lemongrass and lime, others by chilli and medicinal notes of galangal. Keep tissues to hand when eating *tom yam gung* – the take-no-prisoners combination of chillies and lime will get your eyes watering and sinuses tingling.

## Finding it

You can't avoid it – every second restaurant in Southeast Asia serves some interpretation of *tom yam gung*. Restaurants in Bangkok charge around 60B (US$2) per bowl.

---

**\* VARIATIONS \*** Classic *tom yam* gets its mojo from lime juice, but in Thailand, you'll also find *tom khlong*, flavoured with sour tamarind – a near cousin of Malaysia's famous hot-and-sour *asam laksa*. Then there's *tom som*, a lighter version prepared without lemongrass or kaffir lime leaves, popular along the Thai–Laos border.

* By Joe Bindloss *

# Recipe Tom Yam Gung

## INGREDIENTS

750mL fish or chicken stock

4 cloves garlic, crushed

5 shallots, thinly sliced

2 stalks lemongrass, cut into
2.5cm/1in slices

4 thin slices galangal

200g (7oz) straw mushrooms, sliced
lengthways

10 bird's-eye chillies, cut lengthways

3 tbs fish sauce

5 kaffir lime leaves

250g (9oz) raw prawns, washed,
peeled and de-veined

Juice from 1 lime

Handful coriander leaves, chopped

## METHOD

1.  In a pan or wok, bring the stock to the boil and add the garlic,
    shallots, lemongrass and galangal.

2.  Add the straw mushrooms, chillies, fish sauce and kaffir lime
    leaves.

3.  Return to the boil for two to three minutes, then add the
    prawns and cook until just done.

4.  Remove the pan from the heat and add the lime juice, then stir
    and serve, garnishing each portion with chopped coriander.

SERVES 4

# * Tortas Ahogadas *

## GUADALAJARA, MEXICO

**Tortas** are widespread fare throughout Mexico, but only in the city of Guadalajara do these 'Mexican sandwiches' take a dip into a spicy salsa to become a real – drowned – *torta ahogada.*

## What is it?

Think of a sandwich going rogue and joining the X Games of food and what you get is a *torta ahogada*. Basically a crusty roll stuffed with juicy pork confit and a layer of refried beans that is completely drowned in bright red, superpiquant *chile de árbol* salsa.

## Origin

The story goes that a hungry man from Guadalajara came home after a long day of work. All there was for dinner was a piece of old bread, some leftover beans and a couple of pieces of cooked pork. That made a boring, dry-as-the-desert *torta*, so he reached for the spicy salsa his wife had cooked and, without giving it too much thought, submerged the whole *torta* in the salsa. Now, he was onto something…

## Tasting

Connoisseurs insist that what makes a great *torta ahogada* is a good *birote*, the crusty, salty bread characteristic of the region that is able hold the pork and beans AND to retain its crunch in spite of being drowned in salsa. Those new to the *torta* may consider asking for it only 'half-drowned', which means the spicy salsa is diluted with some plain tomato salsa. However, this street food favourite is so full of bravado that going for the fully drowned *torta* is a must, even if it will make your ears sweat. On street stalls in Guadalajara they will serve you the *torta* in a bowl, along with a spoon and a handful of pickled onions. You can eat it with the spoon, which gets awkward, or with your hands, which gets messy, so most people eat it standing up, holding the torta away from their body. Roll up your sleeves and don't wear shoes that you care about.

## Finding it

Visit El Príncipe Heredero, commonly known as '*las tortas atrás de Sears*' (the tortas behind the Sears store). Corner of Manzano and Epigmenio González, Guadalajara, Jalisco. One *torta* is around US$2.50.

**\* TIPS \*** This is the ultimate street food fare. Look on street corners for vendors with long queues and don't waste time finding a chair or a stool. *Tortas ahogadas* are better eaten standing up at a counter. The rice and cinnamon beverage known as *horchata* is the perfect way to cool down after a fiery *torta*.

* Mauricio Velázquez de León *

# Recipe Tortas Ahogadas

## INGREDIENTS

About 30 dried *chiles de árbol*, stemmed and seeded

¾ cup (175mL) cider vinegar

2 tbs pumpkin seeds, toasted

1½ tbs sesame seeds, toasted

1 tsp dried oregano

1 tsp kosher salt or sea salt

¼ tsp ground cumin

⅛ tsp ground allspice

⅛ tsp ground cloves

2 cloves garlic

¾ cup (175mL) water

1 crusty bread roll

1½ cups leftover roasted pork shoulder, shredded

¼ small yellow onion, thinly sliced

1 radish, thinly sliced

## METHOD

1. Combine the chillies, vinegar, pumpkin and sesame seeds, oregano, salt, cumin, allspice, cloves and garlic in a blender and puree until very smooth.

2. Pour through a medium strainer into a bowl, discard solids and stir in ¾ cup (175mL) of water. This is the *chile de árbol* sauce.

3. Heat the oven to 180°C (350°F).

4. Split the roll and fill the bottom half with pork.

5. Place on a baking sheet and bake until warmed through and the bread is toasted, about six minutes.

6. Add the onion and radish and the top bun; pour *chile de árbol* sauce over the sandwich, and let it sit, so that the sauce soaks in.

# * Tteokbokki *

## KOREA

**A dish of rice cakes soaked in a fiery fermented red chilli sauce, once served in Korea's royal courts, has since been transformed into a humble street snack.**

## What is it?

Tteokbokki (tot-pok-ki; literally stir-fried rice cakes) is a street snack of small, cylindrical, chewy rice cakes cooked in a spicy fermented soy bean and red chilli sauce known as gochujang – the same stuff they put in bibimbap. You'll commonly find vats of tteokbokki bubbling away in pushcarts on the streets of Seoul, served on takeaway plates and eaten with chopsticks or a skewer.

## Tasting

As it was served to kings and officials, the original dish was chock-a-block with the good stuff: vegetables, meat, gingko nuts and walnuts. The modern street version has little by way of nutrition, yet the masses love it, and it's easy to see the appeal: Koreans rock up to street carts and are promptly served up a steaming plate of tteokbokki, often to share. Stick your skewer into one of the cylindrical, two-inch-long rice cakes, pop it in your mouth and you'll be hit with a multitude of flavours. The saltiness of the fermented soy bean, the spicy kick of the red chillies and the chewy texture... it's magically warming in winter. Be sure to have a cold drink standing by to douse the flames raging on your tongue though!

## Origin

The first recorded tteokbokki recipe appeared in a 19th-century cookbook, but as a dish served at the royal courts it dates back much further (it also gets a mention in a medical book from around AD 1460). Through the years there have been many recipes made with rice cakes but the current 'street' version was first made in 1953. The Korean War had just ended, Seoul was getting back on its feet and a lady named Ma Bok-rim started selling tteokbokki out of Sindang-dong as cheap comfort food.

## Finding it

Try all variations of the dish in the Tteokbokki Alley, Sindang-dong, Seoul. From W3300 (US$3) per serve.

* **VARIATIONS** * The original *gungjung tteokbokki* (royal *tteokbokki*) is less spicy and cooked with vegetables. These days, you'll find versions stir-fried with noodles, deep-fried *tteokbokki*, *tteokbokki* cooked with pasta, chicken, seafood, in curry... it starts getting pretty, well, inventive. A good time to try these variations is during the Tteokbokki Festival held every October at Sindang-dong, Seoul.

* By Shawn Low *

# Recipe Tteokbokki

## INGREDIENTS

500g (1lb) *tteokbokki tteok* (rice cakes)

100g (3½lb) *eomuk* (fish cake), sliced

150g (5oz) cabbage, chopped

2 spring onions (scallions), chopped

2 garlic cloves, finely chopped

1 tsp sesame oil

1 tsp sesame seeds (optional)

### Sauce

3 cups (750mL) anchovy stock (from stock powder) or water

3 tbs *gochujang* (red chilli paste)

1 tbs *gochugaru* (red chilli pepper flakes) or regular chilli flakes

1 tbs soy sauce, plus additional to taste

1 tbs sugar, plus additional to taste

NOTE These ingredients are all available at Asian or Korean grocers.

## METHOD

1. For the sauce: pour the anchovy stock or water into a medium-sized pan. Add the sauce ingredients and bring to a boil. Make sure the paste is dissolved. Reduce the heat to medium.

2. Add the rice cakes and boil until soft (roughly seven to 10 minutes).

3. Reduce to a simmer to thicken the sauce. Keep stirring to prevent the rice cakes from burning at the bottom of the pan.

4. Add the fish cakes, cabbage, spring onions, and garlic.

5. Simmer for an additional five minutes.

6. Season to taste with additional sugar and soy sauce, bearing in mind that the *gochujang* itself is salty.

7. Add the sesame oil, stir through and dish out in bowls. Top with sesame seeds if desired.

SERVES 4

# * Vindaloo *

## GOA, INDIA

**Often bearing an (undeserved) reputation for extreme heat, a Goanese *vindaloo* is a surprisingly subtle and complex dish that showcases culinary echoes of colonialism across the centuries.**

## What is it?

Pork, chicken or prawns cooked slowly in a spicy curry sauce spiked with vinegar and sugar. The secret to a good *vindaloo* is in the masala (spice blend) that is used; a true Goanese masala blends fenugreek, cumin, roasted chilli, cinnamon, peppercorns and cardamom. Rice or naan bread is also usually served.

## Tasting

Although a dish with a reputation for extreme heat – largely from its popularity in British curry houses – *vindaloo* in Goa is more subtle and balanced. A one-dimensional British *vindaloo* is prepared with a heavy hand on the chilli, but in Goa the dish's historic roots are more evident. Imparting a very distinctive sourness, palm vinegar and garlic replaces the wine vinegar and garlic infusion the Portuguese used to preserve pork on long sea voyages. The all-important masala spices are layered and distinct, their individual flavours released as essential oils during slow roasting. Finally, there's an earthy sweetness from the addition of sugar and ginger.

## Origin

*Vindaloo* is derived from a traditional Portuguese dish called *carne vinha de alhos* – literally 'meat with wine and garlic' – but the dish underwent a subcontinental makeover with palm vinegar, spices and chillies during the time the Portuguese ruled the coast of Goa as a colony for almost five centuries until 1961. An Anglicised version of *vindaloo* is ubiquitous in the Indian restaurants of Britain, but the authentic sweeter and sour version is best eaten in rustic eateries in the backstreets of Panjim in Goa.

## Finding it

Seek out the family-owned Espynick restaurant in a quiet corner of Panjim. A spicy prawn *vindaloo* costs around 450Rp (US$7).

**\* VARIATIONS \*** Other Goan foods influenced by Portuguese cuisine include *balchão*, a Macau-style pickle made from shrimps, Portuguese brandy, laurel, lemon and chilli, and *chouriço*, rustic and spicy pork sausages. For dessert, an iconic dish served at cafes throughout the region is *bebinca*, a baked and layered wonder combining egg yolks, sugar and coconut milk.

* By Brett Atkinson *

# Recipe Pork Vindaloo

## INGREDIENTS

1kg (2lb) pork cut into bite-sized pieces

2 large onions sliced

1 tbs ginger, finely chopped

1 tbs garlic, fincly chopped

1 tsp mustard seeds

1 tbs coriander powder

¼ tsp turmeric powder

4 tbs vinegar

1 tsp brown sugar

salt to taste

2 tbs cooking oil

1½ cups (375mL) of water

### Masala Paste

¾ tsp roasted fenugreek seeds

1 tsp roasted cumin seeds

1 tsp peppercorns

6–8 dried chillies, lightly roasted

4cm (1¼in) stick of cinnamon

2 cardamom pods

2 tsp of water

## METHOD

1. Saute the chopped onions in 1 tbs of cooking oil until caramelised. Using a blender, blitz the onion mixture until it becomes a paste and set aside.

2. Combine the vinegar and brown sugar and set aside.

3. Fry the mustard seeds until they sizzle, then add the chopped garlic and ginger and fry for another two minutes.

4. Mix in the coriander powder, turmeric powder and salt.

5. Add the pork pieces and fry for around six to eight minutes until they have browned. Remove and set aside.

6. Make your masala paste by blitzing all the paste ingredients together in a blender or pestle and mortar.

7. In your original pan, add the remaining oil and saute the chopped onion paste and the masala paste for two minutes.

8. Add in the vinegar and sugar mixture and the 1½ cups of water.

9. Add the browned pork pieces, and cook until the meat softens and a thick gravy is formed.

10. Serve with steamed rice or warm naan bread.

SERVES 4 TO 6

# * Yam Neua *

## THAILAND

**A creation worthy of a celebrity chef, *yam neua* blends grilled beef with Thai herbs, lime juice, palm sugar, fish sauce and lavish quantities of chilli. This is salad for grown ups!**

## What is it?

In its simplest form: grilled beef salad. But this is Thailand, so nothing is ever simple. In place of lettuce, you'll find coriander and mint leaves. In place of tomatoes and cucumber, you'll find sliced shallots and chillies. In place of vinaigrette, you'll find lime juice, palm sugar and fish sauce. It's equally as refreshing as an early morning dip in the Andaman Sea and as fiery as a blast furnace.

## Origin

The model for this supercharged salad was *yam yang nam tok*, aka 'waterfall beef', from Isarn province in northeast Thailand. The waterfall in question is juices dripping from the grilled beef, which blend with lime juice, fish sauce and palm sugar to form a spontaneous dressing.

## Tasting

Whenever you take salad beyond the realms of sliced vegetables, you know something special is going to happen. *Yam neua* is less a side salad than a roast dinner served on a bed of fresh herbs, with a secret chilli payload that will have steam coming out of your ears. As you bite into the first mouthful, fresh herbs and lime juice mingle on the palate, but it only takes a second for the raw power of the chillies and shallots to punch through. Eating *yam neua* is an exquisite balance of pleasure and pain – even after you lay down your fork, the heat of the chilli will linger, seared into your lips. So why put up with this pain? Oh, just those contradictory Thai tastes – hot and sour, sweet and salt – that sound so wrong, but taste so right.

## Finding it

With grilled beef as a core ingredient, this is a dish best sampled in a sit-down restaurant, where you can trust the meat to be freshly prepared. In Bangkok, restaurants charge around 120B (US$4) per portion.

**\* TIPS \*** Don't mistake *yam neua* for a starter or side dish. Served with a ball of sticky rice and a plate piled high with assorted greens (fresh cabbage, yard long beans, Thai basil and mint), it's the perfect light lunch in a country better known for delicious but heavy curries.

* By Joe Bindloss *

# Recipe Yam Neua

## INGREDIENTS

400g (14oz) sirloin steak

1 tbs vegetable oil

Salt and pepper to taste

Juice from 1 lime

4 tbs fish sauce

1 tbs palm sugar

10 bird's-eye chillies, cut lengthways

3 cloves garlic, thinly sliced

5 shallots, sliced

Large handful mint leaves

Large handful coriander leaves, coarsely chopped

1 small cucumber, thinly sliced

## METHOD

1. Rub the meat with vegetable oil, salt and pepper and then grill over high heat in an iron pan to medium rare.

2. Remove from the heat and slice the steak thinly with a sharp knife and set aside.

3. Mix the lime juice, fish sauce and palm sugar in a small bowl, then add the chillies and garlic and set aside.

4. Mix the shallots, mint leaves, coriander leaves, cucumber, and beef slices together in a serving bowl, stir in the dressing and serve.

SERVES 4

# * Yu Xiang Qie Zi *

CHINA

**Curiously named 'fish-fragrant' eggplant, this dish
displays all the hallmarks of classic Sichuanese cuisine –
hot, pungent, sour, sweet and salty.**

## WHAT IS IT?

Despite its name *yu xiang qie zi* does not contain, nor smell of, fish at all. The seemingly simple yet intensely flavourful dish comprises eggplant chunks stir-fried in a fiery chilli bean sauce and mixed with tangy Chinese black vinegar, usually served with plain boiled rice.

## ORIGIN

Sichuanese is one of the world's great cuisines, characterised by strong aromas and unique, robust flavours, as well as the use of indigenous ingredients including pungent pickles and Sichuan peppercorns. What started as a favourite of some of China's royal dynasties who settled in Sichuan province is now popular local fare, with plenty of well-known favourites such as twice-cooked pork, spicy tofu with minced pork and dry-fried green beans. The name *yu xiang qie zi*, which translates to 'fish-fragrant' eggplant, is likely to have originated from the Sichuanese's love of cooking fish and the use of classic Sichuanese ingredients.

## FINDING IT

There is no better place to try this dish than at the many traditional restaurants and teahouses in Chengdu, the capital of Sichuan province and spiritual home of Sichuanese cuisine.

## TASTING

There's not much to fish-fragrant eggplant, other than cubes of eggplant quickly wok-fried in a thick sauce of fermented soybeans in chilli sauce, black vinegar, garlic, ginger, Sichuan peppercorns and lots of dried chillies – yet it packs an unbelievably invigorating and dynamic punch. Perfect for soaking up strong flavours, the humble eggplant is tossed until soft, meaty and golden and then doused in a fiery and aromatic blend of traditional Sichuanese spices. The result is a balanced carnival of hot, sour, sweet and salty. The meatiness of the eggplant means it can stand on its own or as part of a multi-course banquet, eaten with plenty of rice and drowned with cold beer to offset the fiery nature of the dish.

**\* VARIATIONS \* A more substantial version of the dish comes with minced or chopped pork for meat lovers or cubes of tofu for vegetarians.**

* By Johanna Ashby *

# RECIPE Yu Xiang Qie Zi

## INGREDIENTS

4 medium-sized eggplants, chopped into bite-size cubes

2 tbs vegetable oil

1 tbs chilli bean paste

2 tbs soy sauce

2 tbs Chinese black vinegar (balsamic vinegar can be used as a substitute)

1 tbs rice wine or dry sherry

1 tsp sugar

1 tsp cornstarch

2 garlic cloves, crushed

1 tbs ginger, grated

1 tsp Sichuan pepper, ground

Handful of dried whole chillies

Chopped spring onions for garnish

## METHOD

1. Prepare the sauce by combining the chilli bean paste, soy sauce, vinegar, rice wine, sugar and cornstarch in a bowl. Set aside.

2. Heat the oil in a wok and add the eggplant. Fry for a few minutes then add a couple of tablespoons of water and cook until the eggplant is golden brown and soft.

3. Add the garlic, ginger, pepper and chillies and cook for 2 or 3 minutes until fragrant.

4. Stir in the sauce to coat the eggplant and simmer until the sauce starts to thicken.

5. Garnish with the spring onions and serve immediately with just-steamed rice.

SERVES 6

# * Zahtar *

IRAQ AND PALESTINE

**This tasty yet underrated Middle Eastern dip is an intensely flavoured spice-and-nuts combo, a staple of Iraqi and Palestinian cuisines and a signifier of how these Arab nations see themselves as peoples.**

## What is it?

*Zahtar* (also spelled za'atar) is a dry dip ground from a cocktail of spices and nuts, common throughout Arab countries. Eaten as an appetiser or at breakfast and served with *khoubz* (Arab flatbread) and olive oil, it is often prepared in large quantities and kept in the larder. No self-respecting Iraqi or Palestinian kitchen would be without a supply for long.

## Origin

*Zahtar* is both a dish in itself and a herb plant, the purifying properties of which were revered in Roman times and in Ancient Israel under King David. In both manifestations *zahtar* resonates through Arab society as a symbol of home and homeland: it is a reassuring element of one's deep roots in the land, but also, in the case of the Palestinians, a symbol of longing for homelands lost.

## Tasting

The texture of *zahtar* will be unusual for those expecting a smooth, hummuslike dip. Its consistency is more powdery than creamy, which is why unctuous olive oil is as much an essential component as the flatbread, to soak up the powder and take the dry edge off the dish. Cinnamon, cumin and coriander contribute to a sweetness that is invariably the first impression. But there's also a hint of sourness that lingers on the tongue once you're finished, thanks to the deep red berries of the sumac bush. Walnuts add a trace of bitterness for good measure. In this dish's heartland of Iraq and the Palestinian Territories, the soulful stringed oud, earnest conversation about politics and the arts, and contemporary Arab pop music would undoubtedly accompany your time at the table.

## Finding it

As Baghdad and much of Iraq is off-limits, look for Iraqi or Palestinian restaurants across the Middle East. One example is Zaatar w Zeit at Dubai Marina in the United Arab Emirates, where a dish costs 7 to 17 dirham (US$2-4.50).

**\* TIPS \* Praise the chef's *zahtar* and you're likely to be treated like one of the family. It is, however, a delicate balancing act – the greatest sign that you've enjoyed your food is to eat copious quantities of it, so not matching your words with actions may be interpreted as an insult.**

* By Anthony Ham *

# Recipe Zahtar

Sumac powder (a citrus-tinged spice) is widely available from Asian or multicultural grocery stores; in some countries you'll even find it in mainstream stores. Store leftovers in an air-tight jar and they will keep.

## INGREDIENTS

150g (5oz) sesame seeds

60g (2oz) coriander seeds

90g (3oz) walnuts

1½ tbs cumin powder

¾ tbs cinnamon powder

¾ tbs sumac powder

Salt and pepper to taste

## METHOD

1.  Toast the sesame seeds under the grill until they begin to pop and turn golden. Do the same for the coriander, and then the walnuts.

2.  Using a pestle and mortar, crush the seeds and nuts into a powder (but don't pulverise the mixture).

3.  Add the salt and pepper and the remaining spices and mix well.

4.  To eat, dip the bread first in the oil, then in the *zahtar*.

SERVES 6

# Condiments

**Legend**

## Recipe

**E**   **Easy** - A very basic recipe, eg, putting together a sandwich or tossing salad ingredients.

**M**   **Medium** - Suitable for the average home cook.

**C**   **Complex** - Several parts to make, or lots of ingredients to prepare, or a specific technique involved that may take some practice.

**Hot**

**Medium**

**Mild**

**Vegetarian**

**Note** Definitions for words in blue in the recipes can be found in the glosssary on page 214.

# * Green Chile *

NEW MEXICO, USA

**This thick, smoky, mouth-tingling sauce, used as a condiment atop everything from burgers to burritos to scrambled eggs, is synonymous with the southwestern state of New Mexico.**

## What is it?

Roasted Hatch green chillies, grown in the southern New Mexico town of Hatch, are chopped and combined with onions, spices and chicken stock or water, then cooked down to a thick sauce. With added pork or vegetables, it can form the base of a stew. Or, more commonly, it's used as a condiment.

## Origin

Chillies are one of the oldest cultivated crops of the New World. Spaniard Don Juan de Oñate brought green chilli seeds with him from Mexico in 1598 when he settled New Mexico as a Spanish colony, and the chilli became part of the local diet. The recipe for modern-day green chile is likely a combination of Spanish and Native American cooking techniques and tastes.

## Tasting

In late summer, the crisp desert air of New Mexico takes on an exotic smoky scent, as vendors set up shop in empty lots with sacks of fresh green chillies and large metal tumble roasters. Customers buy sacks of chillies, hand them to the roaster, and watch them spin over an open fire until their skins are ashy black. Try green chile at a dusty New Mexican roadhouse, where it oozes out from atop a juicy bison burger; order a green chile–smothered plate of French fries at a fast food joint, trying hard not to drip on your shirt; or dine on grilled prawns with green chile at one of the après-ski restaurants in the arty resort towns of Santa Fe or Taos.

## Finding it

Don't miss the legendary green-chile cheeseburger (US$8) at Bobcat Bite, on the Old Las Vegas Highway outside Santa Fe.

**\* VARIATIONS \* Red chile, made from green chillies that have matured and been dried, gives green chile a run for its money as the state's favourite food. 'Red or green?' your waiter will ask, and your answer is a matter of personal preference (red tends to be smokier and less spicy). If you can't decide, order 'Christmas' – both!**

* By Emily Matchar *

# Recipe Green Chile

## INGREDIENTS

1 tbs olive oil

1 small onion, chopped

1 garlic clove, minced

1 tbs flour

125mL (½ cup) chicken stock (can substitute vegetable stock)

300g (11oz) roast green chillies, peeled, seeded and chopped

1 large tomato, chopped

½ tsp cumin

½ tsp salt

## METHOD

1. Saute onions in the oil over medium heat in a large saucepan.

2. Add the garlic and cook until the onion has softened.

3. Stir in flour and cook for two minutes.

4. Slowly add stock, stirring continuously.

5. Add chillies, tomato, cumin and salt.

6. Cover pan and simmer for 30 minutes, stirring occasionally.

# * Harissa *

## TUNISIA

**Harissa, a thick flaming-red paste, oozes Mediterranean zest with a tantalising clash of bold tastes, uniting crushed garlic, dried chilli and sharp seasonings to embody the essence of Tunisian cuisine.**

## What is it?

The term 'harissa' derives from the Arabic 'to break into pieces', harking back to the crushing of desiccated chillies in a pestle and mortar that gave birth to this fiery condiment. Seasonings typically include caraway, coriander, cumin, garlic, mint and rose petals, but the spiciness of harissa can range from a subtle tingle to a fierce heat. It enlivens many Tunisian dishes, including breads, eggs, salads, pasta and couscous, and is said to aid digestion.

## Origin

The Spanish first introduced the red-hot harissa chilli peppers of the New World to Tunisia in the 1500s, bringing a little more heat to Tunisian cuisine. By this time, the nation's food had already gradually acquired some of its distinctive spices and flavours thanks to its strategic position along spice trade routes between Europe and Asia. It is only in recent years that harissa has made its way into Moroccan dishes, brought by migrants from neighbouring Arab countries who found local cooking a little too bland.

## Finding it

Hunt down the ultimate sizzling harissa for a few Tunisian dinars amid the frenzied crowds of the 19th-century Central Market in the capital, Tunis.

## Tasting

Feast your eyes on seductive mounds of harissa as you meander through a bustling fresh-produce souk (market), before bunkering down for lunch in the heaving heart of an ancient Tunisian medina. Begin with a simple serve of harissa topped with olive oil, inhaling the deceptively sweet chilli scent before plunging a slice of *tabouna* (Tunisian flat bread) into the mix; wait for the kick to come. Savour how garlic granules and chilli chunks fire up the smoky roasted peppers, tomatoes and smooth oils of a scrumptious *salade mechouia*, or drizzle a little harissa over plain couscous and taste those traditionally tame grains spring to life as the spice sinks in. Wash away the burn local-style with an aromatic *thé à la menthe* (mint tea).

**\* TIPS \* Much like baskets of bread in Spain or France, complimentary harissa crops up (unasked for) with dishes of tuna and olives at every meal except breakfast in most restaurants across Tunisia. It's often best enjoyed as a starter by dunking in a chunk of crusty baguette or flat bread.**

# Recipe Harissa

## INGREDIENTS

3 large dried red chillies, stems removed (double the chilli quantity to ramp up the spicy hit)

2 cloves of garlic, chopped

1 tsp ground coriander

1 tsp ground cumin

1 tsp caraway seeds

Salt (to taste)

Olive oil

## METHOD

1. Roughly chop the chillies and soak them in boiling water for about an hour.

2. Drain and dry the chillies with a paper towel before placing them in a blender along with the garlic, coriander, cumin and caraway seeds. Season with a little salt and a dash of olive oil, and blend together until the ingredients become a thick, smooth paste.

3. Spoon the mixture into a clean jar and cover with a 1cm (½in) layer of olive oil. You can store it in the fridge for several weeks.

# * Horseradish *

### EUROPE & USA

**Horseradish is spicy in a totally different way than chilli, but that doesn't mean it's any less intense. The gnarled beige root looks innocuous, but cut it open and the bitter pungency is enough to make your eyes water.**

## What is it?

A cruciferous root vegetable related to broccoli and cabbage, horseradish resembles a thick, creamy-tan carrot. Though the root itself has no smell while whole, cutting it releases its bitter enzymes, a natural defence mechanism against predators. Native to Europe and western Asia, it's a popular condiment across the Western world, often grated and mixed with other ingredients such as mayonnaise to make a sauce.

## Origin

Horseradish has been consumed since the dawn of civilization. Ancient Greeks considered it an aphrodisiac and a painkiller, and legend has it that the Oracle of Delphi told Apollo it was worth its weight in gold. In the first millennium AD, the root spread to Central Europe and Scandinavia, where it was used as both medicine and garnish. By the 1600s, horseradish was an accompaniment to beef and oysters in the British Isles. By the 1850s, it had travelled to America, where Central European immigrants set up horseradish farms in the Midwest.

## Tasting

Horseradish is a root that gets around, and there are infinite ways to sample the spicy stuff. Add zing to your English roast beef with a sauce of grated horseradish and vinegar, or use it to cut the fattiness of your Polish kielbasa. In Germany, take a bracing nip of horseradish schnapps, or wash down your horseradish-topped sausage with some horseradish beer. Add a counterpoint to sharp Wisconsin cheddar with a horseradish-and-cheese sandwich. Or, come brunch time, wake yourself up with a sinus-clearing horseradish-spiked Bloody Mary cocktail. Bottoms up!

## Finding it

The International Horseradish Festival in Collinsville, Illinois, USA, has been celebrating the root every June since 1987.

**\* TIPS \* Horseradish has an important place in Jewish culture. During the holiday of Passover, raw horseradish is eaten to symbolise the bitterness of slavery, while grated horseradish with vinegar is enjoyed year-round with gefilte fish, a mild white-fish ball.**

**\* By Emily Matchar \***

# Recipe Horseradish & Roast Beef Sandwiches

## INGREDIENTS

2 thick slices brown bread

4 slices roast beef

Jarred horseradish (or make your own; see below)

Handful of rocket (arugula)

### Horseradish

1 root of horseradish

2 tbs water

1 tbs white wine vinegar

150mL (5fl oz) double cream

Salt

## METHOD

1.  Peel then roughly chop the horseradish root. Shred it through the grater in a food blender with a little water. Add the vinegar and then the double cream and seasoning to taste.

2.  Spread prepared horseradish on bread to taste. Top with sliced roast beef and salad greens.

SERVES 1

# * Kimchi *

## SOUTH KOREA

**What happens when the world's favorite spicy fruit — the red chilli pepper — meets humdrum cabbage? Kimchi, that's what. It's Korea's iconic staple and every bit as fiery as the people of this tiny Asian nation.**

## What is it?

It's a salty, spicy, fermented vegetable. Preparation is simple, though time consuming: fresh cabbage is salted then smothered with a fiery red paste. Pepper flakes, salt, garlic, ginger and seafood seasoning are the basic ingredients. Usually accompanied by rice, kimchi is eaten at every meal. It's also added to stews, fried rice and *pajeon* (Korean pancake).

## Origin

The origins of kimchi date back to antiquity when vegetables were salted to ensure a winter food supply. Chilli peppers probably came to Korea in the late 16th century when Japan invaded the country. Initially viewed with skepticism, as chilli peppers were thought to be poisonous, spicy vegetables were commonplace by the 1800s, as was the practice of adding salted seafood to kimchi. The final key ingredient in modern day kimchi, napa cabbage, arrived in Korea via China about 100 years ago.

## Tasting

Kimchi is a gastronomic enigma wrapped in a leaf. First encounters are rarely enticing; the acrid aroma can knockback even the most adventurous foodie. Suppress that gag reflex and you'll be rewarded with crunchy leaves covered with a piquant *mélange* of hard-to-identify flavours that vary ever so slightly with each bite.

To experience kimchi's versatility, and Korea's lively dining culture, head to a barbecue meat restaurant. Billowing smoke from charcoal briquettes, the crackle of sizzling pork and the din of soju (distilled alcohol)-inspired chatter all signal the beginning of an exceptional dinner. On your own tabletop BBQ, grill kimchi until golden brown. Use the tongs to place pork, garlic and roasted kimchi on a garden-fresh sesame leaf. *Wrap it. Eat it. Relish it.*

## Finding It

Roasted kimchi on grilled pork at Ham-jeong, opposite Busan's Sajik stadium, costs 8000 W per serving (US$7).

**\* HEALTH \* Koreans love talking up kimchi's health benefits. Eat your kimchi and you might expect (deep breath) fewer digestion problems, lower cholesterol, a clear urinary tract, lower cancer risks, thwarted SARS, a svelte waistline, unblocked blood clots and improved stamina.**

* By Rob Whyte *

# Recipe Kimchi

This is a simplified recipe for fast kimchi. You'll get genuine kimchi with less fuss. All of the speciality ingredients can be purchased at a Korean grocer.

## INGREDIENTS

1 large head of napa cabbage (Chinese cabbage)

½ cup coarse sea salt

### Spicy sauce

½ cup coarse Korean red pepper powder

3 cloves fresh garlic, finely chopped

5cm (2in) piece of peeled ginger root, finely chopped

½ medium pear, peeled and cored

1 tbs sesame seeds

¼ cup (60mL) *jeotgal* (fish juice)

## METHOD

1.  Cut the cabbage lengthwise. Cut each piece again to make four quarters and discard stem. Chop the cabbage into 1 cm pieces.
2.  Place the cabbage pieces in a large stainless steel bowl, sprinkle on the salt and mix together with your hands.
3.  Let it sit 1–2 hours, or until the cabbage is slightly tender, but not wilted.
4.  Wash and drain the cabbage three times.
5.  Place the washed cabbage in a colander and allow the water to drain for 1 hour.
6.  Place sauce ingredients in a blender.
7.  Mix to a fine consistency then let it sit for at least 10 minutes.
8.  Place the drained cabbage in a large stainless steel bowl.
9.  Add the sauce to the the cabbage and mix together with your hands (use plastic gloves to protect your hands).
10. Pack the cabbage into plastic containers (or mason jars) with tight fitting lids. This is fresh kimchi and it's ready to eat.
11. For a deeper, more pungent flavour, let it stand at room temperature for 48 hours. Then refrigerate. The longer it sits, the more pungent and sour the flavour and aroma.

MAKES ABOUT 8 CUPS

# * Lime Pickle *

INDIA, PAKISTAN, BANGLADESH

**Across the Indian subcontinent, spicy lime pickle is
not just a condiment, it's the cornerstone of every meal.**

## What is it?

The preparation is so simple – just pieces of lime, salt, mustard oil, ground chilli, and a sprinkling of Indian spices – yet the taste is so complex. The trick to preparing a good lime pickle is patience. The initial salting of the limes takes two weeks, and you can add another week for the pickle to mature once the ingredients are cooked together to bring out the spicy goodness.

## Origin

Like all pickles, Indian lime pickle is an attempt to preserve summer. Limes are harvested during the cool rainy season, and 'pickled down' to provide that vivid, citrus tang all year round. Every Indian family has a carefully guarded recipe for *nimbu* or *naranga achar* (lime pickle), but pickling is a tradition that dates back to at least Vedic times (1700 BC–150 BC).

## Tasting

Forget everything you know about Indian pickles from eating poppadom in Indian restaurants overseas. Mango chutney is just glorified jam; the real deal in India is lime pickle – the oily, menacing-looking, red condiment that appears on the side of almost every plate served in the subcontinent. This is not just a dip – locals will eat it with *papad* (the real Indian poppadom), with rice, with vegetables, with curry, with just about anything. But be warned, lime pickle packs a punch. The combination of hot chilli, salt and tart lime is vibrant and immediate, like a defibrillator applied directly to the tastebuds. It sometimes contains large chunks of lime – it's wise to chop these down into smaller morsels as the flavours can be overwhelming if you try to chew through a whole quarter lime in one mouthful.

## Finding it

You don't have to find lime pickle: it finds you. Pretty much every meal you order in South Asia will have a tantalising dollop of pickle on the side.

* **VARIATIONS** * India has a rich tradition of pickles and chutneys. As well as lime pickle, you'll find variations made with green mango, ginger, pumpkin, turnip, onion, garlic, even rose petals and lotus roots. In the Indian south, you can't avoid coconut chutney, a cool-yet-hot combo of coconut, mustard seed, red chillies and curry leaves, served on the side with *dosas* (lentil- and rice-flour pancakes), *idli* (steamed rice cakes) and *vadai* (lentil-flour donuts).

* By Joe Bindloss *

# Recipe Lime Pickle

## INGREDIENTS

12 limes, cut into eight segments, then in half again

½ cup of salt (ideally a mix of white sea salt and black rock salt)

6 tsp mustard seeds, ground

6 tsp fennel seeds, roasted dry, then ground

6 tbs ground dried chilli

2 tsp turmeric powder

2 cups mustard oil

2 tsp whole mustard seeds

1 tsp asafoetida

## METHOD

1. Take a sterilised pickling jar and add your chopped limes and salt, then mix together and seal the jar. Keep in a light place for two weeks for the salt to do its work.

2. Once your salted limes are ready, add the powdered mustard seed and roasted fennel, the chilli and the turmeric.

3. Next, heat your mustard oil to smoking point, then add the mustard seeds then the asafoetida, then turn off the heat. Pour the hot mixture over your spiced limes.

4. Allow the pickle to cool, then rest for at least a week before serving.

# * Lutenica *

## THE BALKANS

**Lutenica is the piquant kin of ajvar, Macedonia's ubiquitous sweet red pepper dip. This full-bodied condiment intrigues with its powerful peppers, hints of tomato and garlic zest.**

## What is it?

Crimson and rich, *lutenica* brings the heat to any traditional Balkan meal. Variety is common, as its spiciness can be calibrated by modifying the proportion of sweet to hot peppers and the tomato concentration. Although eaten year-round, *lutenica's* especially connected with the chill of winter; families throughout the region, but particularly in the dish's heartland of Macedonia, prepare it in autumn, bottling up the hot sauce for the cooler months. It is best as an accompaniment to cold cuts and roast meats, or slathered on bread with soft white cheese sprinkled over it.

## Origin

Like everything in the Balkans, the history of *lutenica*, and its next-of-kin *ajvar*, is complicated. *Lut* simply means 'hot' in Macedonian and other Slavic languages, but *ajvar* derives from the Turkish word *hayvar* (and originally, from Persian), meaning 'caviar'. Since the average Balkan peasant was no aristocrat, the key ingredient of this fish-egg delicacy was seemingly substituted for cheaper peppers at some time in the murky Ottoman past. And so the fiery dish was born; today, you'll find *lutenica* throughout the Balkans, from Serbia and Montenegro to Macedonia and Bulgaria.

## Tasting

*Lutenica* is a social dish that sits most comfortably on a long wooden table weighed down with myriad plates, bowls and bottles all fighting for space. Its complex interplay of ingredients strokes your tongue. The enveloping heat of the hot peppers works its way to the fore, mingling with the more delicate tang of sweet red pepper. Neither smooth nor chunky, components such as pepper and garlic compete to distinguish themselves on the palate. Throughout the meal, *lutenica* improvises to match its company; with mild white cheese, its spiciness becomes a tang; with roast suckling pig, on the other hand, *lutenica* emphasises the meat's succulence; spread on rough country bread, you'll need a smoky red wine to round out the condiment's big-hitting flavours.

## Finding it

*Lutenica* is just as likely to be served at a traditional winter carnival as it is a countryside tavern. In a restaurant, it'll set you back 120 to 150MKD (US$2.50-3.20). Try Etno Selo Timcevski, a traditional outdoors restaurant 14km east of Kumanovo, Macedonia.

* **VARIATIONS** * *Lutenica has many relatives across the Balkans, both spicy and sweet. In Bosnia, spicy pindjur is similar but uses eggplant (aubergine) as a base ingredient and includes Bulgarian kyopolou (a type of crushed black pepper). Macedonia has a version of pindjur, too. It doesn't have the eggplant base of its Bosnian cousin and is not too dissimilar to lutenica, though it has a more distinctive tomato flavour, a liquid texture and lacks the trademark zing of lutenica.*

* By Chris Deliso*

# Recipe Lutenica

## INGREDIENTS

3kg (6½lb) sweet red peppers (long peppers, not bell peppers)

1kg (2lb) tomatoes

100mL sunflower oil

2 tsp salt

1 tsp vinegar

3 chilli peppers

2 tsp white sugar

1 small garlic bulb

Parsley

## METHOD

1. Wash the peppers and tomatoes, and finely chop the garlic and parsley.

2. Scald the red peppers on the top of a flat cooker (or an oven burner), at moderate heat, until the skin is blackened. Afterwards, place them under plastic wrap to soften.

3. Peel the softened skins off the peppers and leave them in a colander or spaghetti strainer for 10 minutes, for the residual moisture to drain off.

4. Bake the tomatoes in the oven at moderate heat for 20 minutes. When the tomatoes are soft and the skin has started to wrinkle, remove them from the oven and peel the skins off.

5. Grind the tomatoes in a hand-cranked mincer. (If you don't happen to have a hand-cranked mincer, a pestle and mortar will also work.)

6. Cook the tomatoes in a large pot on the hob at moderate heat, for 10 minutes.

7. While the tomatoes are cooking, cut the peppers into small pieces.

8. Add the peppers and chilli peppers to the pot, as well as the oil, and cook for another 45 to 55 minutes.

9. As the sauce starts to thicken, add the chopped garlic and parsley, along with the salt, vinegar and sugar.

10. When there is about five minutes of cooking time left, warm two empty jars to prepare for bottling.

11. While still hot, pour the finished *lutenica* into the prepared jars or you can enjoy immediately.

12. If bottling, ensure the seals of your jars are airtight. Place the jars in a cool dry place; they only need to be refrigerated after they have been opened.

MAKES 2 JARS OF LUTENICA

# * Muhummara *

## MIDDLE EAST

**This fiery pesto-like paste will set your taste buds tingling. Putting some serious heat into Middle Eastern meze, muhummara is the dip you aren't likely to forget.**

## What is it?

Fresh or roasted red capsicum is pounded together with ground walnuts, olive oil and breadcrumbs to make a paste. Dried Aleppo pepper flakes (known as *pul biber* in Turkey), pomegranate molasses, cumin, salt, garlic and lemon juice are then added according to taste. *Muhummara* is traditionally served as part of a meze spread, scooped up with pieces of bread.

## Origin

Aleppo in northern Syria has been a bubbling cauldron of culinary influences down through the centuries, and hot yet sweet Aleppo pepper has been a favoured spice of the city's chefs since ancient times. *Muhummara* is widely acknowledged to have first been made within the city walls; the recipe then passed down by memory from cook to cook, spreading across the Middle East, long before written recipes became commonplace.

## Tasting

A meze spread is Middle Eastern food at its most flavoursome, with the small morsels of intermingling tastes shared and lingered over. The flashy bowl of potent-red *muhummara* makes its entrance beside the blander shades of dipping staples hummus and baba ganoush. With torn bread, scoop the *muhummara* straight from the bowl – the first taste is all sharp heat, but the sting is soon tempered by the paste's subtle fruity-sour undertones. To complete the experience, do as the locals do and order a milky arak to see how this aniseed-flavoured liqueur compliments *muhummara*'s intense bite.

## Finding it

The riverside Casino Arabi, in the Berdaouni area of Zahle in Lebanon, serves up excellent *muhummara*. Meze dishes cost 5000 LBP to 11,000 LBP (US$3 to US$7).

* VARIATIONS * In Turkey, *muhummara* is sometimes called *acuka*, although the recipe and preparation are the same. A variation of the dish is found in the Caucasus region where it is known as *ajika* and is often made with the addition of coriander and fenugreek.

* By Jess Lee *

# Recipe **Muhummara**

## INGREDIENTS

3 red capsicums

¾ cup fresh, toasted breadcrumbs

¾ cup ground walnuts

2 cloves garlic, minced

2 tbs Aleppo pepper flakes (available at Middle Eastern and Turkish specialty stores and sometimes called *pul biber*)

3 tbs lemon juice

3 tbs pomegranate molasses (available at Middle Eastern and Turkish specialty stores)

2 tbs olive oil

1 tsp cumin

## METHOD

1. Preheat oven to 200°C (400°F).

2. Roast the capsicum in the top tray of the oven, turning occasionally, until the skin is blackened and blistered (approximately 40 minutes).

3. Remove from the oven, seal in a plastic bag and allow to cool.

4. Peel and deseed the capsicum and place into a food processor along with the remaining ingredients. Blend the mixture to a paste.

5. Serve in a central bowl and finish with a drizzle of extra virgin olive oil.

# * Mustard *

## ENGLAND

**Medicine to the Greeks, a spread to the Romans, beloved by Gallic monks – mustard's been popular for millennia, across continents. But it's in England that it's at its fiery best.**

## What is it?

Mustard is a condiment made from the crushed seeds of the mustard plant. It has the power to bring zing to the plainest plate – roast beef with hot English mustard being an all-time classic. The ground seeds of the brown, black and white varieties are used to make this pungent, often lurid-yellow nectar; the secret lies in making it with cold water – not hot – to preserve its natural kick.

## Origin

Northern hemispherians have pepped up their food with mustard seeds for more than two millennia – it added a palate-punch before spices arrived from the East. The Romans made it a condiment, grinding seeds with young wine (*'must'*); they also took it to France, where monks grew it and, in 1777, mild Dijon mustard was born. But it was Jeremiah Colman, a miller from Norwich, who restored mustard's fire – in 1814 he devised a way to powder the seeds without evaporating their heat-giving oils. In 1866 he was appointed mustard-maker to Queen Victoria.

## Tasting

English mustard has a colour akin to the contents of a newborn's nappy. But get over that, this stuff is a taste sensation. Picture the scene: you've rocked up for lunch at a traditional old boozer – one that hasn't gone gastro and still has soggy beermats – and a limp ham sandwich has appeared. Your stomach starts to sink, but then... stuffed amid the sticky sachets you spot it: Colman's English Mustard. A quick squeeze and your snack's transformed. Your nose starts to burn, your eyes to glisten, your tastebuds to declare, 'thank you!' Mustard is the the soulmate of quality produce and the elevator of the mediocre. For the most satisfying combo, eat it with pork pies or cold cuts. Just apply conservatively – remember, it's hot!

## Finding it

Mustard Coffee Bar (www.mustardcoffeebar.com), Bridewell Alley, Norwich. Located in the original Colman's mustard shop it serves mustard-spiced Scotch eggs for £2.50 (US$3.80).

**\* VARIATIONS \*** French Dijon mustard is smooth, pale yellow and doesn't even rank against English on the spiciness scale – it makes a lovely vinaigrette. Wholegrain is a mid-strength, coarser mustard, made using unground seeds – great for adding texture to dressings and other dishes. American mustard – mild, usually sold in a squeezy bottle – is a hot dog essential.

* By Sarah Baxter*

# Recipe Mustard

You can buy it in a jar, but making your own means you can control its kick. Plus, mix in a few extras to give your mustard extra punch – the addition of beer seems especially England-appropriate...

## INGREDIENTS

125g (4½oz) brown mustard seeds

30g (1oz) yellow mustard seeds

275mL (9 fl oz) white-wine vinegar

250mL (8½ fl oz) beer

125g (4½oz) mustard powder

250mL (8½ fl oz) cold water

1 tsp sugar

1 tsp salt

## METHOD

1.  Combine the mustard seeds, vinegar and beer in a bowl. Cover and leave for 48 hours. It does not need to be refrigerated.

2.  Transfer the mix to a food processor; add remaining ingredients.

3.  Process until smooth (about 5 minutes).

4.  Decant into a glass jar; seal and refrigerate.

5.  Allow the flavours to develop for 3-4 weeks.

# * Nam Phrik *

## Thailand

**In Thailand, you're never more than a few feet from *nam phrik*, a pungent, spicy relish that's an essential part of the Thai table.**

## What is it?

The most basic *nam phrik* is simply a paste made from shrimp paste *(gapi)* and chillies, eaten alongside everything from steamed eggs and omelettes to fish cakes, deep-fried prawns and sweet pork. *Nam phrik* is never eaten alone, but is accompanied by side dishes *(kreaung kiam)*, which could be as simple as a plate of raw vegetables or deep-fried pork.

## Origin

Said to be the most ancient among Thai dishes, this paste was, and still is, made with the pestle and mortar. The early versions would mix peppercorns with fermented soy beans and charred shallots, providing heat and salt, alongside some kind of souring agent, such as lime juice or fresh tamarind. As the Thais moved south, they discovered coconuts, palm sugar and fermented fish, which were all added. And as chillies arrived in the 16th century, they too were thrown in.

## Tasting

The classic *nam phrik gapi* is both pungent and delicate, a wonderful melange of raw garlic, shrimp paste, palm sugar, fish sauce, lime juice... and a mind-blowing quantity of bird's-eye chillies. The first taste is deep and resonant, before those tiny fruits kick in and really get the heart beating faster. But as in all Thai food, balance – between the salty, sweet, sour and hot – is everything. This is one relish where all four sit together in beautiful harmony. But you'll find whatever flavours you desire. A bitter version is made with pea eggplants, while you'll find recipes made with coconut in the south. Some have pork as a main ingredient, others green pepper, tamarind, minced prawns and salted duck egg. But remember... *nam phrik* is never, ever eaten alone.

## Finding it

You'll find *nam phrik* in every home and most restaurants. The street food, though, is mainly Chinese in origin, so if you really want authenticity, try David Thompson's brilliant *Nahm* in Bangkok's Metropolitan Hotel.

**\* VARIATIONS \* You'll find *nam phrik* made with crab roe and dried prawns, fermented fish and dried coconut. In Chiang Mai, they do a version with tomatoes and pork, and as you move down to the central plains, this same recipe might have added galangal and sharp Chinese dates. The variations are endless. Another close relative is *lon*, a gentle relish, often pork or prawns simmered in coconut cream.**

* By Tom Parker-Bowles *

# Recipe Nam Phrik Gung

There are dozens of varieties of Nam Phrik in Thailand. This one, adapted from the master Thai chef David Thompson, of Nahm restaurant in Bangkok, features pea eggplants and prawns.

## INGREDIENTS

2 coriander roots

4 cloves of garlic

4 shallots, grilled

8 bird's eye chillis

1–2 tbs palm sugar

2 tbs pea eggplants

½ tsp shrimp paste

½ tbs lime juice

Handful of small prawns

Dash of fish sauce

Some chicken stock

Pinch of salt

## METHOD

1. Grind the garlic, salt and coriander roots into a paste with a mortar and pestle.

2. Peel the grilled (or roasted) shallots and add them, with the chillies and shrimp paste. Pound the mixture, adding stock to keep it moist.

3. Mix in the palm sugar, lime juice and fish sauce to taste.

4. Finally, add the pea eggplants and prawns and crush with the pestle so both are bruised. This coarse, hot, salty condiment can be served with meat or raw / blanched vegetables.

SERVES 8

# * Pepper Jelly *

SOUTHERN UNITED STATES

**As rosy orange as sunset in a jar, sweet-spicy pepper jelly on a tray with crackers and cream cheese is a quintessential part of any proper Southern dinner party.**

## What is it?

Pepper jelly is a spread made from a variety of sweet and hot peppers (chillies), spiced with vinegar and sugar, and set with pectin. The consistency is similar to other fruit jams, and usually contains diced pieces of chilli and chilli seeds. It's commonly served as an appetiser or condiment in the Southern United States.

## Origin

Though the exact origins of pepper jelly are unclear, it was presumably invented by early settlers to the Southern United States looking for a way to preserve the chillies that grew in the region. Different regions have different styles of pepper jelly according to what was commonly grown in the area – Texas pepper jelly usually contains jalapeños, for example, while the north Florida city of St Augustine uses the unique *datil* chillies brought to the area by Chilean immigrants. Most varieties use sweet red bell peppers (capsicums) as the base, though it's not uncommon to see chartreuse jars of green pepper jelly.

## Finding it

A Southern Season, a gourmet megastore in Chapel Hill, North Carolina, has been selling varieties of pepper jelly (US$5–US$10 a jar) since the 1970s.

## Tasting

The classic way to taste red pepper jelly is as an appetiser, served with crackers and cream cheese. The sweet heat of the jelly is a perfect contrast to the cool, creamy cheese. Subbing goat cheese for cream cheese is a slightly more sophisticated take on the concept, bringing an element of tanginess to the party. Pepper jelly also makes an excellent glaze for meats, turning ham, chicken wings or shrimp into instant sweet-spicy delights. The bold may even enjoy slightly softened pepper jelly over vanilla ice cream, the spicy, vinegary kick of the jelly cutting through the richness of the ice cream.

**\* TIPS \*** The mildest jellies typically contain red or green capsicums or raspberry jalapeños, while spicier varieties include *datils*, green jalapeños or chipotles. The hottest of the hot might list *naga jolokia* chillies (aka 'ghost chillies') or habaneros.

* By Emily Matchar *

# Recipe Pepper Jelly

## INGREDIENTS

2 red capsicums, seeded and finely chopped

2 green capsicums, seeded and finely chopped

10 jalapeño chillies, seeded and finely chopped

250mL cider vinegar

1 packet (6g) fruit pectin

1kg (2lb) sugar

## METHOD

1. Place capsicum and chillies in a large saucepan and add vinegar.

2. Stir in pectin.

3. Bring mixture to the boil over high heat.

4. Stir in sugar and return to the boil for one minute, stirring constantly.

5. Remove from the heat and skim away foam with a slotted spoon.

6. Ladle into pre-sterilised glass jars or other heat-proof containers. The jelly will last two to three weeks in the refrigerator.

# * Piccalilli *

## ENGLAND

**This 'Indian pickle' is a gloopy mish-mash of English ingredients and Eastern spices – not much to look at perhaps, but a tasty, tangy addition to many a meal.**

## What is it?

Piccalilli is like edible *potpourri*, a chutney-ish jumble of chopped vegetables and spices, pickled in vinegar. Ingredients vary by season – though cauliflower is usually involved; other common inclusions are green beans, onions and small cucumbers. Turmeric and mustard powder give it its distinctive (alarming?) yellow colour – and a bit of kick.

## Origin

Even the Oxford English Dictionary can't fathom where the word 'piccalilli' comes from, classing it as of 'uncertain origin'. The spelling has varied too: peccalillo, pickalilly, pickylilly... It was also once called Indian pickle, which nods to its roots – it seems to be an Anglicisation of India achar (pickles), mixing the new spices arriving from the Empire with English ingredients. The first known recipe was printed in *Art of Cookery* in 1758; this recommended 'greening' your acidic vinegary mix in a copper pot – no longer advised, as it turns the relish highly toxic!

## Finding it

St Helen's, Lancashire – hometown of Bartons (www.bartonspickles.com), which has been making piccalilli to the same recipe since 1905; a jar costs around £1.30 (US$2).

## Tasting

Fêtes, fairs, country-shows – piccalilli is a stalwart at these traditional affairs; it's the sort of thing your mum would buy from the Women's Institute stall. Certainly, a jar of this garish relish might be found loitering at the back of many an English cupboard or fridge – possibly untouched. It's a bit of a Marmite: most either love or hate its curious, vaguely curried crunch. But order a ploughman's lunch and take the plunge – a platter of English cheese, crusty bread, crisp celery, and perhaps a slab of ham, are the perfect canvas for a daub of piccalilli. Its mild yet discernible tang enhances the satisfyingly simple flavours – not to mention adding a splash of colour too.

* TIPS * The best piccalilli is homemade – factory-churned stuff rarely tastes as good. If you try it, be sure to salt the vegetables first, to ensure they stay crunchy when cooked – do this by soaking them in brine for 24 hours before you start. Also, sterilise your storage jars – wash them in warm soapy water and then heat them for five minutes in a moderate oven.

* By Sarah Baxter *

# Recipe Piccalilli

You can chuck in any vegetables you want – use what's seasonal, and what you like.

## INGREDIENTS

700mL (23 fl oz) malt vinegar

2 tbs coriander seeds

Pinch salt

500g (1lb) cauliflower florets

2 onions, chopped

3 tbs English mustard powder

3 tbs plain flour

1 tbs ground turmeric

2 tsp ground ginger

50mL (1½ fl oz) cider vinegar

100g (3½oz) French beans

2 garlic cloves, crushed

200g (7oz) granulated sugar

## METHOD

1. Soak the vegetables in brine for 24 hours.

2. Put the vinegar, coriander seeds and salt in a large pan and bring to the boil.

3. Add the cauliflower and onion; simmer until slightly softened.

4. Meanwhile, put the mustard powder, flour, turmeric and ginger in a bowl; whisk in the cider vinegar until smooth, then set aside.

5. Add the beans, garlic and sugar to pan; stir until sugar has dissolved then drain over a bowl to collect vinegar.

6. Put the mustard mix and vinegar back into pan; bring to the boil, then simmer for 10 minutes.

7. Return the drained vegetables to the pan; add more sugar and water if necessary to give a thick consistency, then take the pan off the heat.

8. Decant into sterilised, sealable jars; store for three months in cool, dark place before eating.

MAKES 3 TO 4 JARS

# * Pol Sambola *

## SRI LANKA

**This spicy-sweet condiment sums up tropical Sri Lanka. Its tingling heat, tempered by candy-sugar coconut, is sunshine and lazy beach days for your taste buds.**

## What is it?

*Pol sambola* is a coconut-rich spicy *sambol* (Sri Lankan chutney), topped onto other dishes for extra zing. The main ingredient is freshly grated coconut, blended with a mixture of ground, dried hot red chillies, red onion, salt, chilli powder and lime juice. Often tamarind juice or Maldive fish (cured tuna) is added as well.

## Origin

Although the origins of *pol sambola* aren't known, the dish encompasses two of the country's most famed cuisine components: coconut and chilli. Coconuts have been a staple crop for the island since at least the Rohana Kingdom (210–161 BC). Sri Lanka became an important stop on the trade routes in the 7th century when Arab merchants discovered the country's glut of pungent chilli and spice. It's not surprising that Sri Lankan cooks combined these two easily sourced ingredients to make what is today one of the nation's most popular condiments.

## Tasting

A sticky-looking orange side dish appears without fanfare on your table. Under the rhythmic thwack-thwack of the restaurant's wobbling ceiling fans, the Sri Lankans at the table next to yours are spooning generous dollops of this stuff onto their rice. Do as they do to discover why the *pol sambola* bowl is often the first one emptied. The initial taste is the fruity sweetness of coconut, but a powerful punch of chilli soon makes its presence known. There's sourness as well, thanks to a generous dousing of lime and, if the cook has used Maldive fish, a wonderfully salty note adds a final bite. Sweet, salty, sour and spicy, *pol sambola* is the piquant antidote to a humid Sri Lankan day.

## Finding it

Chettinad Restaurant in the Pettah district of Colombo serves up excellent *pol sambola* with its vegetarian feasts. Around Rs 500 (US$4) for a meal).

* TIPS * *Sambols* are Sri Lankan side dishes that add extra flavour to the main curry-and-rice meal. It's also completely normal to just scoop the *pol sambola* straight from the plate using a roti or paratha (Sri Lankan flatbreads). Remember to use only your right hand when eating.

* By Jess Lee *

# Recipe Pol Sambola

## INGREDIENTS

3 cups grated flesh of fresh coconut

½ red onion, finely diced

3 dried red chillies

1 tsp chilli powder

1 tbs Maldive fish (optional)

Juice of 1 lime

Salt to taste

## METHOD

Using a mortar and pestle (or a food processor) grind up the red onion, dried red chillies, chilli powder, Maldive fish and half of the lime juice until it becomes a paste. Add the coconut and the rest of the lime juice and combine by hand until mixture is an even orange-red colour. Add salt to taste.

# * Salsa Xnipec *

**Salsa Xnipec means 'the dog's nose' in Mayan so prepare for some nose-tingling snuffles after tasting this fiery salsa!**

## What is it?

This table salsa is the archetypal condiment in the Yucatán region. Served with almost every meal, brave Yucatecos use it over any food in need of a burst of flavour. It can be smooth or chunky: the one constant is the presence of blazing habaneros, the exceptionally hot peppers that define much of the cuisine of this Mexican region.

## Origin

*Xnipec* has been prepared in the Yucatán peninsula for more than 8000 years, since the first habanero peppers were grown domestically. Habaneros come from the Amazonia region in South America and it is believed they reached Mexico via Cuba (hence the name habanero for Habana, the Cuban capital). But its scientific name is *Capsicum chinense* thanks to a Dutch botanist named Nikolaus J von Jacquin, who mistakenly believed that habaneros originated in China.

## Tasting

*Xnipec* goes best with food from the Yucatán region. At the Lucas de Vargas Market in Mérida, people sprinkle *xnipec* over freshly made *panuchos* (black-bean-stuffed tortillas topped with chicken or turkey), and tacos with *cochinita pibil* (slow-roasted, marinated pork, sour oranges and annatto seeds wrapped in banana leaves). Although the kick from the *xnipec* can be extreme, it is tamed with pickled red onions which give a cool contrast to the spicy habaneros. Luckily, you don't have to travel far to get a *xnipec* hit. If you find habaneros in your local market you can easily make your own. But beware, *xnipec* is not for the faint of heart and if you go too far you may find your nose getting as wet as your dog's!

## Finding it

There will be a dish of *xnipec*, or a version of it, on the table at any traditional restaurant or market stall on the Yucatán peninsula, from Chiapas to Mérida. In Mérida try it at restaurant Los Almendros, Calle 50. No 493.

* **VARIATIONS** * One of *Xnipec*'s advantages is its simplicity: just three ingredients plus salt. However, you can find variations that include tomatoes, roasted garlic, onions or spring onions. All is good, so long as you keep the habaneros as the main attraction. There are also bottled versions but these are much more vinegary and watery than the real, made-by-hand, stuff.

# Recipe Salsa Xnipec

## INGREDIENTS

4–5 habanero peppers

⅔ cup (170mL) sour orange juice or use a combination of lime juice, lime zest and grapefruit juice

¼ cup coriander leaves (cilantro), chopped

Salt to taste

## METHOD

1. Over an open flame on the stove or a barbecue, roast the habaneros until the skin blackens. In Yucatán cooks often roast the habaneros by placing them directly over hot charcoal coals.

2. Using a pestle and mortar crush the habaneros, adding enough juice to make a salsa. Add the coriander and salt to taste.

3. Adjust the seasoning and let it rest for half an hour or so.

4. Use it over scrambled eggs, grilled meats, rice and beans, and, why not, a good slice of pizza.

# * Sambal Ulek *

## MALAYSIA & INDONESIA

**No, that innocent blob of red sauce isn't ketchup, it's *sambal ulek* – Indonesian chilli paste, a fiery mix of chillies and toasted shrimp paste.**

## What is it?

The core ingredients for *sambal ulek* are crushed raw red chillies and *terasi* (*belacan*) – toasted shrimp paste. Ground in a pestle and mortar with garlic and shallots, this mix is preserved with the addition of oil, salt and palm sugar. It's essentially chopped chilli made easy. Chefs keep a jar on hand to spice up soups and stir-fries, and a generous spoonful is added to the side of each plate so that diners can add extra spice as required.

## Origins

Sambal was originally an Indonesian word, but today the term is used across the region, and even as far afield as Sri Lanka and the Philippines. Now integral to Indonesian cooking, the condiment owes its existence to the spice trade from South America to Spain and Portugal and on to Spanish and Portuguese colonies in Southeast Asia. This was how the chilli first arrived in Asia, and Asian cooking was never the same again.

## Tasting

Taste it tentatively, is our advice. You may find a dollop of this culinary napalm on the side of your plate, or in a bowl or dish on your table. Do not let the bright red colour or the wholesome appearance lull you into false sense of security. This is not the local ketchup, this is preserved fire. As you deposit the first morsel into your mouth, you can expect a hammer-blow hit of chilli, and the heat will be even more ferocious if the sambal is freshly prepared. Then you'll notice the other flavours: the salt, and sugar, the garlic, and the curious, fishy tone added by the *terasi* (*belacan*). The trick is to take small blobs with each forkful as you eat; stirring a big spoonful into your meal is likely to lead to sudden, unexpected pools of explosive heat.

## Finding it

It will find you! Most meals in Indonesia or Malaysia come with a complimentary dollop of *sambal ulek* on the side.

**\* VARIATIONS \* *Sambal ulek* is the starting point for a vast family of other sambals, prepared with everything from fish to fruit. As well as the core ingredients of chilli, shrimp paste, sugar and salt, popular additional ingredients include peanuts, tomatoes, lemongrass, lime juice, pineapple, tamarind pulp, ginger, anchovies, beans, unripe banana, and even fermented durian!**

* By Joe Bindloss *

# Recipe Sambal Ulek

## INGREDIENTS

20 fresh red chillies, sliced

10 shallots, chopped

4 cloves garlic, peeled and chopped

1 fresh tomato, chopped

1 tsp toasted shrimp paste (*terasi/ belacan*)

1 tsp salt

1½ tsp palm sugar

4 tbs vegetable oil

## METHOD

1. Heat oil in a wok and add the chilli, shallots and garlic; fry until the chillies and shallots are soft.

2. Add the tomato and continue to fry for another minute, then transfer the mixture to a pestle and mortar.

3. Crush and grind the ingredients together with the toasted shrimp paste, salt and palm sugar, and work the mixture into a coarse paste.

4. Transfer to a jar and keep in the fridge until needed.

# * Wasabi *

JAPAN

One of Japanese cuisine's magical ingredients, the indigenous wasabi has a unique and pungent yet refreshing taste that elevates raw fish dishes to dizzying heights.

## WHAT IS IT?

Contrary to popular belief, wasabi is not the synthetic condiment in paste or powdered form, nor is it the same as the sharper-tasting and cream-coloured horseradish, but rather a knobbly, pale green root vegetable with bright green flesh. When grated, wasabi yields a biting and 'nose-clearing' effect yet with a remarkably cleansing taste, making it a perfect accompaniment to sashimi.

## ORIGIN

It is believed that wasabi was originally used for medicinal purposes in medieval Japan and it was not until the Edo period that wasabi's popularity as a condiment and ingredient in Japanese cookery grew due to its formal cultivation. In addition to its flavour and ability to disguise the strong smell of the sea, wasabi's anti-bacterial and deodorising properties likely led to its use with raw fish.

## TASTING

Wasabi thrives on Japan's cold, pure running water, which is why it remains a difficult ingredient to source outside Japan. Those used to the ubiquitous sachets in takeaway sushi or the powdered pastes served in sushi restaurants might be surprised to learn that the hotness of such condiments is due to the harsher horseradish, which is often used to supplement the more expensive wasabi. Fresh wasabi root on its own is rather bitter but the taste of freshly grated wasabi is truly a revelation – more delicate and fragrant than horseradish, the initial pungent 'hit' lasts only a few seconds after grating and delivers a surprisingly refreshing taste. Fresh wasabi is best eaten on its own, and not mixed with soy sauce, requiring the merest blush on sushi or sashimi or as a palate cleanser between different types of raw fish dishes.

## FINDING IT

Try it at one of Tsukiji Fish Market's sushi bars for the unforgettable taste sensation of incredibly fresh sashimi and wasabi.

* VARIATIONS * Wasabi is used as an ingredient in dressings, sauces, and even ice cream! The leaves of the wasabi plant can also be eaten, having the same bitey flavour as the ground root.

* By Johanna Ashby *

# Recipe Salmon Tartare with Wasabi Mayonnaise

If you are unable to find fresh wasabi, powdered or paste versions are an acceptable substitute for this elegant starter. The wasabi mayonnaise can also be used as a dipping sauce for grilled meats and vegetables.

## INGREDIENTS

1 part freshly grated or pre-prepared wasabi

10 parts whole-egg mayonnaise

300g (11oz) sashimi-grade salmon, chopped in small cubes

1 medium avocado, diced

1 shallot, finely diced

Juice of 1 lime

Handful of dill

Salad leaves for serving

## METHOD

1. To make wasabi mayonnaise, mix the freshly grated wasabi with the mayonnaise.

2. For salmon tartare, mix the wasabi mayonnaise with the salmon, avocado, shallot, lime juice and dill.

3. Using a round cookie cutter, or mould, pack the salmon mixture in the mould on a plate.

4. Carefully lift the mould, season the salmon mixture with salt and pepper and garnish with salad leaves to serve.

SERVES 4

# * Glossary *

**acuka** Turkish name for *muhammara*.

**ají amarillo** A Peruvian yellow chilli pepper, turning orange as it matures.

**ají limo** A Peruvian chilli with a spicy, yet distinctive citrus flavour when cooked. It's commonly used in *ceviche*, salsa and rice dishes.

**Aleppo pepper** Commonly used in Middle Eastern/ Mediterranean cuisine, it has a moderate heat with a bit of a cumin, fruity undertone.

**allspice** Not to be confused with mixed spice or five-spice, allspice is a key ingredient in Caribbean jerk seasoning and made with the dried, unripe berries of a pimento tree.

**amchur** Ground mango powder used in Indian cooking.

**annatto paste/seed** Used primarily in Mexican and Caribbean cooking to give a rich, saffron-like colour. Try a blend of turmeric and paprika as a substitute.

**añejo** A sharp Mexican cheese made from either goats' or cows' milk, flavoured with paprika. Good for grilling or baking. Parmesan or feta can be used as a substitute.

**árbol** see *chile de árbol*

**atchar** Spicy pickles – a South African condiment usually made with unripe green mangoes and chillies and served with curry.

**baharat** An Arabian spice blend consisting of allspice, cardamom seeds, cassia bark, cloves, coriander seeds, nutmeg, dried red chilli/paprika and peppercorns.

**belacan** Malay shrimp paste. Used widely in Asian countries and purchased in blocks.

**berbere** An exotic spice mixture from Ethiopia and Eretria, *berbere* features the rare Ajwain seed, along with chilli, garlic, ginger, dried basil, cloves, fenugreek, cardamom and coriander among other ingredients.

**bird's-eye chilli** A small chilli found in Southeast Asia, technically medium in heat, but more than hot enough for most people.

**candlenuts** A staple of Indonesian food used to thicken spice pastes. Candlenuts look similar to hazelnuts, but macadamia nuts would be the best choice if a substitute is required.

**cassareep** A key ingredient in Guyanese pepperpot, this is a thick black liquid made from cassava.

**cassava** A tuberous root and major source of carbohydrate in the developing world. Has a delicate flavour and accompanies meat. Boiled or fried potatoes could be a fair substitute.

**cayenne pepper** Used powdered, whole, in dried flakes or in a thin, vinegar-based sauce, cayenne pepper is a hot, pungent chilli. Widely available, but red chilli powder or paprika could be used as a substitute.

**ceviche** A dish of fresh, raw fish marinated in citrus juice (lemons or limes) until 'cooked' by the acid. Unlike *escabeche*, *ceviche* is not cooked prior to marinading, so the freshness of the fish is paramount.

**chile de árbol** A small Mexican chilli pepper also known as bird's-beak chilli/rat's-tail chilli. Can be substituted with cayenne pepper.

**Chinese five-spice** A classic mixture of spices used in Chinese cooking, ingredients usually comprise star anise, cloves, fennel seeds, Sichuan pepper and Chinese cinnamon.

**Chinese cinnamon** Also known as cassia cinnamon. Has a more pungent, stronger taste than Ceylon (real) cinnamon, as Chinese cinnamon contains 5% cassia to Ceylon's milder 0.4%.

**chipotle** A smoke-dried jalapeño chilli – used primarily in Mexican cooking, with a mild, earthy spiciness. Ideal in salsas, for meat marinades or added whole to soups and stews.

**çiğ köfte** Translates as 'raw meatballs' in Turkish. Çiğ köfte is the finest lean raw beef (sometimes lamb), ground with onions, tomato paste and bulgur (cracked wheat) and laced with *isot* pepper.

**cloves** A very strong spice, native to Indonesia. Commonly available, but try a mixture of allspice, cinnamon and nutmeg if a substitute is required.

**cumin** An aromatic spice available whole (as a dried seed) or ground; it's traditionally used to flavour curries and soups. Use caraway seeds (half as much) as a substitute if required.

**doro wat** An Ethiopian stew or curry, traditionally prepared with chicken, egg and onion laced with *berbere* spice mixture.

**epazote** A herb with a strong, acidic taste used to flavour Mexican dishes. Can be difficult to source/substitute – try combining cumin, oregano and coriander.

**escabeche** Poached/fried fish marinated in an acidic mixture (usually vinegar/citrus juice) and served cold. Also the name of the marinade itself. See also *ceviche*.

**fenugreek** Available in seed or dried herb format, or as a fresh vegetable. The yellow seeds are a popular feature of Ethiopian and Indian cooking, particularly in dhals and spice mixes.

**five-spice powder** See *Chinese five-spice*.

**fufu** A staple in West African cooking – yams or cassava pounded into a dough. Pinch off a bit of fufu with your right hand and dip into soups.

**galangal** A rhizome, similar in appearance to ginger, though darker. It can be purchased fresh (use a very sharp knife to slice) or powdered. Ginger can be used in its place, but it is much milder than galangal.

**garam masala** A 'sweet' blend of spices including cardamom, cloves, cumin, pepper and star anise.

**ghee** Clarified butter.

**ginger flower** Also known as torch ginger. In Southeast Asia the bud of this beautiful flower is used to make laksa. Can be purchased frozen from large Asian grocery stores.

**gochujang** A savoury Korean condiment of red pepper paste, comprising red chilli, rice, fermented soybeans and salt.

**guajillo chilli** A Mexican chilli pepper, reddish-brown in colour and moderately hot in flavour. Used in salsas, pastes and meat rubs.

**guaque chilli** A Guatemalan chilli pepper.

**gula melaka** The Indonesian name for palm sugar.

**habanero chilli** An intensely hot chilli pepper that can vary in colour (unripe are green, other colours include orange, red, white, brown and pink).

**hae ko** Prawn paste – a common ingredient in Asian cuisine.

**harissa** A hot chilli sauce from Tunisia.

**hawaji** A Yemeni spice mix incorporating peppercorns, caraway seeds, saffron, cardamom and turmeric.

**huajiao** See *Sichuan pepper*.

**huoguo** Translates as 'fire pot' in Chinese – a simmering broth of chillies and Sichuan peppercorns in which various meat, seafood and vegetables are cooked, 'asian-fondue' style.

**ika mata** A raw fish salad with coconut, originating in Rarotonga (Cook Islands).

**injera** An Ethiopian fermented pancake with a spongy texture, traditionally eaten with wat or doro wat.

**isot pepper** A dried Turkish chilli pepper with a smoky, sultry taste. Used in meat and savoury foods with an initially mild heat that builds deceptively over time. Also known as Urfa biber.

**jalapeño pepper** A medium-sized chilli pepper, usually picked green.

**jerk** A style of Jamaican cooking (where meat is dry-rubbed with hot spice and turned – 'jerked' – regularly over heat) and also the name given to the seasoning, which features allspice and Scotch bonnet peppers.

**jjigae** A Korean dish similar to a stew, typically served in a communal dish with meat and vegetables.

**Kampot pepper** Available as green, black, red or white peppercorns, originating from the southern province of Kampot in Cambodia.

**kecap manis** Indonesian sweet soy sauce, extra syrupy with the addition of palm sugar. Regular soy sauce mixed with honey or molasses can be used in its place.

**kerisik** A dense paste used in Malaysian and Indonesian cuisine – made from coconut roasted in a dry pan and ground in a mortar and pestle.

**kimchi** A Korean side dish of vegetables with a variety of seasonings. Has a spicy/sour flavour.

**kitfo** An Ethiopian dish consisting of raw minced beef that has been blended with a chilli-based spice mix and doused in melted, clarified butter.

**la douban jiang** A hot paste of red chilli peppers, fermented broad beans, soy beans, salt, rice and spices, popular in Sichuan cuisine.

**lajiaojiang** Chinese hot chilli paste.

**laksa leaves** A weirdly metallic tasting mint, with strong pepper notes. Use mint and coriander as a substitute. Also known as Vietnamese mint.

**leaf masala** A blend of cumin, coriander, fennel, paprika and bay leaves. Ideal for curries.

**lemongrass** A popular herb in Asian cuisine and can be purchased whole, dried or powdered. As the name suggests, it has a citrus flavour.

**lontong** Compressed rice cake, usually served cold or room temperature with Indonesian dishes.

**machaca** A Mexican dish of dried, spiced and shredded beef or pork jerky, usually served with flour tortillas.

**ma-la** Meaning numbing and spicy – the repercussions of eating *ma-la* sauce; the numbness created by Sichuan peppercorns.

**mirchi ka pakoda** An Indian snack of whole chillies in batter.

**mole** A slow-cooked savoury Mexican sauce featuring chilli peppers, herbs, spices and occasionally dark chocolate.

**muhummara** A spicy Syrian dip, using fresh or roasted red capsicum pounded with ground walnuts, olive oil and breadcrumbs along with dried Aleppo pepper, pomegranate molasses, cumin, salt, garlic and lemon juice.

**'nduja** A Calabrian spicy, spreadable salami. Substitute with chorizo or any spicy Italian sausage.

**nit'r qibe** An Ethiopian spiced butter consisting of unsalted butter, black cardamom seeds, fenugreek powder and ground nigella seeds.

**okra** Small, five-sided pods with a zucchini/ eggplant taste. Used as a thickening agent in soups and stews due to the gelatinous substance released when cooked.

**omo tuo** A Ghanese dish consisting of balls of sticky pudding rice – often accompanies soups.

**otak-otak** A Southeast Asian cake made with spiced fish paste, wrapped in a banana leaf and grilled over a charcoal fire. Also sold frozen or in canned varieties in Asian stores.

**Padrón peppers (pimentos de Padrón)** Small Spanish peppers – considered the Russian Roulette of peppers; while the taste is generally mild, there are a few that are really hot!

**pandan leaves** Long green leaves used in Southeast Asian cuisine for their sweet, toasted coconut/ pecan/basmati flavour.

**pepperoncino** An Italian mild chilli, slightly bitter.

**petai** Known as the 'stink bean', not because it has a particular odour, but you will after consuming it. Used in Southeast Asian cooking in combination with other strongly flavoured foods.

**pico de gallo** Mexican salsa made from uncooked chopped tomato, white onion and chillis.

**pul biber** see *Aleppo pepper*.

**queso fresco** A Mexican fresh cheese, either made from raw cow's milk or a combination of cow and goat milk. Use feta or goat's cheese as a substitute.

**ras el hanout** A complex Moroccan spice blend (can feature up to 50 spices) commonly used in tagines and meat rubs.

**sambal** A particularly fiery salsa-like condiment featuring tomato, onion, carrot and chilli. Buy ready-made sambals at food markets or Asian grocery stores.

**Scotch bonnet pepper** A variety of chilli pepper found mostly in the Caribbean islands – popular in hot sauces and condiments. Also has some sweet varieties.

**serrano pepper** A popular chilli pepper used in Mexican cuisine. Similar in appearance to a jalapeño chilli pepper but spicier.

**Sichuan pepper** A popular spice in Asian cuisine. Can be used whole or, more commonly, the powder features in Chinese five-spice. Not as hot as chilli pepper but has slightly zesty, lemony overtones.

**star anise** A star-shaped spice closely resembling liquorice in flavour, it's a traditional component of Chinese five-spice and garam masala. If a substitute is required, try anise seed, allspice or fennel seeds.

**suanmiao** A Chinese vegetable also known as garlic leeks. Use baby leeks or spring onions as a substitute.

**sumac** A citrus-tinged spice used in Middle Eastern cuisine.

**Szechuan pepper** see *Sichuan pepper*.

**tai plaa** A very hot Thai paste made with fermented fish innards.

**tamarind juice** Made from the mashed, ripened pulp of the tamarind pod. Used as a base in Southeast Asian dishes, it has a distinctive sweet and sour flavour. Can be bought in Asian markets or use lemon or lime.

**teff** An Ethiopian grain used to make *injera*. It's high in iron, protein and calcium, and similar in texture to quinoa or millet, but with a smaller seed that cooks faster.

**tinga poblana** A classic stew from the Puebla region of Mexico: shredded pork shoulder cooked with chipotle chillies.

**tomatillo** A light-green-husked Mexican fruit and a key ingredient in thickening sauces. Use green salsa or underripe tomatoes with lime juice as a substitute.

**torch ginger** see *ginger flower*.

**turmeric** This is a rhizome, like ginger but usually smaller. Beneath the dull orange peel, you'll find brilliant gold. Available fresh in Asian grocery stores, and as a ground spice almost everywhere.

**Urfa biber** see *isot pepper*

**Vietnamese mint** A weirdly metallic tasting mint, with strong pepper notes. Use mint and coriander as a substitute. Also known as laksa leaf.

**water spinach** A popular vegetable for stir-frying in Southeast Asian countries. Look for it in Asian markets or substitute with watercress, snow pea leaves, or even regular spinach.

**zaatar/zahtar** The name of a Middle Eastern mixed herb and also a spice mixture, generally made from ground thyme, oregano and marjoram combined with toasted sesame seeds, sumac and salt.

# Authors *

## Tom Parker Bowles

Tom Parker Bowles is a food writer with an ever-expanding gut. He has a weekly column in *The Mail on Sunday*, as well as being Food Editor of *Esquire*. He is also a Contributing Editor to *Departures* magazine. His first book, *E is for Eating: An Alphabet of Greed* (2004) was an opinionated romp through the world of food. His next, *The Year of Eating Dangerously* (2006) explored the more weird and exotic delicacies of the world. And his third, *Full English: A Journey Through the British and Their Food* was published in 2009 and won the Guild of Food Writers 2010 award for best work on British food. *Let's Eat – Recipes from My Kitchen Notebook* (2012), is a collection of his favourite recipes, gathered from around the world and recreated in his own kitchen. His latest book, *Let's Eat Meat*, hits the shelves in 2014

## * Contributing Authors *

**Abigail Blasi** Specialises in writing on Italy, and is dedicated to sampling the country's dazzling gastronomy and hunting down its spiciest flavours.

**Anthony Ham** Writer and photographer with a passion for food from Africa to the Arctic and from Spain to Syria.

**Brett Atkinson** Frequent traveller to Australia, Turkey and Southeast Asia, restaurant reviewer for viewauckland.co.nz, and incorrigible street food and craft beer fan.

**Caroline Veldhuis** Contributor to Lonely Planet travel/culture books, lifelong vegetarian and international culinary student who has been declared a 'messy' cook in both Vietnam and Turkey

**Chris Deliso** Travel writer covering Southeast Europe for Lonely Planet, long residing in the Balkans, where he finally learned to eat (and even enjoy!) his vegetables.

**Daniel McCrohan** Peppercorn-addicted British writer, living in chilli-laced China since 2005. Author of multiple Lonely Planet guidebooks and creator of the iPhone app Beijing on Budget. Visit danielmccrohan.com.

**Emily Matchar** Writes about culture for magazines and newspapers. She's contributed to more than a dozen Lonely Planet titles. Nashville-style 'hot' fried chicken would be her jailhouse last meal.

**Ethan Gelber** Founder/editor of TheTravelWord. com; AFAR Ambassador; agitator for responsible, sustainable and local travel; voracious consumer of culture, especially the edible kind.

**Isabella Noble** London-based lifelong vegetarian, with a fervent fear of tomatoes and an insatiable hunger for exploring the world, one beach at a time.

**Jessica Lee** Co-author of Lonely Planet's *Turkey* and *Egypt*, Middle Eastern food-nut, once challenged a Turkish waiter to a hot pepper eating competition and won.

**Johanna Ashby** Food and travel freelance writer and specialist author for Lonely Planet, keen on street food to fine dining and everything in between.

**Joshua Samuel Brown** Purveyor of good eats from Singapore's hawker centres to Taiwan's night markets to Portland's food-truck scene, Joshua is co-author of a dozen-plus Lonely Planet guides.

**Karyn Noble** A London-based editor, writer and shameless epicurean. Australian by birth, she will happily debate the merits of Vegemite as a condiment.

**Kate Thomas** Lonely Planet West Africa author with a magic compass for tracking down fresh and fiery dishes from Liberia to Mali – and a firm belief that nothing beats the oysters in Guinea-Bissau.

**Kate Whitfield** Sometime Lonely Planet editor, freelance writer, contributor to the since-departed *Wine X* magazine and *Black Book* restaurant guide, voracious traveller.

**Lucy Corne** Blogger on all things beer-related, co-author of Lonely Planet's *South Africa, Lesotho & Swaziland*, cake devourer and offal avoider.

**Luke Waterson** Co-author of Lonely Planet's *Mexico*, *Peru* and *Cuba*, contributor to *The World's Best Street Food*, Food/Travel writer for the BBC. Addicted to Oaxaca's chillies.

**Mark Beales** Co-author of Lonely Planet *Thailand*, dedicated foodie and curry connoisseur. Visit markbeales.com.

**Mauricio Velázquez de León** Regular contributor to Lonely Planet guides on Mexico and *Saveur* magazine. He lives in the United States, thousands of miles from his favorite taquería.

**Paul Bloomfield** Contributor to *The Times*, *Daily Telegraph*, *Wanderlust* and *BBC Wildlife*, Asia obsessive, man on a mission to track down the perfect noodle soup.

**Penny Watson** Based in Hong Kong, Penny writes food and travel articles for newspapers, magazines, guidebooks and coffee table tomes in Australia, Asia and the UK. Some like it hot; Penny is one of them.

**Piera Chen** Travel addict, sometime poet, (co-) author of Lonely Planet's books on Hong Kong and China, Piera takes her rice with a baby-fistful of fresh chillies, finely chopped.

**Rob Whyte** Long-time resident of South Korea, contributor to Lonely Planet books about Korean food and travel, intrepid countryside backpacker and Korean barbecue meat connoisseur.

**Sarah Baxter** Travel writer, Associate Editor of *Wanderlust* magazine and runner of marathons – to counterbalance the global eating (faves: Nova Scotia lobster roll, Cornish cream tea).

**Shawn Low** Growing up in food-crazy Singapore endowed Lonely Planet travel editor Shawn with a glutton complex and a tongue-of-steel that can withstand the fieriest of spices.

**Stuart Butler** A frequent visitor to Ethiopia and author of the Lonely Planet Ethiopia guide. He has written about things foodie for *Olive* magazine and a number of in-flight magazines.

**Tienlon Ho** Enjoys travelling to places where she can eat innards and heads, and no one cares, and has written about that and other things for Lonely Planet.

**Virginia Jealous** Has been travel writing for Lonely Planet since 1999. She's also a poet; her second collection, *Hidden World*, was published in 2013.

**Will Gourlay** Long-time Lonely Planet editor, and writer with a particular focus on the many delights of Turkey, often seen loitering near kebab stands.

# * Index *

## Type of Dish

**The World's Best Spicy Food**
March 2014
Published by Lonely Planet Publications Pty Ltd
ABN 36 005 607 983
90 Maribyrnong St, Footscray,
Victoria, 3011, Australia
www.lonelyplanet.com
10 9 8 7 6 5 4 3 2 1

**Printed in China**

ISBN 978 1 74321 976 8
© Lonely Planet 2014
© Photographers as indicated 2014


**Publisher** Piers Pickard
**Associate Publisher** Ben Handicott
**Commissioning Editors**
Will Gourlay, Robin Barton
**Art Direction** Mark Adams
**Layout Designers** Adrian Blackburn, Leon Mackie
**Editors** Bridget Blair, Sam Forge, Lorna Goodyer,
Kate James, Saralinda Turner, Tasmin Waby, Kate
Whitfield, Tracy Whitmey
**Image Research** Rebecca Skinner
**Pre-Press Production** Ryan Evans
**Print Production** Larissa Frost
**Thanks to** Sam Forge

**Lonely Planet Offices**
**Australia**
Locked Bag 1, Footscray, Victoria, 3011
Phone 03 8379 8000 Fax 03 8379 8111
Email talk2us@lonelyplanet.com.au

**USA**
150 Linden St, Oakland, CA 94607
Phone 510 250 6400 Toll free 800 275 8555 Fax 510
893 8572
Email info@lonelyplanet.com

**Europe**
UK Media Centre, 201 Wood Lane, London,
W12 7TQ
Phone 020 8433 1333 Fax 020 8702 0112
Email go@lonelyplanet.co.uk